New Documentary

New Documentary: A Critical Introduction provides a contemporary look at documentary and fresh and challenging ways of theorising the non-fiction film. This engaging textbook brings the study of documentary up to date by examining critical issues of performance, gender, authorship and spectatorship and suggests how these are important to an understanding of documentary cinema. Areas addressed include:

- key texts such as Zapruder's film of Kennedy's assassination, *Shoah*, *The Leader, His Driver and the Driver's Wife* and *The Atomic Café*;
- the work of filmmakers such as Emile de Antonio, Chris Marker, Nicholas Barker, Nick Broomfield, Molly Dineen and Patrick Keiller;
- an analysis of key aspects of documentary such as the use of voice-over and archive, American cinéma vérité, docusoaps and political image-making;
- an innovative examination of the importance of performance to documentary;
- interviews with contemporary documentary filmmakers.

Stella Bruzzi is Senior Lecturer in Film and Television at Royal Holloway College, London. She is the author of *Undressing Cinema: Clothing and Identity in the Movies* (Routledge 1997).

Critical responses to *Undressing Cinema* by Stella Bruzzi

'One of the year's best scholarly undertakings', Jonathan Romney, *The Guardian*

'A must for any serious film course reading list', Nick Roddick, *Sight and Sound*

'An important intervention. Meticulous in its research, fascinating in its breadth of approach and elegantly written', Pamela Church Gibson, *Screen*

'Fascinating to fashion victims as well as film buffs', Tom Dewe Matthews, *Independent on Sunday*

New Documentary

A critical introduction

Stella Bruzzi

Routledge
Taylor & Francis Group

LONDON AND NEW YORK

First published 2000
by Routledge
11 New Fetter Lane, London EC4P 4EE

Simultaneously published in the USA and Canada
by Routledge
29 West 35th Street, New York, NY 10001

Reprinted 2003, 2004

Routledge is an imprint of the Taylor & Francis Group

© 2000 Stella Bruzzi

Typeset in Galliard by Taylor & Francis Books Ltd
Printed and bound in Great Britain by Biddles Ltd, King's Lynn, Norfolk

British Library Cataloguing in Publication Data
A catalogue record for this book is available from the British Library

Library of Congress Cataloging in Publication Data
Bruzzi, Stella
New documentary : a critical introduction / Stella Bruzzi.
    p. cm.
Includes bibliographical references.
1. Documentary films – History and criticism. I. Title.

PN1995.9.D6 B78 2000
070.1′8–dc21   00-036637

ISBN 0–415–18295–6 (hbk)
ISBN 0–415–18296–4 (pbk)

Contents

Figures

Acknowledgements

Thanks once again to Rebecca Barden for her encouragement and patience. Many friends and colleagues helped, in different ways, with this book and I am particularly grateful to Pamela Church Gibson, Barry Langford, Carol Lorac, Susannah Capon and Dan Rebellato. Many thanks also to Nicholas Barker, Chris Terrill, Rachel Bell, Nick Shearman and Mark Fielder for giving me invaluable interviews. I am most in debt to my family who have supported me throughout the three years – off and on – that it has taken me to complete this book: to my mother Zara for looking after my son Frank whilst I wrote the final chapter, and to my husband Mick, without whose advice, help and kindness the book would never have been completed. As the birth of Frank made it more difficult to write the text than it might otherwise have been, I dedicate this book to him.

Introduction

The aim of this book is twofold: to invite the reader to reassess some of the ways in which documentary film has been theorised and to bring the theoretical discussion of documentary practice up to date by focusing on output from the 1980s and 1990s. Even when older non-fiction material is examined, the intention is to introduce the significant antecedents to this more modern work. There are very simple reasons for this bias towards the modern: those interested in documentary find films that are familiar and relevant to them more engaging than older texts, and theoretical writing on documentary has, by and large, not kept pace with developments in critical and cultural theory. Not enough writing on documentary has tackled readily accessible, contemporary examples, nor has it advanced the manner in which non-fiction film has traditionally been discussed. The prime motivation for this book is to introduce an alternative way of discussing documentary; to initiate this, this Introduction is largely given over to outlining the shortcomings and preoccupations of documentary's theorisation.

Theory

The first issue of documentary's theorisation that needs to be tackled is the imposition on documentary history of a 'family tree'. The most influential genealogy is Bill Nichols' chain of documentary 'modes', which are assumed to beget and in turn be superseded by those that follow. There are others, such as Paul Rotha's early 'evolution of documentary' outlined in *Documentary Film* in 1936 or Erik Barnouw's genealogy of sorts in *Documentary: A History of the Non-fiction Film* (1993), but Nichols' 'family tree' is the one that has stuck, although hybrid, eclectic modern films have begun to undermine his efforts to compartmentalise documentaries. Nichols has, to date, identified five modes: the Expository; the Observational; the Interactive; the Reflexive; and the Performative. He is keener on some modes than on others (the Interactive and the Reflexive, particularly) but his categories have increasingly become negatively and weakly defined by what they are not.[1] The premise is that documentary has evolved along Darwinian lines, that documentary has gone from being primitive in both form and argument to being sophisticated and complex; as a general rule, his modes suggest a progression towards introspection and personalisation. Although Nichols' descriptions of various documentary modes are illuminating (his use of terms such as 'interactive' and 'performative' will, unfortunately, mean something quite different to most readers), the rigid use to which they have been put is not. The fundamental problem with his survival-of-the-fittest 'family tree' is that it imposes a false chronological development onto what is essentially a theoretical paradigm. So, because the Expository mode is primitive and didactic, Nichols maintains that it is also the earliest, rather arbitrarily attributing it to the 1930s. It is simply not tenable to maintain that voice-over (the *sine qua non* of the Expository mode) is any less popular a device in non-fiction film now than it was; narration is everywhere, likewise observation – frequently in the same documentary. If Nichols' genealogy holds, then what about the very self-conscious, reflexive films of Vertov or Vigo in the 1920s and 1930s? Or contemporary didactic documentaries? A further problem with this 'family tree' is that, in order to sustain itself, wildly heterogeneous documentaries are forced to co-exist, very uncomfortably at times, within one mode – a dilemma that is examined more specifically in Chapter 2 of this book.

Documentary has not developed along such rigid lines and it is unhelpful to suggest that it has. In fact, Nichols himself now acknowledges this, commenting (in parentheses, though) 'None of these modes expel previous modes; instead they overlap and interact. The terms are partly heuristic and actual films usually mix different modes although one mode will normally be dominant' (Nichols 1994: 95). If this is the case, then what is the point of constructing genealogical tables? The result – whether conscious or not – of having imposed this 'family tree' on documentary history is the creation of a central canon of films that is deeply exclusive and conservative. With this in mind, this book stresses the development of a dialectical relationship between more innovative non-fiction films and the established documentary canon and considers the many ways in which rigid classifications of documentary have been repeatedly problematised, though this debate is at times more emphatically entered into than at others and an alternative canon will certainly not be supplied.

An insistent implication of Nichols' 'family tree' is not merely that documentary has pursued a developmental progression towards greater introspection and subjectivity, but that its evolution has been determined by the endless quest of documentary filmmakers for better and more authentic ways to represent reality, with the implied suggestion that, somewhere in the utopian future, documentary will miraculously be able to collapse the difference between reality and representation altogether. Documentary and fiction are forever the polarities that are invoked in this debate: Nichols' latest genealogy bizarrely begins (that is, pre-Expository) with 'Hollywood fiction' whose deficiency is the 'absence of "reality"' (Nichols 1994: 95). The inverted commas around 'reality' are telling here, as if the real can never be authentically represented and that any film, whether documentary or fiction, attempting to capture it will inevitably fail. Michael Renov (1986: 71–2) likewise asserts it is important to recall that the documentary is the cinematic idiom that most actively promotes the illusion of immediacy insofar as it forswears 'realism' in favour of a direct, ontological claim to the 'real'. Every documentary issues a 'truth claim' of a sort, positing a relationship to history which exceeds the analogical status of its fictional counterpart.

Not only is Renov's claim naïve (that documentary has the capacity to bypass its own representational tools and establish a direct relationship with reality) but he instinctively distrusts what he is saying by perpetually placing that elusive realm beyond the image again in inverted commas. Sometimes it seems necessary to remind writers on documentary that reality does exist and that it can be represented without such a representation either invalidating or having to be synonymous with the reality that preceded it. Later, Renov returns to this differentiation between fiction and documentary when he comments

> There is nothing inherently less creative about nonfictional representations, both [fiction and nonfiction] may create a 'truth' of the text. What differs is the extent to which the referent of the documentary sign may be considered as a piece of the world plucked from its everyday context rather than fabricated for the screen. Of course, the very act of plucking and recontextualising profilmic elements is a kind of violence.
>
> (Renov 1993: 7)

It is very odd to suggest, as Renov does here, that not only is documentary as creative as fiction but that its 'truth' (that is that murky half-truth that lives between inverted commas) is the '"truth" of the text', the real world having got lost along the way. Particularly devilish is Renov's final aside that 'of course' the act of representation is automatically a violation of the truth (without inverted commas, presumably). Continuously invoked by documentary theory is the idealised notion, on the one hand, of the pure documentary in which the relationship between the image and the real is straightforward and, on the other, the very impossibility of this aspiration. In this vein Brian Winston somewhat hysterically suggests that, in the future, documentary will simply be mounting a panicked rear-guard action against marauding fakery:

> It seems to be likely that the implications of this technology [for digital image manipulation] will be decades working themselves through the culture. However, it is also clear that these technological developments, whatever else they portend, will have a profound and perhaps fatal impact on the documentary film. It is not hard to imagine that every documentarist will shortly (that is, in the next fifty years) have to hand, in the form of a desktop personal video-image-manipulating computer, the wherewithal for complete fakery. What can or will be left of the relationship between image and reality?
>
> (Winston 1995: 6)

This is a case of throwing the baby out with the bath water: that is, that every-thing authentic about documentary is thrown into doubt because a couple of charlatans could conceivably create *faux* documentaries. 'Fakery' has always been a possibility, it does not require a Harry, as Richard Dimbleby's April Fool's Day 'pasta grows on trees' documentary (that apparently had some non-Italians fooled) amply demonstrated. Its presence similarly does not invalidate legitimate documentaries nor does it mean that the spectator will, from now on, dismiss all documentaries as 'fake'.

All too often, documentary is seen to have failed (or be in imminent danger of failing) because it cannot be decontaminated of its representational quality, as Erik Barnouw (1993: 287) suggests when declaring

> To be sure, some documentarists claim to be objective – a term that seems to renounce an interpretative role. The claim may be strategic, but it is surely meaningless. The documentarist, like any communicator in any medium, makes endless choices. He (sic) selects topics, people, vistas, angles, lens, juxtapositions, sounds, words. Each selection is an expression of his point of view, whether he is aware of it or not, whether he acknowl-edges it or not.

Barnouw's claim is simple but erroneous: that the minute an individual becomes involved in the representation of reality, the integrity of that reality is irretrievably lost. What is, time and time again, entered into is the perennial Bazin vs Baudrillard tussle, both of whom – from polar perspectives – argue for the erosion of any differentiation between the image and reality, Bazin because he believed reality could be recorded, Baudrillard because he believes reality is just another image. Because the ideal of the pure documentary uncontaminated by the subjective vagaries of representation is forever upheld, all non-fiction film is thus deemed to be unable to live up to its intention, so documentary becomes what you do when you have failed. The purpose of the ensuing discus-sions is to suggest, from a variety of perspectives, that the pact between documentary, reality and spectator is far more straightforward than these theo-rists make out: that a documentary will never be reality nor will it erase or invalidate that reality by being representational. Furthermore, the spectator is not in need of signposts and inverted commas to understand that a documen-tary is a negotiation between reality on the one hand and image, interpretation and bias on the other.

Documentary is predicated upon a dialectical relationship between aspiration and potential, that the text itself reveals the tensions between the documentary pursuit of the most authentic mode of factual representation and the impossi-bility of this aim. This is not a new phenomenon – the fissures are there in Huston's war documentaries, for instance, or the 'collage junk' films of Emile de Antonio – it just has not been talked about much within the parameters of documentary theory, a body of work that has concentrated upon the desire (really only articulated fully by the American founders of direct cinema) to attain the 'grail' of perfect authenticity. Many antecedents of the modern documentary were not so haunted by issues of bias, performance and authorial inflection – Esfir Shub did not consider the fact/fiction divide between her portrayal and Eisenstein's of Russia's recent political history to be particularly significant, identifying the fictionalised *Battleship Potemkin* as the catalyst to her search for newsreel material with which to compile another film to 'show the revolutionary past' (Jay Leyda, quoted in Macdonald and Cousins 1996: 58). In this frame of mind, the repeated use of Eisenstein's dramatisation of the storming of the Winter Palace in *October* as a piece of newsreel is not so anachronistic. The suspicion and cynicism with which Robert Flaherty's reconstructions in *Nanook of the North* or *Man of Aran* are now treated stem not from an understanding of why he reconstituted an Arran family or recorded their dialogue in a studio (technical limitations, a desire to make a record of a lost way of life, and so on) or of how such films may have been understood for what they were by contemporary audiences. Likewise, John Grierson's early definition of documentary in light of Flaherty's work as 'the creative treatment of actuality' (Rotha 1952: 70) has been viewed as contradictory. As Winston (1995: 11) suggests: 'The supposition that any "actuality" is left after "creative treatment" can now be seen as being at best naïve and at worst a mark of duplicity.'

And yet, as Winston later points out, Grierson himself differentiated between documentary and other, lesser, forms of non-fiction film, and openly acknowledged the 'contradictions' in his definition by stressing repeatedly that the element which documentaries possessed but which other forms of non-fiction film lacked was 'dramatisation' (Winston 1995: 103). Grierson, the Soviets, Paul Rotha and other early practitioners and theorists were far more relaxed about documentary as a category than we have become.

Worries over authenticity and the evolution of documentary are frequently linked to the increasing sophistication of audio-visual technology. Whereas technical limitations certainly influenced the kinds of documentaries that were feasible in the 1930s when Grierson was first writing, this is no longer the case, so the return we are currently witnessing to a more fluid definition of documentary must have another root. The role of American *cinéma vérité* has proved the crucial historical factor in limiting documentary's potential and frame of reference, and it is significant that, although many theorists suspect and criticise direct cinema, most of them dedicate a large amount of time to examining it. Richard Leacock and his fellows believed that the advancements in film equipment would enable documentary to achieve authenticity and to collapse the distance between reality and representation, because the camera would become 'just a window someone peeps through' (Donn Pennebaker quoted in Winston 1993: 43). As Errol Morris has bluntly put it:

> I believe that cinema vérité set back documentary filmmaking twenty or thirty years. It sees documentary as a sub-species of journalism. ... There's no reason why documentaries can't be as personal as fiction filmmaking and

bear the imprint of those who made them. Truth isn't guaranteed by style or expression. It isn't guaranteed by anything.

(Quoted in Arthur 1993: 127)

As Morris's timescale suggests, it has taken time for documentary filmmaking to rid itself of the burden of expectation imposed by direct cinema; furthermore, virtually the entire post-*vérité* history of non-fiction film can be seen as a reaction against its ethos of transparency and unbiased observation. Obviously the problem now is not a lack of technical equipment capable of recording actuality: DVD cameras, hidden cameras and self-authored diary television have all been hurled at documentary to prove this. It is no longer technical limitations that should be blamed for documentary's 'contradictions' but rather the expectations loaded onto it by its theorisation. It can legitimately be argued that filmmakers themselves (and their audiences) have, much more readily than theorists, accepted documentary's inability to give an undistorted, purely reflective picture of reality. Several different sorts of non-fiction film have now emerged that propose a complex documentary truth arising from an insurmountable compromise between subject and recording, suggesting in turn that it is this very juncture between reality and filmmaker that is the heart of any documentary.

The most sustained questioning of American *vérité*'s fantasy has emerged through the examination of films based on performance and authorship. Documentary practice and theory have always had a problem with aesthetics, as John Corner observes, 'The extent to which a concern with formal attractiveness "displaces" the referential such as to make the subject itself secondary to its formal appropriation has been a frequent topic of dispute' (Corner 1996: 123). The discussion in Chapter 1 of Abraham Zapruder's 8-mm recording of the assassination of President Kennedy posits that there is an inverse relationship between style and authenticity: the less polished the film the more credible it will be found. Performative documentaries, a discussion of which concludes this book, confront the problem of aestheticisation, accepting, as does Nick Barker, authorship as intrinsic to documentary, in direct opposition to the exponents of direct cinema who saw themselves as merely the purveyors of the truth they pursued. Likewise, the role performance plays in documentary has become, in several instances, not the death of documentary but rather a crucial way of establishing its credibility, as the dialogue on the subject of control between Molly Dineen and Geri Halliwell in *Geri* illustrates. The later films of Nick Broomfield take this notion of constructed truth a stage further as they build themselves around the encounters between subjects and Broomfield's on-screen alter ego – encounters that, in turn, form the basis for a reflexive dialogue with the spectator on the nature of documentary authenticity. What emerges is a new definition of authenticity, one that eschews the traditional adherence to an observation or Bazin-dependent idea of the transparency of film and replaces this with a performative exchange between subjects, filmmakers/apparatus and spectators.

When arguing against Bill Nichols' presupposition that objectivity in the documentary is impossible, Noël Carroll points out that, because documentaries do not, on the whole, reveal the process of their construction, this does not mean that they automatically deny the existence of these processes (Carroll 1996b: 293). To conclude, Erik Barnouw's assumption is that the intervention of the camera necessarily distorts and alters human behaviour, *ergo* that the resulting piece of film cannot be objective or truthful so that film is deemed to have failed. Why failure? It is perhaps more generous and worth while to simply accept that a documentary can never be the real world, that the camera can never capture life as it would have unravelled had it not interfered, and the results of this collision between apparatus and subject are what constitutes a documentary – not the utopian vision of what might have transpired if only the camera had not been there. If one is always going to regret the need for cameras and crews and bemoan the inauthenticity of what they bring back from a situation, then why write about or make documentaries? Instead, documentaries are performative acts whose truth comes into being only at the moment of filming – a moment that, in turn, signals the death of the documentary pursuit as identified by critics such as Erik Barnouw. The paradox that now dominates – as documentaries such as Broomfield's seem more spontaneous and authentic because they show the documentary process and the moment of encounter with their subjects – is that they also flaunt their lack of concern with conforming to the style of objectivity dictated by documentary history and theory. This is, erroneously, taken by many as a sign of the performative documentary's fictiveness; Izod and Kilborn, for instance, refer to the 'denial of realism' (Izod and Kilborn 1997: 78) that ensues with the intrusion of the *auteur*, as occurs in the films of Morris, Broomfield and Moore. A final difficulty arises, from many performative documentary filmmakers citing direct cinema as the biggest influences on their films. Perhaps what Broomfield *et al.* mean by this is that they have realised that American *vérité* produced such powerful films not because of what Leacock and his colleagues believed in, but because their films are the ultimate expression of how hard it is to disguise the impossibility of what they were trying to achieve. The link between the observational and the performative is just one of the ways in which documentary can be seen to be going against both the 'family tree' structure and, conversely, proving the notion that documentaries will always tread the line between intention and execution, between reality and the image.

Organisation and structure

Although the above introduction to documentary theory has touched on some of the ways in which this book has structured its arguments, I will conclude by outlining briefly its organisation of material. Part I comprises two chapters: the first deals with the issues of film as record or archive, the second with documentary's use of narration. These discussions are intended to function as a polemical introduction to the problems posed by seeing documentary as an eternal conflict between objectivity and subjectivity, positing that accidental film, such as Abraham Zapruder's home movie footage of Kennedy's assassination, exemplifies non-fictional film at its most objective, whilst the use of narration – an overt intrusion of the filmmaker's bias and didactic point of view – exemplifies documentary at its most subjective. As both discussions conclude, such categorical definitions are crude and invalid, Chapter 1 by focusing on the dialectical re-use of archive material in documentaries such as *The Fall of the Romanovs*, *Millhouse: A White Comedy* and *The Atomic Café*, and Chapter 2 by pointing out the very different relationships established between the voice-over and the image in films such as *The Times of Harvey Milk*, *Hôtel des invalides* and *Sunless*. Chapters 3 and 4 follow on from an introduction that looks in more depth at the problems posed to an understanding of documentary practice by direct cinema – or more precisely the way in which the exponents of direct cinema defined their achievements. The discussions of 1990s' British observational documentary and of documentaries that adopt the structure of a journey serve as illustrative examples of the ways in which documentary centred on observation has moved on since the 1960s and how the moment of encounter – so key to direct cinema – has become the starting point for a varied reassessment of the aims of the observational mode. The particular emphasis of Chapter 3 will be the phenomenal success of docusoaps, whilst the journey documentaries to be discussed in detail are Claude Lanzmann's *Shoah* and Patrick Keiller's *London*. Part III tackles the question of performance in documentary, from, broadly speaking, the perspectives of the subject-performer and the director-performer. Chapter 5 examines the ways in which the American presidential image has evolved from the era of Kennedy in the early 1960s to Bill Clinton in the 1990s. The starting point for this discussion is the representation of Kennedy in the direct cinema documentaries *Primary* and *Crisis*, progressing to the disillusionment with the presidential image that follows Nixon's use of the television broadcast as a platform for lying and concluding with an examination of *The War Room*, *Feed* and Clinton's Grand Jury testimony against a backdrop of presidential politics dictated by spin and image-making. Chapter 6 looks at documentaries that are themselves performative, adopting as its point of departure the use of the term by J.L. Austin and Judith Butler (thereby understanding the term 'performative' in a very different way to Bill Nichols in *Blurred Boundaries*). The films of Nicholas Barker, Molly Dineen and Nick Broomfield are examined as exemplary of the thesis that underpins this whole book: that documentaries are inevitably the result of the intrusion of the filmmaker onto the situation being filmed, that they are performative because they acknowledge the construction and artificiality of even the non-fiction film and propose, as the underpinning truth, the truth that emerges through the encounter between filmmakers, subjects and spectators.

Documentaries will continue to evolve and continue to re-visit old terrain. Who would have thought that, at the very end of the twentieth century, even the methods of Robert Flaherty would be revived? But that is exactly what has happened with a film such as *Twockers* in which real people are rehearsed to play themselves as if in a drama.

Part I

Ground rules

To initiate an analysis of documentary as a perpetual negotiation between the real event and its representation (that is, to propose that the two remain distinct but interactive) this opening section will juxtapose the notion of film as record with the use of voice-over. This is not an arbitrary selection, but a decision to establish this book's underlying thesis that documentary does not perceive its ultimate aim to be the authentic representation of the real through an examination of (a) the component of documentary that uniquely exemplifies the ideal of a non-fictional image's 'purity' (film as record), and (b) the component that most overtly illustrates the intrusion of bias, subjectivity and conscious structuring of those 'pure' events (narration). In 1971 the German documentary dramatist Peter Weiss offered a definition of documentary theatre that is pertinent to this argument. In 'The Materials and the Models', Weiss argues that, whilst documentary theatre 'refrains from all invention; it takes authentic material and puts it on the stage, unaltered in content, edited in form' (Weiss 1971: 41), it also 'presents facts for examination' and 'takes sides' (p. 42). Weiss manifestly does not automatically perceive the imposition of a structure (whether through editing or other means) to mean the loss of objectivity, instead he advocates documentary theatre rooted in dialectical analysis, the principal components of which are the raw material and the theatrical model. His intention in a play such as *The Investigation* – as he intimates later in 'The Materials and the Models' – is to extract from the material 'universal truths', to supply 'an historical context' and to draw attention to 'other possible consequences' (p. 43) of the events encompassed by the play. The raw material is incapable of drawing out or articulating the truths, motives or underlying causes it both contains and implies, so it falls to the writer to extract this general framework. Weiss's notes towards a definition of documentary theatre suggest that documentary is born of a negotiation between two potentially conflicting factors: the real and its representation; but rather than perceive this to be a problem that must be surmounted – as is perceived in much documentary film theory – Weiss accepts this propensity towards a dialectical understanding of the factual world to be an asset and a virtue.

The intention here is to examine documentary film along the lines that Weiss uses to examine documentary theatre. Although theoretical orthodoxy stipulates that the ultimate aim of documentary is to find the perfect way of representing the real so that the distinction between the two becomes invisible, this is not what one finds within the history of documentary filmmaking. Part of the intention behind these opening paragraphs is thereby to reconsider the documentary 'canon' as it has been laid out by reinstating some of the influential figures who have not conformed to the history imposed by much documentary theory, and who have adopted an attitude to their filmmaking comparable to that of Weiss towards the creation of documentary theatre. Both the discussion of film as record and the discussion of voice-over conclude by suggesting that the dialectical relationship between the event and its representation is the backbone of documentary filmmaking.

1   The event
Archive and newsreel

Documentary is persistently treated as a representational mode of filmmaking, although at its core is the notion of film as record. In its examination of documentary's purported struggle for objectivity, this opening chapter will be concerned with the relationship between film as record and as representation, centred on the idea – or ideal – of an original unadulterated truth; although many of the films to be cited also contain a voice-over, this analysis will focus on the use of newsreel and other raw or accidental footage and archive. The material to be considered will be the Zapruder footage of the assassination of President Kennedy, the compilation films of Emile de Antonio and *The Atomic Café*.

The crux of the problem when considering the potential differences between film as record and as representation, is the relationship between the human and the mechanical eye. Dziga Vertov posited a relationship between the eye and the kino-eye (the latter he referred to as the 'factory of facts' [Michelson 1984: 59]), espousing the idea that cinema's primary function was to show what the human eye could see but not record:

> In fact, the film is only the sum of the facts recorded on film, or, if you like, not merely the sum, but the product, a 'higher mathematics' of facts. Each item of each factor is a separate little document, the documents have been joined with one another so that, on the one hand, the film would consist only of those linkages between signifying pieces that coincide with the visual linkages and so that, on the other hand, these linkages would not require intertitles; the final sum of all these linkages represents, therefore, an organic whole.
>
> (Michelson 1984: 84)

For a compiler of images and a recorder of life, such as Vertov, the recording procedure is always subservient to the facts being committed to film; the mechanical eye is simply capable of showing and clarifying for its audience that which initially stands before the naked eye. The act of filming concretises rather than distorts and is in itself a way of comprehending the world. Later the French documentarist and theorist Jean-Louis Comolli returns to the relationship between the human eye and its mechanical counterpart, but reaches very different conclusions, believing that, through the advent of photography

> the human eye loses its immemorial privilege; the mechanical eye of the photographic machine now sees *in its place*, and in certain aspects with more sureness. The photograph stands as at once the triumph and the grave of the eye.
>
> (Comolli 1980: 122–3)

Comolli, from a perspective that acknowledges the ambivalence of the mechanical eye, argues that Bazin, for one, is naïve to think that, because the camera records a real event, 'it provides us with an objective and impartial image of that reality' as 'The *represented* is seen via a *representation* which, necessarily, transforms it' (p. 135).

The underpinning issue is whether or not the intervention of the filmmaker and, therefore, the human eye renders irretrievable the original meaning of the events being recorded. Linda Williams, like many others currently writing on documentary, detects a loss of faith 'in the ability of the camera to reflect objective truths of some fundamental social referent', a loss which she goes on to say 'seems to point, nihilistically … to the brute and cynical disregard of ultimate truths' (Williams 1993: 10). Later Williams comments that 'It has become an axiom of the new documentary that films cannot reveal the truth of events, but only the ideologies and consciousness that construct competing truths – the fictional master narratives by which we make sense of events' (p. 13), so doubting entirely that the image-document itself can mean anything without accompanying narrativisation and contextualisation. The problem with Williams' analysis is that it expediently singles out examples (such as *The Thin Blue Line* and *Shoah*) rooted in memory and eye-witness testimony, films that intentionally lack or exclude images of the events under scrutiny, thus making a plausible case for a 'final truth' (p. 15) to be dislodged in favour of a series of subjective truths.

Whilst not advocating the collapse of reality and representation, what this chapter will attempt is an analysis of film as record from an alternative perspective to the one implicitly proposed by Williams here or Renov, Winston and Barnouw in the Introduction, namely that documentary has always implicitly acknowledged that the 'document' at its heart is open to reassessment, reappropriation and even manipulation without these processes necessarily obscuring or rendering irretrievable the document's original meaning, context or content. The fundamental issue of documentary film is the way in which we are invited to access the 'document' or 'record' through representation or interpretation, to the extent that a piece of archive material becomes a mutable rather than a fixed point of reference. This is not, however, to imply that a filmmaker such as de Antonio disregards the documentary source of his films, or that his films are mere formalist exercises that tread the post-modern path of disputing the distinction between the historical/factual and the 'fake' or fictive. Rather his films and those, such as *Atomic Café*, which have been overtly influenced by his 'collage junk' method, play on the complexity of the relationship between historical referent and interpretation; they enact a fundamental doubt concerning the purity of their original source material and its ability to reveal a truth that is valid, lasting and cogent. De Antonio's films do not simply deny or suppress the existence of an independent truth contained within the raw footage they re-edit and comment upon, and it is perhaps this sort of equivocation that problematises the perception of archive's role in documentary.

Film as accidental record: 'the Zapruder film'

To test some of the assumptions about film as record and its transmutation into archive it seems appropriate to turn to the most notorious piece of accidental footage: Abraham Zapruder's 22 seconds of 8-mm film showing the assassination of President Kennedy, 22 November 1963, in Dallas, Texas. Several factors make 'the Zapruder film', as it is commonly known, an interesting example. The film is the work of a very amateur cameraman, a classic piece of home movie footage that Zapruder simply intended as a family record of the President's visit. The discrepancy between quality and magnitude of content and the Zapruder film's accidental nature make it particularly compelling. The home movie fragment almost did not happen as Abraham Zapruder, a local women's clothing manufacturer, had left his Bell and Howell camera at home on the morning of 22 November because of the rain, but had been persuaded by his secretary to go back and fetch it; it also almost looked quite different, as Zapruder found his position on the concrete block just in front of the 'Grassy Knoll'[1] at the last minute. Additionally, as illustrated in the film itself, it is evident that this position gave Zapruder a view of the motorcade that was partially obscured by a large road sign, tantalisingly blotting out certain details of the assassination. In keeping with this accidental quality is Zapruder's own tentativeness when discussing the film before the Warren Commission, commenting humbly, 'I knew I had something, I figured it might be of some help – I didn't know what' (quoted in Wasson 1995: 7). Similarly important is Zapruder's lack of expertise as a camera operator. The silent film jolts in response to the shots and Zapruder finds it difficult to keep Kennedy centre frame: at the crucial moment when the fatal head shot hits him, the President has been allowed to almost slide out of view, leaving the most famous frames of amateur film dominated, almost engulfed, by the lush green grass on the other side of Elm Street. 'Zapruder' became shorthand in American film schools in the years following the assassination for a piece of film of extremely low technical quality whose content was nevertheless of the utmost significance.[2] For Bazin, the apotheosis of the photograph is the similarly artless family snapshot whose documentary equivalent would be the home movie. So it was that students and others sought to emulate the style of the Zapruder footage; as Patricia Zimmerman comments with reference to home movies, 'the American avant-garde has appropriated home-movie style as a formal manifestation of a spontaneous, untampered form of filmmaking' (Zimmerman 1995: 146). The home movie is, virtually by definition, the documentation of the trivial, the personal and the inconsequential, events of interest only to the family group involved. What makes Zapruder's home movie exceptional is that it happens to capture an event that is not private and trivial but public and of huge importance. Footage that by accident rather than design captures material this monumental transgresses the boundaries between the official and unofficial uses of broadcast film, offering an alternative point of view, a perspective that is partly predicated upon the absenting of the film *auteur*, the conscious creator of the images. Zapruder's accidental home movie, like George Holliday's similarly spontaneous video recording of the beating of Rodney King by members of the LAPD in March 1991, became the official text of the events it recorded.

Why is this combination of the accidental, the amateur and the historically significant event so engaging? If one were to devise a method for classifying archive material in accordance with its purity or level of distortion, the Zapruder film would be at the top of the scale. Paul Arthur comments on the 'mutual agreement' between film theorists such as Siegfried Kracauer and Bela Balazs that 'newsreels and documentary reportage in general are "innocent" or "artless" due to their lack of aesthetic reconstruction' (Arthur 1997: 2). Arthur goes on to quote Siegfried Kracauer when positing that 'it is precisely the snapshot quality of the pictures that makes them appear as authentic documents' (p. 3), concluding that 'the absence of "beauty" yields a greater quotient of "truth"' (p. 3), thereby establishing an inverse ratio between documentary purity and aesthetic value. The Zapruder film, by these criteria, is exemplary in its rawness, innocence and credibility as a piece of non-fiction evidence or documentation. Zapruder, unlike those who copied him, is not consciously manipulating his amateur status, and it is this naïveté that audiences still find compelling, as exemplified by the preponderance of 'the accidental video witnessing of spectacular events' (Ouellette 1995: 41) that dominates the American series *I Witness Video*. Andrew Britton mentions, as if it is a foregone conclusion, that 'there can be no such thing as a representation of the world which does not embody a set of values', so ensuring that the documentary's 'greatest strength is its availability for the purpose of analysis and ideological critique' (Britton 1992: 28). There is no space in this claim for non-fiction images such as the Zapruder film, accidental footage that is not filmed with a conscious or unconscious set of determining values – 'value', in Britton's estimation, being automatically attached to the author/filmmaker as opposed to a film's content. Yet historical documentaries are made up of such non-critical fragments as the Zapruder footage. Within such a context, the film's 'value' is presumed to be that, because of the singular lack of premeditation, intention and authorship, it is able, unproblematically to yield the truth contained within its blurry, hurried images; but therein lies its problem and the factual film's burden of proof.

The Zapruder footage very quickly became an object of fetishistic fascination. As film that shows the moment of Kennedy's death, its 'imagery operating as the equivalent of the snuff film', the Zapruder frames bear uneasy comparison with the pornographic ideal of 'going all the way' to the moment of death (Simon 1996: 67). However, the fact that for twelve years the images were only known as single frames published in the Warren Commission Report[3] into the assassination or *Life* magazine, which secured the rights to the Zapruder film on the night of the assassination for $150,000, inevitably rendered them mysterious. By 1975, when the film was first broadcast, the rights had been returned to the Zapruder family, although the original footage now belongs to the US government, which paid the heirs of Abraham Zapruder £10million to keep it in the national archives (a deal that was agreed on the day John Kennedy Jr died in a plane crash). In the immediate aftermath of the assassination, the Zapruder film was thus not available as film, although the surrounding events were: the arrival of the motorcade at Parkland Memorial Hospital, Jackie Kennedy accompanying her husband's coffin on Air Force One's flight back to Washington, the funeral, the arrest and subsequent murder live on television of Lee Harvey Oswald. The absence of the key assassination images was exacerbated by the presence of these surrounding pieces of tape and film and by the knowledge that the Zapruder film was all the time being examined, re-examined and re-enacted by the Warren Commission. Such absence or lack was especially marked when considering the fatal shot to Kennedy's head, as these frames (Nos. 313–15) were deemed too traumatic to show (*Life* omitting them from early publications of the film), or, as occurred in the published Warren Commission Report, were distorted, as two frames (314 and 315) were 'accidentally' reversed, which gave the impression that Kennedy's head was thrust forward by the impact of the bullet, thus supporting their lone gunman theory. When these frames did become readily accessible, the 'involuntary spasm' shown as the bullet hits Kennedy itself 'became the site of an investigatory fetish' (Simon 1996: 68), the Zapruder film's most over-scrutinised images.

Although the Warren Commission said that 'Of all the witnesses to the tragedy, the only unimpeachable one is the *camera* of Abraham Zapruder' (my italics; *Life* Magazine, 25 November 1966, quoted in Simon 1996: 41), its status as evidence is ambiguous: it can show that President Kennedy was assassinated but is unable to show how or by whom, because Zapruder's camera (and it is revealing that the apparatus is singled out for unimpeachability and not the man) is effectively facing the wrong way – at the President and not at who shot him. Other photographic material, taken from the opposite side of Elm Street, which could potentially reveal more about the positions of the assassins – such as Orvill Nix's film and Mary Moorman's photograph – has been allegedly subjected to greater Security Services intervention and violation,[4] although the Warren Commission did omit Zapruder frames 208–11 from its final report, despite the assertion that the first bullet struck Kennedy at frame 210 (Simon 1996: 40).

If documentary putatively aspires to discover the least distortive means of representing reality, then is not footage such as the Zapruder film exemplary of its aim? It is devoid of imposed narrative, authorial intervention, editing and discernible bias and yet its contents are of such momentous significance that it remains arguably the most important piece of raw footage ever shot. The Zapruder film as a piece of historical evidence has severe limitations. Despite its value as explicit raw footage, the truth that its frames can reveal is restricted to verisimilitude of image to subject; the non-fictional image's mimetic power cannot stretch to offering a context or an explanation for the crude events on the screen, thus proposing two levels of truth: the factual images we see and the truth to be extrapolated from them. Or is that 'truths'? One of the consistently complicating aspects of the Zapruder film is that it has been both 'unimpeachable' and 'constantly open to multiple interpretations' (Simon 1996: 43), an open series of images that can be used to 'prove' a multitude of conflicting or divergent theories about the assassination. This is the footage's burden of proof: that, as an authentic record, it functions as incontrovertible 'evidence', whilst as a text incapable of revealing conclusively who killed President Kennedy it functions as an inconclusive representation. What the Zapruder film demonstrates, is an irresistible desire (on the part of theorists and probably practitioners as well) for manipulation, narrativisation or conscious intervention, despite the avowed detestation of such intrusions upon the factual image. The Zapruder footage has, for example, led Heidi Wasson to speculate wildly that the footage 'becomes the threshold to an imaginary and real space where seemingly contradictory rituals are re-enacted' (Wasson 1995: 10). Exemplifying this duality, the Zapruder footage's continuous paradox is that it promises to reveal what will always remain beyond it: the motivation and the cause of the actions it depicts. This has, in turn, led consistently to two impulses, the first being to focus obsessively on the source material itself, to analyse, re-analyse, enhance, digitally re-master Zapruder's original in the vain hope that these images will finally reveal the truth of who killed Kennedy, the second being to use the same sequence of images as the basis for an interpretation of the assassination that invariably requires and incorporates additional, substantiating material, usually drawing from an ever-dwindling number of eye-witnesses and an ever-increasing pool of conspiracy theorists. Although Zapruder's footage is an archetypal example of accidental, reactive and objective film, it has rarely been permitted to exist as such because, as Bill Nichols comments, 'To re-present the event is clearly *not* to explain it' (Nichols 1994: 121).

It is this central inadequacy that has led to a peculiar canonisation of certain emotionally charged pieces of film and video, images that could be termed 'iconic'. Recently the transmutation occurred with the endlessly repeated and equally endlessly inconclusive shots of the mutilated car in which Princess Diana and others were killed in a Paris underpass on 31 August 1997. Although these images could really only tell us that Diana, Dodi Fayed and Henri Paul had died, they were, alongside the hastily edited compilation documentaries that started running on the afternoon of the crash, played again and again as if, miraculously, they would suddenly prove less inconclusive, or indeed that looking at them hard enough would enable us to reverse the events they confirmed. The iconic status afforded the Diana and Zapruder footage, is the result of other factors; imbuing the images with significance beyond their importance as mere film or video, they function as the point where diverse and often conflicting mythologising tendencies, emotions and fantasies collide. A comparably hyperbolic and intense language was adopted to describe both deaths – 'the day the dream died', 'the end of Camelot' – and the mass outpouring of grief that followed them more than adequately repressed the shortcomings and failings of the individuals struck down. The Zapruder film has become the dominant assassination text, onto which is poured all the subsidiary grief, anger, belief in conspiracy and corruption surrounding the unresolved events it depicts. The text is simple, its meaning is not; as Roland Barthes observes, 'Myth is not defined by the object of its message, but by the way in which it utters this message: there are formal limits to myth, there are no "substantial" ones' (Barthes 1957: 117).

With each repeated viewing of the Zapruder film, do we still simply see it for what it is, see the death? This question might seem needlessly obfuscating, but at issue is how we look at any image that is so familiar that we already know it intimately before we begin the process of re-viewing. Iconic documentary material such as this is, in part, forever severed from its historical and narrative contextualisation. The killing of President Kennedy is perpetually reworked in the present; each theory about who killed Kennedy and why urges us to impose a closure on these malleable images, adopting the language of certainty ('who killed Kennedy will be shown here for the first time'[5]) whilst knowing presumably that they will be superseded in due course by a new theory, a new set of certainties. The Zapruder film remains the core text of the Kennedy assassination, 'invisibly back-projected on all the other film evidence' (Simon 1996: 47), and our obsession with it is in no small part due to our ambivalent desire to have it both reveal and keep hidden the truth behind the 'world's greatest murder mystery'.[6] Its iconic and fetishistic status is due to its familiarity and its instability as evidence; Zapruder captures a public death and presents us with a personal viewing experience (a home movie) – as Errol Morris comments, 'we're there … it's happening before our eyes'.[7] If a piece of archive footage becomes so familiar that a mere allusion to one detail or one frame triggers off a recollection of the whole, then the experience of watching that film is not simply that of observing the representation of an actual event. The Zapruder film has significance beyond the sum of its parts; despite its subject matter, it begins to function like a melodrama, to comfort the viewer almost with its known-ness, its familiarity. Knowing the end ironically frees us to speculate upon alternatives ('what if ?', 'if only'), to reconstruct the sequence just as we see it relentlessly repeating the very events we are trying to suppress. This is particularly the case when it comes to the frames immediately prior to the shot hitting Kennedy's head; the pause (even at real speed) between gun shots always seems implausibly long, Kennedy is slumping into his wife's arms and Zapruder has almost lost him from view when suddenly the right side of his head explodes. In that hiatus between points of intense violence, the impulse is to re-imagine history.

The Zapruder film shows us everything and it shows us nothing; it is explicit but cannot conclusively confirm or deny any version of the assassination. Perhaps, cynically, one could proffer this as the reason for its enduring mystique, that because it will never solve the murder mystery it is a perfect fantasy text. Too often the indissoluble ambivalence of the Zapruder film is forgotten in favour of an 'anything goes' approach to it as a historical document that has no meaning until it has been interpreted or given a story, an attitude that Wasson succumbs to when treating the footage as just another cultural artefact, suggesting that the 'film *qua* film quickly dissolves, becoming intimately linked to the cultural phenomena which infuse it' (Wasson 1995: 10). This conclusion resembles the inflexible formalism of Hayden White (1987: 76) as he says that 'any historical object can sustain a number of equally plausible descriptions or narratives'. The essential ambiguity surrounding Zapruder's images hinges on the awareness that their narrativisability does not engulf or entirely obscure their veracity. Nichols is thereby wrong to believe that inconclusive pieces of film record such as Zapruder's leave the event 'up for grabs' (Nichols 1994: 121–2); what is 'up for grabs' is the interpretation of that event. If the footage's realness is merely to be fused with its imaginative potential, then why is the actual Zapruder film so different from and more affecting than its imitators, all of which effectively represent the same event? There have been countless reconstructions of the home movie fragment, from a dream sequence in John Waters' *Eat Your Makeup* (1966) in which Divine parodies Jackie Kennedy reliving the day of the assassination, to the countless more earnest versions made for quasi-factual biopics, to the documentary restagings of the events undertaken (from the Warren Commission onwards) to attempt to establish the facts. One anomaly is that the closer or more faithful the imitation is to the Zapruder original, the more it emphasises its difference from it. An interesting example of a Zapruder re-enactment is the accurate reconstruction undertaken for *The Trial of Lee Harvey Oswald* (David Greene, 1976), a film made before copies of the Zapruder were widely available. The Zapruder simulation is repeatedly used during the hypothetical trial of the film's title, and those in the courtroom are shocked by what they see. But whilst Oliver Stone's *JFK*, in a comparable courtroom situation, uses the real Zapruder footage digitally enhanced, enlarged and slowed down (thus compelling the cinema spectator to identify directly with the diegetic audience's horror), the reconstruction for *The Trial of Lee Harvey Oswald* differs from its prototype in one crucial respect: it omits the blood and gore of the fatal shot to Kennedy's head. This is citation, not replication – a mythologised rendering of the original, brutal snuff movie.

The ultimate, uncomfortable paradox of the Zapruder film as raw evidence is that the more it is exposed to scrutiny, with frames singled out and details digitally enhanced, the more unstable and inconclusive the images become. The industry of what Don Delillo has termed 'blur analysis'[8] has always flourished, but the results are confusing and frequently fanciful, despite Simon's assertion that

The film must be slowed down to be legible; its twenty-two seconds go by too fast for its vital content to be adequately studied. As a result, it speaks its own impossibility as film. ... Its status as evidence relies simultaneously on duration and its arrest, film and still frame.

(Simon 1996: 48)

Run at proper speed, the Zapruder footage is brief and incomplete; the action starts and stops convulsively, in mid-action. This indeterminacy is the overriding characteristic of accidental footage, its jolting, fragmentary quality not only producing an unfinished narrative, but also preventing a conscious viewpoint from being imposed on the images by either the person filming or the audience. The speed with which the assassination occurs is thereby a crucial factor, as Noël Carroll (1996a: 228), intimates: 'Unexpected events can intrude into the viewfinder – e.g., Lee Harvey Oswald's assassination – before there is time for a personal viewpoint to crystallize.'

The paradox remains, however, that it is only when viewed at proper speed that the true impact of Kennedy's death becomes apparent. In his analysis of the trial of the LAPD officers accused of beating Rodney King in March 1991, Bill Nichols suggests that, far from being an elucidating technique, the slowing down of the original George Holliday video tape could be used to distort the facts, as the LAPD defence team demonstrated with their assiduous dissection of the same footage that the prosecution alleged proved their case for police brutality to corroborate their case for acquittal. The defence argument

appeared to fly in the face of common sense. But it took the *form* of a positivist, scientific interpretation. It did what any good examination of evidence should do: it scrutinised it with care and drew from it (apparent) substantiation for an interpretation that best accounted for what really happened.

(Nichols 1994: 30)

Similar distortions have occurred around the Kennedy assassination. Two examples are the magnifications of a piece of film and a portion of a photograph – Robert Hughes's film showing the Texas School Book Depository and Mary Moorman's photograph showing the Grassy Knoll. Both have been digitally enhanced to the point of allegedly revealing shady figures at a window or crouched behind a picket fence. The evidence, in the enhanced versions, might be convincing, but played at real speed or unmagnified these two records of the assassination day appear inconclusive, the results of a desperate desire to find something plausibly human amidst the play on light and shade. One person's figure is another person's shadow.

The Zapruder film (and Holliday's video of Rodney King) make us perhaps question 'the truth-bearing capacities of film' (Simon 1996: 48). This returns us to the notion that Abraham Zapruder's camera, though able to produce an unfailingly authentic record of the Kennedy assassination, is pointing the wrong way, that the film may just be one of many texts that can be used to explain the assassination, not the only one. Still one of the most compelling investigative films made about the assassination and its aftermath is Emile de Antonio's *Rush to Judgement* (1966) on which he collaborated with lawyer Mark Lane. Lane had written a book of the same name, published on 15 August 1966, that took issue with key areas of the Warren Commission Report, made public on 27 September, 1964. Neither the book nor the film attempts to solve the 'murder mystery' of the assassination, but merely to insinuate that the Warren Commission's conclusions are unconvincing and that there are grounds for arguing that there had been a conspiracy to kill Kennedy; hence the adoption in both of an examination/cross-examination structure. As Lane stipulates in the documentary's first piece to camera, the film will be making 'the case for the defence'. More tantalising than the inconclusiveness of the Zapruder footage is the lack of testimony from Lee Oswald, Oswald having been shot in the basement of the Dallas police headquarters by Jack Ruby on 24 November as he was being escorted to the County Jail. *Rush to Judgement* is the first of several television and film attempts to give Oswald's defence a 'voice'.[9] The majority of the film's interviewees support the theory that Kennedy was shot at least once from the front as seems logical from the movement backwards of the President's head in the Zapruder footage; it is ironic and apposite, therefore, that the majority of de Antonio's witnesses are facing the Grassy Knoll, and so literally looking the other way from Zapruder. With the absence of any archive material of the assassination itself, *Rush to Judgement* is reliant on memory presented, within its prosecutional framework, as testimony. The difference between the Zapruder film and *Rush to Judgement* is the difference between the event and memory, between a filmed representation of a specific truth and the articulation of a set of related, contingent versions. In a film such as *Rush to Judgement* the human eye replaces the mechanical eye as the instrument of accurate or convincing memory; as the photographic evidence yields fewer rather than more certainties, the eye-witnesses interviewed by de Antonio and others usurp its position. The obvious problem with the growing dependency (from the 1960s onwards) on interviews as evidence not (supposedly) overly manipulated by the *auteur*-director, is that what can too easily be revealed is a series of truths (or what individuals take to be truths) not a single, underpinning truth. Just as the Zapruder film remains an inconclusive text, so *Rush to Judgement* ensures that the assassination inquiries are not closed by the appearance of one hastily compiled report, having one interviewee, Penn Jones, state directly to camera at the end of the film:

> I would love to see a computer, faced with the problem of probabilities of the assassination taking place the way it did, with all these strange incidents which took place before and are continuing to take place after the assassination.[10] I think all of us who love our country should be alerted that something is wrong in the land.

The fundamental discrepancy between 'raw' archive material as exemplified by the Zapruder film and a memory/interview-based documentary such as *Rush to Judgement* highlights the source for the growing disillusionment with the notion of image as document. If pieces of unpremeditated archive as ostensibly uncontaminated and artless as Zapruder's or Holliday's home movies can produce contradictory but credible interpretations, then the idea of the 'pure' documentary which theorists have tacitly invoked is itself vulnerable. In *Il Giorno della Civetta* the Sicilian writer Leonardo Sciascia adopts the artichoke as a metaphor for describing the authorities' pursuit of the Mafia: that no matter how many leaves the police or the judiciary tear away, they never reach its heart, or if they do, its heart proves to be a strangely inconclusive place. Likewise the hounding of the 'pure' documentary; for is it not the case (as with gruesome and ubiquitous reality television or the stop-frame 'blur analysis' to which the Zapruder and Holliday films have both been subjected) that the closer one gets to the document itself, the more aware one becomes of the artifice and the impossibility of a satisfactory relationship between the image and the real? Not that reality television should be doubted and immediately classified as manipulative fiction, but even the least adulterated image can only reveal so much. The very 'unimpeachability' or stability of the original documents that form the basis for archival non-fiction films is brought into question; the document – though showing a concluded, historical event – is not fixed, but is infinitely accessible through interpretation and recontextualisation, and thus becomes a mutable, not a constant, point of reference. A necessary dialectic is involved between the factual source and its representation that acknowledges the limitations as well as the credibility of the document itself. The Zapruder film is factually accurate, it is not a fake, but it cannot reveal the motive or cause for the actions it shows. The document, though real, is incomplete.

The compilation film and Emile de Antonio

As a consequence of this, archive material has rarely been used unadulterated and unexplained within the context of documentary film, rather it has primarily been deployed in one of two ways: illustratively, as part of a historical exposition to complement other elements such as interviews and voice-over; or critically, as part of a more politicised historical argument or debate. The former usage, as exemplified by series such as *The World at War*, *The Vietnam War*, *The Nazis: A Lesson From History*, *The People's Century* or *The Cold War* is straightforward in that it is not asking the spectator to question the archival documents but simply to absorb them as a component of a larger narrative. Within this category of archive reliant documentary, the origin of the footage is rarely an issue, as the material is used to illustrate general or specific events and is usually explained by a voice-over and interviewees. The alternative political approach to found footage – for which the derivation of such archive is a significant issue and which frequently uses such material dialectically or against the grain – has a long-standing history and is more complex. The 'compilation film' (a documentary constructed almost exclusively out of retrieved archive) was pioneered by

Soviet filmmakers Esther Shub and Dziga Vertov in the 1920s, both of whom worked within a revolutionary tradition which believed in political, instructive and inspirational cinema. The importance of Shub particularly was that she applied to non-fiction film (although the Soviets endlessly debated the validity of the fiction/non-fiction divide – see Tretyakov *et al.* 1927) the 'montage of attractions' most readily associated with Sergei Eisenstein, whom she had employed as her editing assistant. Jay Leyda comments of Shub's films that they

> brought back to life footage that had hitherto been regarded as having, at the most, only the nature of historical fragments. By the juxtaposition of these 'bits of reality', she was able to achieve effects of irony, absurdity, pathos and grandeur that few of the bits had intrinsically.
>
> (Leyda 1983: 224)

Two stages of 'compilation' are indicated here, one which involves collation and discovery and another which requires assimilation and analysis. Shub's method was to both focus on the original footage and recontextualise it. Exemplary of Shub's way of working is the film she made to commemorate the February 1917 overthrow of the imperial family, *The Fall of the Romanovs* (1927) – a revolutionary, pro-Bolshevik film that was, nevertheless, largely dependent on antipathetic, pro-Tsarist material. It thereby exhibits the dependency upon dialectical collision between the inherent perspective of the original archive and its radical re-use that remains a characteristic of the compilation documentary. In the summer of 1926, Shub travelled to Leningrad where she found that much of the relevant pre-Revolutionary newsreel footage had been damaged or had disappeared, although she did come across the private home movies of Nicholas II and some 60,000 metres of film, of which she chose 5,200 metres to take back to Moscow (Leyda 1996: 58–9). Of her structuring of this found footage, Shub says:

> In the montage I tried to avoid looking at the newsreel material for its own sake, and to maintain the principle of its documentary quality. All was subordinated to the theme. This gave me the possibility, in spite of the known limitations of the photographed events and facts, to link the meanings of the material so that it evoked the pre-Revolutionary period and the February days.
>
> (Leyda 1996: 59)

The significant observation here is the idea that a clear distinction exists between 'newsreel' and 'documentary', and, following on from this, that whilst the newsreel is limited to showing events, it is the function of a documentary to provide structure and meaning. A documentary, a structured and motivated non-fiction film, does not aspire to convey in as pure a way as possible the real material at its core because this is what newsreel or other comparable forms of amateur, accidental and non-narrative film do.

Shub's compilation film technique conforms to the tradition of dialectical, political filmmaking, to the idea expressed by Eisenstein that 'the expressive effect of cinema is the result of juxtapositions' (Eisenstein 1926: 147). The events retraced in *The Fall of the Romanovs* do not just 'speak for themselves', and Shub's intention is to use archive material extrapolated from its original context to offer a reinterpretation of events and to effect 'the politicised activation of "suppressed" ideas or the inversion of conventional meanings' (Arthur 1997: 2). In *The Fall of the Romanovs*, Shub both straightforwardly tells the story of the events leading up to the revolution and passes commentary on why it occurred. Juxtapositions are frequently set up via the film's brief intertitles. Near the beginning, one such intertitle draws attention to the vast expanses of land owned and overseen by a wealthy few, followed by a piece of film illustrating this claim that concludes with an exterior shot of what we subsequently learn is the sumptuous residence of the governor of Kaluga. Following the exterior shot, there is an intertitle 'And next to them – this', followed by images of tiny peasant mud huts. The implications of social injustice are quite obvious, but, like Eisenstein, what Shub then does, once the initial juxtaposition has been established, is to intercut a variety of images that further illustrate this social difference without feeling the need to explicate them. Shub's method is not to disappear the archive's origins and potential original meaning as Arthur implies (it remains significant that the images of the governor of Kaluga descending the steps of his vast residence with his wife on his arm is home movie footage – personal material that, of itself, signals immense privilege) but rather to preserve that meaning whilst simultaneously imposing a fresh interpretative framework. Hayden White dwells on the idea that it is narrative that gives the real historical event cogency, arguing that it is only through the presence of a story that the inherent meaning of events can be revealed or understood and that 'To be historical, an event must be more than a singular occurrence, a unique happening. It receives its definition from its contribution to the development of a plot' (White 1987: 51). Conversely, Shub and others who followed her do not condemn the unnarrativised event as indecipherable until it has been positioned within a developmental structure, rather they posit that there is a fruitful dialogue to be had between original newsreel, home movie footage and the like and the critical eye of the filmmaker (and the implied new audience). A documentary, as Tretyakov and others intimate, will never be merely the Zapruder film or the Kaluga governor's home movie, it will always be, to some degree, the creative treatment of actuality.

The most important compilation documentary filmmaker is the American Emile de Antonio, who made a series of documentaries, from *Point of Order* (1963) to *Mr Hoover and I* (1989), that scrutinised and assessed recent American history. His films are notably Soviet in their intent: formally radical and rooted to the idea that meaning is constructed through editing, they mirror de Antonio's Marxist intentions and his distrust of more conventional documentary modes such as observational cinema and the use of didactic narration; they use archive material provocatively and dialectically and compel audiences to think, to question and to seek change.[11] De Antonio is a strong advocate of bias and of the foregrounding of opinion, thereby undermining the notion that documentary is principally concerned with transparency and non-intervention. It is therefore ironic that the question of authorship has frequently plagued compilation filmmakers: Shub found that critics considered *The Fall of the Romanovs* not to be her film and de Antonio had *Point of Order* (a re-editing of the televised 1954 McCarthy vs Army hearings) excluded from the 1963 New York film festival on the grounds that 'it was television and not film' (Weiner 1971: 10).[12] De Antonio's work offers the most comprehensive articulation of the ideas first expressed by Shub about the polemical potential of archive film. One interviewer terms de Antonio's method 'radical scavenging' (Weiner 1971): revisiting existing footage to construct out of it an alternative and maybe even directly oppositional narrative from that which it inherently possesses.

Just as Shub and those who follow her create a dialectical relationship between original film and its recontextualisation, so they do not believe that the marked clarity of their own political position will stand in the way of audiences formulating their own opinions. In one interview, whilst attacking American *cinéma vérité* ('Only people without feelings or convictions could even think of making *cinéma vérité*'), de Antonio states: 'I happen to have strong feelings and some dreams and my prejudice is under and in everything I do' (Rosenthal 1978: 7). This 'prejudice' informs de Antonio's treatment of his audience; his films are difficult, they 'make demands on the audience' (Weiner 1971: 13), thus immediately recalling Eisenstein's view, with reference to *Strike*, that film should plough the audience's psyche. Like Eisenstein's, de Antonio's films are furtively didactic. Despite his films' democratic intention (not wanting to teach but to reveal) de Antonio wants his audience to arrive at the same conclusion as himself, a method he calls 'democratic didacticism' (Waugh 1985: 244). This term neatly embodies de Antonio's particular brand of archive documentary that instructs without divesting the spectator or the re-edited archive of independence of thought. De Antonio's films aim to convince the audience of the arguments put forward, they are passionate as well as intellectual and articulate, constructed around 'a kind of collage junk idea I got from my painter friends' of working with 'dead footage' (Rosenthal 1978: 4).[13] 'Collage junk' is central to de Antonio's notion of 'democratic didacticism' as it is through the juxtaposition of 'people, voices, images and ideas' that he is able to develop a 'didactic line' that nevertheless eschews overtly didactic mechanisms such as voice-over (Weiner 1971: 6). De Antonio refutes entirely the purely illustrative function of archive material, instead the original pieces of film become mutable, active ingredients. Imperative to de Antonio's idea of 'democratic didacticism', though, is that the innate meaning of this original footage, however it is reconstituted, is never entirely obscured. One vivid, consistent facet of de Antonio's work is that his collage method does not attack hate figures such as Richard Nixon, Joseph McCarthy or Colonel Patton directly, but rather gives them enough rope by which to hang themselves – turning often favourable original footage in on itself.

To witness McCarthy's demise on live television is far more effective (both live in 1954 and in 1963, the date of *Point of Order*'s release) than being told, with hindsight, that the American political establishment finally realised that the junior senator was a bigoted, drunken liar. De Antonio is fond of recounting how, despite years of trying, McCarthy's counsel, Roy Cohn, was unable to nail de Antonio for manipulation of the facts: 'There is no finer flattery nor more delicious treachery than verbatim quotation' (Tuchman 1990: 66). Several of the sequences in *Point of Order* belie this innocence, the most ostentatious example being the end of the film. In this sequence de Antonio imposes a narrative structure that shows McCarthy continuing a bumbling, verbose diatribe against Senator Symington, while those present pack their bags and clear the chamber, concluding with a final shot – a photograph – of the empty committee chamber. De Antonio constructs this sequence using a collage of disparate, not necessarily sequential images, using such non-synchronous material to suggest that the establishment, who previously had sustained him, finally turns its back on McCarthy. The duality of *Point of Order* is that de Antonio constructs its narrative and meaning out of footage over which, in the first instance, he had no authorial control, hence Cohn's distrust of de Antonio as well as his inability to find libellous bias in the film. De Antonio succinctly identifies the mechanism whereby this duality is possible when commenting, 'Honesty and objectivity are not the same thing. Nor are they even closely related' (Weiss 1974: 35). *Point of Order* is 'honest' in that all the images it collates are irrefutably real, and yet it is not 'objective' because those same images have been resituated to suit and argue de Antonio's perspective of the events they show. What a film like *Point of Order* elucidates very clearly is the problem of equating the image ostensibly without bias with the truth (and the cameras deployed for the McCarthy vs Army hearings are as non-interventionist as possible, simply focusing on who is speaking). His 'collage junk' films are an astute, ironic dismantling of this assumption.

De Antonio's work clearly illustrates not only that original footage is open to interpretation and manipulation, but that general theses can be extrapolated from specific historical images and that the historical event does not only reside in the past but is inevitably connected to the present. De Antonio's Marxism thus underpins all his documentaries. Walter Benjamin in 'Theses on the Philosophy of History' suggests that historical materialists should disassociate themselves from the victors of history and the maintaining of the status quo and instead 'brush history against the grain' (Benjamin 1955: 259). A similar stance is adopted by de Antonio, whose films seek to draw out the subsidiary, buried, unofficial text of American history. In certain instances the link between past and present is explicitly made, as in *In the Year of the Pig* (1969) in which de Antonio, in a documentary which spans the years between French colonial rule of Vietnam and the Tet Offensive of 1968, examines the (then) contemporary war in direct relation to the history of imperialist intervention in Indochina. De Antonio's intention is to offer the 'intellectual and historical overview' (Rosenthal 1978: 9) lacking, he argued, from the blanket but unanalytical

Figure 1.1   In the Year of the Pig

Source: Courtesy of BFI Stills, Posters and Designs

newsreel coverage of the war. Whereas so many subsequent films about Vietnam (*Dear America*, for instance) marginalise the problem of American intervention in Vietnam by stressing the personal effect of the war on the GIs, *In the Year of the Pig* dwells almost exclusively upon historical contextualisation. The photo montage sequence which opens the film, contrasts (with black leader in between) the image of a Civil War soldier who died at Gettysburg with a photograph of a GI in Vietnam with 'Make war not love' daubed on his helmet (Figure 1.1). This counterpointing highlights the imminent loss of life awaiting the troops in Vietnam; it also represents the immorality, as de Antonio sees it, of the American position, that 'our cause in Vietnam was not the one that boy had died for in 1863' (Crowdus and Georgakas 1988: 168), hence the reprise of the Gettysburg image – in negative and accompanied by a scratchy version of *The Battle Hymn of the Republic* – at the end of the film. Both *In the Year of the Pig*'s cumulative structure and its use of individual images, serve the desire to endlessly contextualise and reassess the present. A universal truth that emerges through the film via the many images of cultivation and farming, Ho Chi Minh walking through the jungle and GIs lying dead amidst the undergrowth is that any attempt to defeat the North Vietnamese will always be futile, for not only have they suffered and recovered from a cycle of attacks and invasions throughout history, but their endurance is symptomatic of their lifestyle, their affinity with the land and the American inability to conquer it. Vietnam in this context represents stability. Complementing this overall argument are the potent specific images, such as the sequence showing French colonisers in white hats and suits being pulled in rickshaws by some Vietnamese, getting out at a café where a Moroccan in a fez brusquely dismisses the Vietnamese when they hold out their hands for payment. For de Antonio this 1930s scene 'encapsulates the whole French colonial empire' (Crowdus and Georgakas 1988: 167), and is 'the equivalent of a couple of chapters of dense writing about the meaning of colonialism' (Crowdus and Georgakas 1988: 167). This may be an overestimation of its capacity (much of the scene's impact stems from its contextualisation within a confrontational and polemical film), but the sequence nevertheless reflects upon itself as a historical document and upon its contemporary relevance to the much later American aggression.

The most enduring aspect of de Antonio's work is its use of collage techniques to offer an ironic and humorous critique of American history – a quality directly echoed by *The Atomic Café*, to be discussed at the end of this chapter. *Millhouse: A White Comedy* (1971), notable as a pre-Watergate anti-Nixon film, is, as the title suggests, a documentary comedy. Like most of de Antonio's films, how *Millhouse* came to be made is just as important as what it says or how it says it. The film was the major reason for de Antonio's presence (on whom the FBI had already amassed a substantial file) on Nixon's 'enemies' list, something of which he was inordinately proud, claiming that the ten White House files on him were, above the film awards he had won, his 'ultimate prize' (Rosenthal 1978: 8). Whilst he was cutting *Painters Painting*, de Antonio received an anonymous telephone call from someone saying he had stolen all the Nixon footage from one of the television networks and that he was willing to give de Antonio the material for nothing if he would make a film out of it. De Antonio agreed, and 200 cans of films were dropped off one night at the building where he was editing. In order to preserve the anonymity of his source and to ensure that the FBI could not trace the material, de Antonio had all the film's edge numbers erased. This is characteristic de Antonio 'derring-do'. Because of the sensitivity of their subject matter, most of his films attracted secret service or police attention (which never ultimately prevented their release): whilst setting up *Rush to Judgement* witnesses were intercepted and scared off before de Antonio could interview them; the film, tapes and negatives of his interview with the Weathermen (the basis for *Underground*) were subpoenaed by the FBI – an action which prompted many from Hollywood to rally to his support; he was arrested, along with the Ploughshares 8, for demonstrating outside a nuclear plant during the production of *In the King of Prussia*. The documentaries are an audacious fusion of intention, content and form; they are both personal and universal. *Millhouse*, on a basic level, is an expression of de Antonio's own personal hatred for Nixon's 'essential creepiness' (Weiner 1971: 4–5) which he always thought would be Nixon's final undoing.[14] In addition, the film is a complex attack on the political system that sustained Nixon and permitted him to repeatedly resuscitate his career despite his endless shady dealings. The comic and political elements are necessarily intertwined, as Nixon afforded so many opportunities for satire; *Millhouse*'s 'Six Crises' structure, for instance, ironically mimics Nixon's pre-presidential memoirs, *Six Crises*. From the early years spent hounding Alger Hiss in 1948 (and the absurd discovery of some incriminating film in a pumpkin in Whittaker Chambers' garden)[15] or smearing his opponent Helen Gahagan Douglas's name during their 1950 senatorial contest, Nixon's 'creepiness' and comic potential serially endangered his progression as a politician.

An essential component of the dialectics that inform *Millhouse* is the tussle at its heart between its comic and its serious political tendencies. Nixon (as opposed to his manipulation by de Antonio) is frequently the direct source of the film's comedy. *Millhouse* consistently focuses upon and derives humour from Nixon's painstaking and painful reconstructions of his own media persona, particularly at moments of crisis. As de Antonio comments:

> What Nixon has been able to do in his political life is totally transform his exterior, his external personality. ... Nixon is packaging himself, and that is the importance of the Checkers speech. The Nixon of Checkers is a different creature than the Nixon of Cambodia 1970, or the Nixon of the 1968 campaign, or the Nixon who went to China.
>
> (Weiss 1974: 32)

The power of *Millhouse* is that it makes a logical link between Nixon's perpetual reinvention of himself (his courting of the media and his superficiality) and the appropriateness of the 'collage junk' method that fabricates meaning from juxtaposing an eclectic group of images. De Antonio observed that Nixon was paradoxically obsessed with the media and overly preoccupied with 'shielding himself from the American people' (Weiss 1974: 32), of hiding his innate untrustworthiness behind a faltering masquerade of Horatio Alger little-man-made-good sincerity. Satirical compilation films are inherently dependent upon the surface value of archive, and the opening sequence of *Millhouse* establishes the tone for much of the ensuing attack on Nixon's superficiality and the values it represents, as Nixon's wax effigy in Madame Tussaud's is assembled to the announcement 'The President of the United States' and the bombastic strains of *Hail to the Chief*. *Millhouse* dismantles Nixon's self-created image, piecing together an excruciating caricature of the 'poor, wretched, clumsy mixed-up man' as de Antonio calls him (Crowdus and Georgakas 1988: 174). De Antonio's Nixon resembles a puppet, a dummy that has learnt a series of mannerisms. There are, for example, the two rapid montages of Nixon executing his most memorable gesture of raising both hands above his head in a V and the overlapping of Nixon's 1968 'I see a day' convention speech with Martin Luther King's earlier 'I have a dream' (from which, *Millhouse* insinuates, it was plagiarised). Nixon's performances masked a vacuum at their core – a point underlined in an interview specially shot for *Millhouse* with a high school companion who, despite being his friend, 'can't think of an anecdote' to tell about Nixon.

The comic moments of *Millhouse* often centre upon Nixon's perception and performance of himself. An exemplary sequence would be the one centring on Nixon's arrival at the White House after his victory in 1968. The sequence is as follows:

Part of a specially shot interview with an aide explaining how Nixon described himself as 'an intellectual' and 'called himself at one point the egg-head of the Republican party'. Cut to:

Archive of an early presidential press conference at which Nixon, flanked by his family, itemises his hobbies as reading and history, stressing that he does not read Westerns or watch much television, in the process making a dig at his predecessor Lyndon Johnson by quipping, 'we've removed some of the television sets', an aside that is greeted with laughter. Cut to:

A continuation of the first interview in which the aide, barely able to suppress a smirk, recounts how Nixon told him he would rather be teaching 'in a school like Oxford' and writing books. Cut to:

Lengthy sequence showing an evening of White House entertainment comprising an instrumental, expressive dance version of *Satisfaction*, a song to Nixon ('Mr Nixon is the only one'), a homophobic joke by Bob Hope (who is also the MC), Nixon thanking Hope by quoting James Thurber who 'once wrote that the oldest and most precious national asset of this century is humour' and wishing him well for the show's overseas tour (presumably of Vietnam).

In this sequence, the comedy results from de Antonio's juxtaposition of collated material to ridicule Nixon's pompous opinion of his own intellectuality. The attacks on him are direct (as in the interview) and indirect (as in the juxtaposition of Nixon's self-aggrandisement with some particularly tawdry White House entertainment); Nixon also shows himself up by quoting James Thurber during

Figure 1.2 Millhouse: A White Comedy
Source: Courtesy of BFI Stills, Posters and Designs

a sequence putatively illustrative of his intellectuality (Figure 1.2). The power of a sequence such as this resides in its effortless ability to make us laugh at Nixon and signalling a very clear point of view without resorting to direct authorial intervention or overtly didactic means. The analytical montage in this sequence also serves to demonstrate de Antonio's (and our) intellectual superiority to Nixon, a patronising tone that characterises many comic compilation films.

This analytical, intellectual approach to historical documentary filmmaking is manifested not merely in the way Nixon the individual is reassessed, but in how the system he epitomises is also scrutinised. As de Antonio comments, 'This film [*Millhouse*] attacks the System, the credibility of the System, by focusing on the obvious and perfect symbol for that system' (Weiner 1971: 4). Repeatedly, what de Antonio attempts in his documentaries is not the articulation of a solution to a problem but the exposure of what is wrong, the infinitely corruptible and corrupting political and ideological system that dominated America during the period he was making films (1963–89). In this, the films remain both democratic and radical. Through charting Nixon's shady history and through the comic analysis of Nixon's chaotic relationship with his image, the successful 1968 presidential candidate comes to be depicted as a puppet, a figurehead of a machine.[16] The serious political intent of *Millhouse* is most clearly manifested in sequences that focus upon Nixon's role as leader; this is when de Antonio vents his political hatred, as exemplified by the documentary's sequence concerning Vietnam and the escalation of the conflict under the Nixon administration. The sequence, near the end (like Eisenstein, de Antonio increases the complexity and aggression of his montage sequences progressively through his films), begins with a résumé of the history of American interference in Vietnam, subsequently arriving at the present. The contemporary section of the sequence is as follows:

A speech by Nixon in which he comments, 'In the previous administration we Americanised the war in Vietnam. In this administration we are Vietnamising the search for peace.' Cut to:

A map of Indochina being gradually shaded black – North and South Vietnam followed by Cambodia and then Laos, over which a woman's voice quotes Mao Tse Tung: 'The people may be likened unto water and the guerrilla band unto fish'. Cut to:

Graphic stating the South Vietnamese casualties of war to date (1,000,000) and the number of refugees (6,000,000). As this graphic fades, the woman's voice quotes from the *New York Times*: 'In this year, 1971, more civilians are being wounded in the three countries of Indochina and more made refugees than at any time in history', a statement that continues over the same Nixon speech as before, this time mute.
   Nixon's speech continues, this time with synch sound, as he pledges that his aim is for South Vietnamese forces to 'assume full responsibility for South Vietnam', a comment overlaid onto footage of South Vietnamese soldiers marching. Cut to:

The filled in map of Indochina accompanied by the woman's voice-over: 'Two and a half Hiroshimas a week.' Cut to:

Another Nixon speech in which he promises that the US stand to gain nothing from the Vietnam war except 'the possibility that the people of South Vietnam will be able to choose their own way in the world'. Superimposed onto Nixon as he speaks is a long list of American companies who are profiting from the war. Cut to:

A protest march.

The target here is Nixon's mendacity concerning the escalation of the war in Indochina under his administration, each image and piece of sound (and it is interesting that the narrated quotations function as components of the collage) being used to embellish this point. The sequence is raw and intense, reaching a crescendo with the significantly uncredited piece of voice-over making the elliptical comment 'two and a half Hiroshimas a week' and the scrolling list of

American companies sustaining the war. Illustrative of the dangerous as opposed to comic potential of Nixon's untruthfulness, this sequence also emphasises his part in history and his political role; the moment at which Nixon is mute as the voice-over recounts the South Vietnamese casualties of the conflict so far being a reminder of both his untrustworthiness and his impotence.

As exemplified by *Millhouse: A White Comedy*, de Antonio's style combines comedy with acute and angry political commentary. His documentaries are overtly confrontational, radical in both form and content. De Antonio's preoccupation was American post-war political history; he distrusted politicians and sought an intellectual mode of filmmaking capable of magnifying their flaws and exposing both the shortcomings of the electoral system and the inadequacy (as de Antonio saw it) of conventional documentary forms to radically reassess notions of factual representation and analysis. His ethos of 'collage junk' has been copied and reworked many times, and has become an instrumental component of documentaries of historical analysis. From it can be taken several things, most importantly the twin notions that all documentaries, because the product of individuals, will always display bias and be in some manner didactic, and that there is no such thing as incontrovertible truth, as each document or factual image, when made to conflict with another, finds its meaning irretrievably modified. Contextualisation, not merely the image itself, can create meaning; history, which de Antonio refers to as being the theme of all his films (Crowdus and Georgakas 1988), is perpetually modified by its re-enactment in the present.

Modern examples: Historical television documentaries; The Atomic Café

De Antonio saw himself as a pioneer of a 'new' documentary form that prioritised the compilation and juxtaposition of interviews and archive. The 1960s was very much the era of the observational documentary (and drama documentary) focusing upon the present, on actions that were unfolding contemporaneously with the filmmaking process. By the 1970s, more emphasis was placed upon contextualisation and history, and with this arrived an increased dependency on compilation and interviews. The two traditions of archive documentaries have persisted: the historical television series or strand that uses archive material illustratively and films such as *The Atomic Café* (which thanks de Antonio in the end credits), which adopt the polemical, confrontational style of de Antonio.

The conventional television use of archive is largely non-dialectical, the purpose of its retrieved archive being to demonstrate what has already been or is in the process of being signalled by other information sources such as the voice-over or the words of interviewees. Arguably it is thus the more didactic, formal aspect of a series such as *The Cold War* (Jeremy Isaacs, 1998), namely its voice-over, that defines its identity. Within this hierarchy, words guide the audience's responses to the archival image, whether this is Kenneth Branagh's voice-over or the words of eye-witnesses and the testimonies of experts. During Episode 2 ('Iron Curtain, 1945–1947') there is a short sequence that exemplifies both uses of the voice to determine and define our interpretation of found footage. Telling the story of the immediate aftermath of World War Two at the time of the British, American and Soviet control of Germany, a terse piece of narration ('Berlin – the final battlefield') prefaces familiar aerial shots of a devastated German capital (endless rubble, buildings reduced to shells), followed by a more personalised account of the period by a German female interviewee recounting being raped by a Russian soldier which, in turn, is intercut with footage of women hanging their heads or looking pleadingly at the camera. Within this short *Cold War* sequence there are two distinct uses of archive. The Berlin footage (which one could term 'iconic' in that it has become so much part of the way in which we collectively recall the end of the war) is inserted to substantiate the information, already elliptically given in the voice-over, that the city, in 1945, had been the site of the Nazis' final resistance and capitulation against the Allied forces. In this the visual material performs a corroborative, illustrative function within what is effectively a documentary lecture on the beginnings of the Cold War; the images are contextualised and explained even as they appear, and their viewing, whilst enhancing our assimilation of the events under discussion, does not promote debate or argument. The audience is not invited to speculate upon the origins of the material or any possible discrepancy between original and current meaning; this use of archive is not combative or political, and the edits between images and voice offer a cumulative as opposed to a dialectical understanding of the event they represent.

The second use of archive exemplified by the above sequence (in a similarly non-interventionist vein) is the insertion of general or non-specific images to accompany the distressing recollection by the woman interviewee of her first experience of rape. Although, once more, the archive is used illustratively, the relationship between word and image differs from that of the preceding example in that there is only an inferred or contrived correlation between the two. We have no means of knowing what the actual motivation for the women's despair in these images is, they are only given a specific connotation (that women were regularly raped by the occupying Russian soldiers in Berlin) by being juxtaposed with the interviewee's personal account. It is often the case that there is no footage available to illustrate a verbal description of a past event, so a filmmaker must resort to generic images that offer an approximate representation. This use of generic archive provokes a common slippage in historical documentaries, namely that the non-specific image ('desperate women' in Berlin circa 1945) has imposed upon it a new, precise and, by definition, transient signification that may or may not correlate with its original meaning. The 'generic' use of archive is an economic measure used in *The Cold War* and other similar documentaries to convey to the audience the memories invoked by eye-witness or expert accounts; the raped woman herself is not represented by the images, but her trauma and its potential emotive effect on us is. An audience understands this convention which, in turn, suggests that the same archival images could be recycled again and used as the 'figurative' representation of an entirely different story or situation. Paul Arthur sheds doubt upon the entire enterprise of using archive footage within a documentary context, when commenting that the dissonance between personal recollection and images

> raises the spectre of ... partiality. Documentarists who would never dream of restaging an event with actors do not hesitate in creating collages that amount to metaphoric fabrications of reality. The guarantees of authenticity ostensibly secured by archival footage are largely a myth.
>
> (Arthur 1997: 6)

As de Antonio's films showed, it is possible for re-used footage to retain vestiges of its original meaning, however reconfigured, a potential that Arthur's blanket condemnation excludes, although it remains legitimate to argue that the use of generic footage in *The Cold War* is manipulated into illustrating a memory which is imposed rather than innate, and so retains a mythic quality.

The People's Century (BBC/WGBH, 1997) is an example of a series that uses archival images differently, despite its stylistic similarities with other big historical series. *The People's Century* sticks by one important device: the direct linking of interviewees and archive, so the eye-witness testimonies are specifically and graphically correlated to the images used as illustration. When the subject is the student anti-war demonstrations at the end of the 1960s, it would not, one assumes, have been difficult to find images of Jeff Jones of the Weathermen to accompany his interview for the series. Others interviewed for the same episode, however, were not known figures but just happened to have been captured on film and subsequently tracked down by the filmmakers. Within the framework of *The People's Century*, the original footage is not treated as neutral or as generically figurative, instead it becomes concretely illustrative of what is being said around it. *The People's Century* constructs a bridge between personal history, oral history and the official history of the historical image, a link that is, in the use of generic archive, almost assumed not to exist. As is the case with the Berliners in the images used to accompany the woman's account of her rape, the figures in the original archive are depersonalised, extricated from their original circumstances, and find themselves condemned to perpetual anonymity and worse, in a sense, to have never existed. Most significant in *The People's Century*, therefore, is the reinstatement of these 'anonymous' individuals captured on camera into the official recorded history of this century; the ultimate verification of the notion that archive functions as the substantiation of memory.

A series such as *The People's Century* retains the idea that historical footage possesses an inherent meaning, although this signification is not positioned within a dialectical framework as it might be in 'collage junk' documentaries. The continuation of de Antonio's style of politicised compilation film is better exemplified by a film such as *The Atomic Café* (Kevin Rafferty, Jayne Loader, Pierce Rafferty, 1982), a satirical indictment of American Cold War propaganda in the 1950s that owes much to the comic montage conventions of a film such as *Millhouse*. *The Atomic Café* is predicated upon a simple central thesis: that the government's and the establishment's deliberately misleading and scare-mongering representation of the threat of nuclear war in the 1950s is ripe for ironic reassessment, and as such the film offers a distillation of de Antonio's 'collage junk' method. It is a film which had a huge impact at the time of its release, is still (with its release on video and the appearance of Loader's accompanying CD-ROM *Public Shelter*) widely viewed, and has exerted considerable influence on how 1950s Cold War America is represented. *The Atomic Café*, like de Antonio's documentaries, is exhaustive; it took five years to compile and edit, and makes substantial use of forgotten film from obscure 1950s government film catalogues. It uses official material to subversive ends, consistently imposing on the archive an opinion and meaning that is completely at odds with its original intention. Out of propaganda, *The Atomic Café* constructs ironic counter-propaganda; out of compiled images from various sources it constructs a straightforward dialectic between the past and the present. *The Atomic Café* operates a similar duality to that found in the majority of politically motivated compilation films, that the archive documents are respected on their own terms as 'evidence' at the same time as they are being reviewed and contradicted by their recontextualisation. As a result, the original material, despite the montage editing techniques deployed, is what remains memorable about the film; it is significant, for example, that many of the reviews from the time of the film's release focus on the 1950s propaganda rather than the film's formal qualities.

Broadly speaking, there are two types of sequence in *The Atomic Café*: those that leave the original archive relatively unadulterated and those that more overtly play around with different pieces of footage to create, through contrapuntal editing, a distinct narrative structure and ideological point. One section of *The Atomic Café* that is frequently remarked upon intercuts the cartoon 'Burt the Turtle' with the informational film 'Duck and Cover' in which children and families are instructed to follow the turtle's example and cover themselves with whatever is to hand if the bomb strikes. The immediate response to this sequence is to laugh, primarily at the comic ineptitude and naïveté of the notion that cowering under a picnic blanket or tucking oneself under a school desk is adequate protection against an atomic blast, but also at the government's belief that anyone would find this propaganda credible. There are several official films throughout *The Atomic Café* that provoke much the same response: the cartoon film about a doctor and his patient suffering from 'nuclearosis'; the nuclear family (sic) at the end who, after surviving a bomb in their shelter, re-emerge with father saying stoically that they have not suffered that badly and now have 'nothing to do except await orders and relax'. In these instances it might be overly simplistic to state that 'the documents speak for themselves' (Titus 1983: 6), for the pleasure derived from merely observing the archive that Pierce Rafferty has found is necessarily modified or compromised by what it is immediately or generally juxtaposed against. The 'Duck and Cover' sequence, for example, runs into a more formally radical and manipulative sequence. First, there is part of a televised (and one presumes rigged) question-and-answer session about the nuclear threat between members of the public and 'experts'. A woman asks how far from the centre of the blast would one have to be to survive, to which the reply given is 12 miles. This is juxtaposed with another contemporary 'expert' (presumably not a government stooge) describing how it would be futile (a word he repeats) to think of survival even in a bomb shelter within a 2,000 square mile radius of the blast, which in turn is juxtaposed with the 'nuclearosis' cartoon making assurances about the effectiveness of small shelters within the home. After a piece of similar archive showing homes being built with shelters and proudly displaying a 'we are prepared' sticker, there appears another sceptical academic remarking that shelters, far from acting as a deterrent, will ironically prompt the USA and the USSR to contemplate the possibility of nuclear conflict all the more readily. Within these five minutes, reconstituted footage is used in both ways hitherto mentioned: it is left relatively unadulterated and is overtly manipulated to construct an argument. What is strikingly presented in the latter part of the sequence (in the clear knowledge that 'Duck and Cover' and the laughter it provoked will impinge on this) is the idea that archive can be recontextualised to produce a counter-argument, or in this instance a piece of counter-propaganda. Within this there is a dominant text suggesting that the government fabricated an unrealistic image of nuclear war and the possibilities of survival alongside a subtext revealing that this was done not naively but in full possession of the available scientific facts about nuclear blasts and fall-out (it is hugely important in this respect that the realistic opinions are put forward by academics of the time not by individuals speaking with hindsight).

A sequence that has prompted some questioning of documentary method has been *The Atomic Café*'s opening, which concerns the first hostile nuclear strikes against Japan. After opening with footage of the first ('Trinity') atom bomb test in the New Mexico desert, *The Atomic Café* begins its examination of Hiroshima. The sequence starts with an interview with Paul Tibbets (captain of the Enola Gay, the American plane carrying the atomic bomb) and a fighter plane taking off, intercut with Japanese civilians walking through city streets and a single, sharply dressed Japanese man filmed from a low angle as he looks up at a brilliant blue sky. Subsequently, the film returns to Tibbets' voice overlaid onto footage of a bomber plane (not identified as the Enola Gay) manoeuvring itself out of the line of the atomic blast; Tibbets is explaining his decision to leave the area as quickly as possible when he realised the extent of the damage, a level of destruction represented by some intensely familiar footage of a city flattened except for a few isolated shells of buildings. After the subsequent American nuclear attack on Nagasaki, film of burnt and maimed survivors being subjected to physical examinations follows on from a perhaps unintentionally critical Tibbets stating that the US forces sought 'virgin targets' which had not suffered previous bomb damage in order to carry out 'classroom experiments' on the effects of radiation, – an interview that culminates in the pilot's throwaway speculation that the guilt engendered by these atomic attacks was possibly the catalyst for the US government's subsequent decision to say as little as possible about the reality of nuclear war. Paul Arthur is one of those to have taken issue with the opening of *The Atomic Café*, seemingly particularly preoccupied with the use of the isolated, 'generic' Japanese man in the Hiroshima section:

> In context, the montage sequence makes a discursive leap that frays our intuitions of documentary protocol, adopting a narrative editing trope that both heightens dramatic anticipation and elicits pathos for a specific individual. Since we may reasonably doubt that this man was an actual victim of the bombing, his function within the sequence is confusing. The fact that he does not belong to the scene portrayed becomes important, and misleading, in ways that related substitutions do not.
>
> (Arthur 1997: 5)

Arthur's contention appears to be that the conventions of generic archive somehow are not appropriate to individuals for whom we may feel pathos. It is dubious that an audience for *The Atomic Café* would be troubled by the likelihood that the Japanese man was not a victim of the Hiroshima bomb; instead, this sequence would probably be viewed as symbolic as opposed to accurately representative, but Arthur's problems with the sequence are interesting because of what they suggest about the political manipulation of images. Arthur would presumably feel happier with a comparable sequence in Barbara Margolis' *Are We Winning, Mommy?: America and the Cold War* (1986), another epic documentary about America in the nuclear age in which the start of the Cold War is far less elliptically portrayed. *Are We Winning, Mommy?* views the bombing of Hiroshima as a direct result of President Truman's growing conviction, after the Potsdam conference, that Stalin, like Hitler, was bent on world domination. The Trinity test and the subsequent attacks on Japan are thereby placed within a clear political framework, whilst *The Atomic Café* eschews such linearity of argument and, like de Antonio, seeks to be democratic and not overly guiding. *Are We Winning, Mommy?* offers an often brilliant historical overview of the Cold War (and likewise took five years to make), whereas *The Atomic Café* is an agitational film, a piece of counter-propaganda that does more than observe the post-war nuclear escalation. *Are We Winning, Mommy?* elects to make its position explicit, whilst *The Atomic Café* works through insinuation.

To return to the opening of *Atomic Café*. The unsuspecting, smart Japanese man is an Everyman figure, a representative character who not only functions as a cog within the Hiroshima narrative – a personalised reaction to the imminent arrival of the Enola Gay – but as a more abstract presence within the subliminal subtext underpinning the whole film: that what was being practised in the 1950s was an elaborate form of disavowal whereby the American government knew but denied and actively suppressed the true horrors of nuclear arms under a ludicrously inane arsenal of propaganda films. The inevitable destruction of

Figure 1.3   The Atomic Café
Source: Courtesy of BFI Stills, Posters and Designs

any individual caught by a nuclear blast is the knowledge that informs the rather beautiful shots of the lone Japanese man (brought back for *The Atomic Café*'s final vitriolic montage as he is juxtaposed with a reprise of 'Duck and Cover'); Americans – like him – would stand no chance if directly hit, and it is one of the documentary's poignancies that the largely American audience is compelled to identify with someone who is effectively 'the enemy'. Within a collage film such as *The Atomic Café* some of the archival documentation has a dual contextuali-sation, being given an immediate meaning and one that pertains to the overall perspective of the film. If the documentary is to work as an agitational text (as one that provokes its audience into awareness and action as well as increasing its historical knowledge) it has to be able to use or manipulate its original docu-ments into a polemical thesis. This would be impossible if, as Arthur would have it, every piece of archive was forced to perform a denotative function. The implied target of *The Atomic Café* is the actively repressive American govern-ments and authorities of the 1950s; like de Antonio before them, Rafferty, Loader and Rafferty are attacking the system that, in this case, fabricated the Cold War, forcing a parallel with the similarly nuclear-obsessed Reagan govern-ments of the 1980s. Like the wiser contemporary audiences of *The Atomic Café*, it is also suggested that the original viewers of the 1950s propaganda were not so gullible that they believed Burt the Turtle; they too denied what they had known since the end of the war: the blanket destruction of Hiroshima and

Nagasaki. It is imperative to consider the opening Japan sequence, complete with all its strongly manipulative editing, as the basis for the remainder of the film, as the mini text which informs the whole. With disavowal, acknowledgement precedes repression. In *The Atomic Café* the documentation (made accessible to Americans at the time) of the destruction of Hiroshima and Nagasaki precedes the propaganda for the building of bomb shelters (later renamed fall-out shelters when the position that one could survive the bomb itself became untenable) and other measures to ensure survival. Just as it is unlikely that Americans truly believed that consuming tranquillisers and tinned food in a subterranean bunker would save them, so we, the current audience, have the Japan footage as the images which shape our responses to the silliness that ensues. *The Atomic Café* is more than a clever piece of counter-propaganda that reverses the original meaning of the archive it uses, it confronts its audience with the complex series of manoeuvres that sustained the Cold War and its accompanying propaganda (Figure 1.3).

Conclusion

This chapter has taken issue with the central tenet of much theoretical writing on documentary, namely that a successful documentary is contingent upon representing the truth at its core as objectively as possible. Documentary film is traditionally perceived to be the hybrid offspring of a perennial struggle between the forces of objectivity (represented by the 'documents' or facts that underpin it) and the forces of subjectivity (that is the translation of those facts into representational form). The discussion of the Zapruder film of Kennedy's assassination posited the impossibility that a single piece of film, even one as accidental and unpremeditated as it is, can be a full and intelligible record of an event without being in some way contextualised or set alongside other sources of information. The realisation, however, that the authentic document might be deficient or lacking should not precipitate a representational crisis as it too often does. As the compilation films discussed for the remainder of this chapter exemplify, documentaries are predicated upon a negotiation between the polarities of objectivity and subjectivity, offering a dialectical analysis of events and images that accepts that no non-fictional record can contain the whole truth whilst also accepting that to re-use or recontextualise such material is not to irrevocably suppress or distort the innate value and meaning it possesses. These 'collage junk' films are ostensibly democratic in that they do not overtly intervene upon original film material. In the next chapter voice-over narration is examined as arguably the most blatant example of intervention on the part of the documentary filmmaker. As de Antonio sees it, narration is a fascist act that proclaims a film's didacticism.

2   Narration
The film and its voice

How and why did documentary narration acquire its miserable reputation, whilst still remaining one of the most commonly used devices in non-fiction filmmaking? Voice-over, in both documentaries and fiction films, is an extra-diegetic soundtrack that has been added to a film. On the whole such a voice-over gives insights and information not immediately available from within the diegesis, but whereas in a fiction film the voice-off is traditionally that of a character in the narrative, in a documentary the voice-over is more usually that of a disembodied and omniscient narrator. The negative portrayal of voice-over is largely the result of the development of a theoretical orthodoxy that condemns it for being inevitably and inherently didactic. Within this book's critique of the manner in which documentary's history has been depicted as an endless pursuit of the most effective way of representing the 'purity' of the real, this analysis of voice-over will question its condemnation as the imposed destroyer of the 'pure' film image, questioning along the way the over-simplified perception of voice-overs as all in some manner pertaining to the most basic 'voice of God' model. We have been 'taught' to believe in the image of reality and similarly 'taught' how to interpret the narrational voice as distortive and superimposed onto it. The endpoint of this discussion will be the various ways in which the classic voice-over has been modified and its rules transgressed through the insertion of ironic detachment between image and sound, the reflexive treatment of the narration tradition and the subversion of the archetypal solid male narrator in a documentary such as *Sunless*. The diversity of the form strongly suggests that an overarching definition of voice-over documentaries is distortive in itself.

The 'problem' at the heart of discussions of narration is the question of how one views the relationship between sound and image. In 1930 filmmaker and theorist Paul Rotha argued that sound films were 'harmful and detrimental to the culture of the public' (Rotha 1930: 408). Rotha, long before Christian Metz, automatically classified film as a purely visual medium to which sound could do irreparable damage, stating that, 'Immediately a voice begins to speak in a cinema, the sound apparatus takes precedence over the camera, thereby doing violence to natural instincts' (Rotha 1930: 406). The 'one legitimate use for the dialogue film' according to Rotha was the topical newsreel, for here the appeal was not aesthetic or 'dramatic' but factual. Underpinning Rotha's objections is a belief in the purity of film predicated upon its visual impact alone, arguing that a silent film has a more lasting effect on its audience than a sound film and displaying an undeniable romanticism when positing that 'No power of speech is comparable with the descriptive value of photographs' (Rotha 1930: 405). Unlike the Soviets who, at the end of the 1920s, supported sound if deployed as another tool with which to 'strengthen and broaden the montage methods of influencing the audience', but warned against the 'commercial exploitation' of synchronised sound which would instead 'destroy the culture of montage, because every mere *addition* of sound to montage fragments increases their inertia' (Eisenstein *et al.*, 1928: 234), Rotha is troubled by the idea that sound will contaminate the image. So it is with documentary: whereas what could be termed the alternative narration tradition, like the Soviets, advocates a 'contrapuntal use of sound vis-à-vis the visual fragment of montage' (Eisenstein *et al.*, 1928: 234), most of the time voice-over is perceived as a threat, as didactic and anti-democratic.

Voice-over is the unnecessary evil of documentary, the resort of the 'unimaginative and incompetent' (Kozloff 1988: 21). Direct Cinema pioneer Robert Drew, in an article combatively entitled 'Narration can be a killer', contends that only documentaries that eschew narration as a structuring device can 'work, or are beginning to work, or could work, on filmic-dramatic principles', that only films that tell a story directly (without voice-over) can 'soar' into a utopian realm 'Beyond reason. Beyond explanation. Beyond words'. As Drew dogmatically concludes, 'words supplied from outside cannot make a film soar', so 'narration is what you do when you fail' (Drew 1983: 271–3). Drew's objections to narration are echoed by the majority of theoretical writing about documentary, which, along with certain practitioners, has cemented the view expressed above by promoting the idea that the term 'voice-over', when applied to documentaries, signifies only the didactic single, white, male tones of *The March of Time* and its sorry derivatives. Most to blame for this negative perception of voice-over documentaries has been Bill Nichols' 'family tree' representing documentary genealogy as starting with the 'expository mode' (commentary-led, didactic), the oldest and most primitive form of non-fiction film. The fundamental problems with Nichols' 'family tree' are that it elides differences between films that fall firmly within one of the identified categories and imposes onto documentary history a false chronological structure dictated by an obsession with the linearity of documentary's theoretical evolution. As he comments, the direct address/expository style was 'the *first* thoroughly worked out mode of documentary' (my italics; Nichols 1983: 48). It serves Nichols' (but not documentary history's) ends to maintain that this is so. The non-fiction films of the silent era (or as Nichols no doubt perceives it: the era of documentary chaos) are too numerous to list here, but the work of Dziga Vertov, for one, was neither didactic and voice-over led nor under-theorised.

The coherent history of documentary film is thus deemed to have begun around the time of the Second World War. The most oft-cited example of the narration-led documentary form is Louis de Rochemont's *The March of Time*, a monthly film magazine that ran from 1935–51 and used archive and dramatisation in the reconstruction of what it deemed to be significant current events. In the episode recounting the Battle of Britain, for example, this pivotal confrontation is re-enacted using a handful of bomber planes, newsreel footage and reconstructions. Above all *The March of Time* offered a synthesis, a viewer's digest of a cycle of events that had already reached a conclusion, and within this strict, instructional framework its booming, relentless voice-over ('Time marches on!') inevitably took on the role of teacher. This sort of commentary was dubbed the 'voice of God', with all the insinuations of patriarchy, dominance, omniscience that term harbours. The standard assumption as far as documentary theory is concerned is that whereas synch sound 'helps anchor the meaning of the images' (Nichols 1981: 200) thereby preserving their dominance, narration is an intrusion which interferes with this automatic prioritisation of the image whilst concomitantly immobilising and distancing the spectator through its dictatorial methods. Documentary's 'tacit proposal' to its audience is, as Nichols sees it, 'the invocation of, and promise to gratify, a desire to know' (Nichols 1981: 205), a function exemplified by the use of direct address, readily characterised as instructive and 'overwhelmingly didactic' in its domination of the visuals (Nichols 1983: 48) and of audience response. The omniscient narrator offers the dominant – if not the only – perspective on the footage on the screen. Nichols is worth quoting at length on what he terms 'The expository mode' as inherent within much of his seminal writing on the subject are the dangerous assumptions and slippages that colour much theorisation of documentary's deployment of commentary:

> The expository text addresses the viewer directly, with titles or voices that advance an argument about the historical world. ... The expository mode emphasises the impression of objectivity, and of well-established judgement. This mode supports the impulse towards generalisation handsomely since the voice-over commentary can readily extrapolate from the particular instance offered on the image track. ... Exposition can accommodate elements of interviews but these tend to be subordinated to an argument offered by the film itself, via an unseen 'voice of God' or an on-camera voice of authority who speaks on behalf of the text. ... Finally, the viewer will typically expect the expository text to take shape around the solution to a problem or puzzle: presenting the news of the day, exploring the working of the atom or the universe, addressing the consequences of nuclear waste or acid rain, tracing the history of an event or the biography of a person.
>
> (Nichols 1991: 34–8)

As identified in this passage, the primary features of narration-led documentaries are: that, by blending omniscience and intimacy, they address the spectator directly; they set out an argument (thus implying forethought, knowledge, the ability to assimilate); they possess a dominant and constant perspective on the events they represent to which all elements within the film conform; they offer a solution and thereby a closure to the stories they tell. It is hardly surprising, therefore, that Nichols, in the earlier *Ideology and the Image* had made a direct comparison between the Expository documentary form and 'classical narrative cinema' (Nichols 1981: 97). Carl Plantinga is one of the many subsequent critics to have accepted the chronology supplied by Nichols, thus conflating the direct address form's simplicity with being 'naïve and politically retrograde' (Plantinga 1997: 101). Although Plantinga – unlike Nichols – subsequently identifies variants within the expository mode, differentiating between formal, open and poetic exposition, he is ultimately only providing subdivisions within Nichols' monolithic category, as, predictably, the 'formal' submode is the most rigid whilst the other two are more experimental and by implication 'better' and more advanced (pp. 106–18). Any attempt at rigid classification seems bound to dismiss or find fault with voice-over documentaries more readily than with any other mode. To such an extent has the conventional trajectory dominated, that the differences between narration-led documentaries are simply elided, and even a film as unconventional as Buñuel's *Land Without Bread* is assumed to conform to the traditional 'narration is bad' model. Not only does Nichols arbitrarily decide that voice-over is the dominant feature of otherwise vastly divergent films, but he creates a definition of expository documentary that fits only a portion of the films that might reasonably be assumed to conform to that category. *The March of Time* or *The Times of Harvey Milk* might explain, solve and close a sequence of events, but the same cannot be said of Franju's *Hôtel des invalides*, Chris Marker's *Sunless* or even more straightforward films such as Joris Ivens' *The Spanish Earth* and John Huston's *The Battle of San Pietro*. In bracketing together *Night Mail* and *The Battle of San Pietro* as prime examples of films utilising a 'voice of God' commentary (Nichols 1991: 34), despite Auden's scripted narration for the former being conspicuously poetic and Huston's voice-over in the latter being equally conspicuously ironic, Bill Nichols is only classifying (or condemning) the documentaries through their appropriation of one distinctive formal device. However varied the use of narration has been both before and after *The March of Time*, the overriding view is that the documentary voice-over is the filmmakers' ultimate tool for telling people what to think. This gross over-simplification covers a multitude of differences, from the most common use of commentary as an economic device able to efficiently relay information that might otherwise not be available or might take too long to tell in images, to its deployment as an ironic and polemical tool.

Conventional 'voice of God' narration: *The World at War*, *The Times of Harvey Milk*

Two examples of conventional 'voice of God' documentaries are *The World at War*, Thames Television's 24-part series about World War Two, and *The Times of Harvey Milk* (1984), Robert Epstein's emotive, Oscar-winning film about the gay San Francisco supervisor who was shot dead on 27 November 1978 by fellow Supervisor Dan White. Big, historical series such as *The World at War* or, more recently, *The Nazis: A Warning from History* (BBC, 1997) and *The Cold War* (Jeremy Isaacs/BBC, 1998) are, by nature, instructive, in that they have taken an event or a series of events from history which they subsequently 'tell' the television audience about. This approach to documentary is compatible with – and in some manner is an extension of – John Reith's conception of public service broadcasting in the UK. Reith's dictum that factual broadcasting in this country should both educate and entertain came from an elitist conception of the role of the media, that the BBC had a sense of moral obligation to its audience to impart worthwhile information. This is the 'filmmakers as teachers and audience as willing pupils' model of documentary, very much dependent on the understanding that the former have dedicated a substantial amount of time and resources to acquiring the requisite knowledge (historical information, interviewees, archive, etc.) to assume their academic superiority over the latter. There are various common factors that link historical series such as those cited above: the use of actors' voices for the narration, the deceptively simple compilation of archive to illustrate specific points (often belying the assiduous research that has gone into the selection),[1] the interviewing of 'experts' and eye-witnesses. One of the most famous recent voice-overs is Laurence Olivier's for *The World at War*. Olivier, unlike the younger and less well known Sam West, for instance, who narrated *The Nazis*, has the particular seniority that results from having been England's most universally acclaimed and respected classical actor.[2] This 'star' persona is exploited by Jeremy Isaacs' series, especially when it comes to Episode 20: 'Genocide', the programme which tackles the Final Solution. This episode opens with Olivier (for the only time in the series) delivering a scripted, formal piece to camera, in which he warns 'you will find it [the ensuing programme] grim viewing, but watch if you can. This happened in our time, but must not happen again', and in which he also asserts that the following film 'shows *how* it was done and *why* it was done'. There are several underlying issues that colour this opening address, the first being the suggestion that Olivier, however sincere, is 'acting', performing pre-scripted lines. Here he has broken one of the 'rules' of documentary voice-over which is to remain separate and disembodied from the images commented upon.[3] The issue of subjectivity is also present in the ideological implications of Olivier's words: that the events about to be shown form part of a closed historical sequence by which the audience will be moved and which, if they look and listen attentively, they will be able to prevent from recurring. What 'Genocide' implicitly offers, therefore, is the surety that it can contain and explicate the 'truth', and this it does by adopting a classic and simple cause–effect linear structure guided by Olivier's voice-over.[4]

The methods deployed for telling the story of the Final Solution are exemplified by the opening sequences. The first images of 'Genocide' (immediately following Olivier's piece to camera and prior to the title sequence) are two tracking shots following the railway lines either side of the Auschwitz gates. The immediate point of spectator-identification is thereby with the victims of the Nazi extermination programme, and what the film subsequently seeks is an explanation for this final journey. The film adopts two structuring strategies or routes of inquiry, the first is to have the narration 'interpret' the events depicted, the second is to chart a linear historical trajectory through these events, from the late 1920s to the final liberation of the camps. The former is an example of the most common deployment of voice-over as a means of making sense of a montage of images that otherwise would not be explicable; the latter is a frequently adopted measure for telling such a monumental story. The voice-over in *The World at War* makes sense of, and creates links between, the images it is covering. An early example in 'Genocide' is the archival sequence that begins with footage of Himmler attending skiing championships and a Nazi youth camp, followed by neo-Darwinian Nazi propaganda films showing animals demonstrating the 'survival of the fittest' laws of nature, and concluding with images of race and plough horses, medical examinations of 'perfect' humans and a variety of group sporting activities. Without Olivier's narration outlining and offering an opinion on Nazi racial philosophy which sought a 'race of supermen' and 'pedigree humans', these images could arguably be open to interpretation, or at least the logic binding them together might be obscured. The pivotal narrative figure for the episode is Heinrich Himmler, appointed by Hitler as Reichsführer of the SS, whom the voice-over describes at the outset as the one who 'refines the philosophy of Nazism'. The selection of Himmler is not arbitrary but expedient and to a degree reductive, as what happens through this episode of *The World at War* is that all the historical events represented in terms of narrative unity refer back, however tangentially, to this one individual. The conventional cause–effect structure pursued by 'Genocide' is in danger of permitting the inference that, had Himmler not existed, the Final Solution would not have happened, or more generally of conforming to what Marxist historian E.H. Carr derogatorily labels the 'bad King John theory of history', whereby history is interpreted as 'the biography of great men' and their evil counterparts, and that 'what matters in history is the character and behaviour of individuals' (Carr 1961: 45). The voice-over in *The World at War* steers the telling and thereby the comprehension of its subjects and abides by a determinist view of history whereby 'everything that happens has a cause or causes, and could not have happened differently unless something in the cause or causes had also been different' (Carr 1961: 93). *The World at War* as a series does not follow a strictly chronological structure, although each episode is set out in a linear fashion. In 'Genocide' this means that the interviews with SS officers, camp survivors, Anthony Eden and all the other figures are in some way related to Himmler and the blame attached to him as the key architect of the Final Solution at the outset of the film. A residual effect of this is to stop the audience from probing deeper into less straightforward issues such as Nazi ideology and the practicalities of the mass exterminations. The programme likewise shies away from taking issue with its subjects as it maintains its supposedly objective stance. Eden, for example, is not made to confront the inadequacy of being more concerned with the reception in the House of Commons to his 1943 statement regarding the treatment of the European Jews than with the issue of why, despite this information, the Allies did so little to intervene. The version of the Holocaust offered in 'Genocide' is simplified but not distorted.

As Jeffrey Youdelman remarks at the outset of 'Narration, Invention, and History', the common (but he argues misguided) reaction to documentary narration is that the use of a voice-over necessarily suppresses the voices of the documentary subjects themselves, that narration-led films are directly opposed to films which, using 'oral history interview techniques', capture 'for the first time the voice of the people who have shared in the making of working-class history and culture' (Youdelman 1982: 454). Youdelman ends his article by not reviling but praising those filmmakers who advocate the use of 'commentary, intervention, and invention', and who believe in 'taking responsibility for the statement the film was making' (Youdelman 1982: 458). Youdelman here envisages the dialectical co-existence of an authorial 'voice' and factual representation.

The 'voice' of a documentary such as *The Times of Harvey Milk* is easily discernible: supportive of Milk, his politics and his sexuality; saddened by his death; angered by the law's treatment of his murderer. As with the choice of Olivier for *The World at War*, the decision to use Harvey Fierstein as the narrator for *The Times of Harvey Milk* is indicative of the film's stance towards its subject. Fierstein, a well-known gay writer and actor, has an immensely distinctive voice (gravel mixed with treacle) that immediately makes the film into a statement about gay politics. The question of bias, however, is astutely handled by the film. Although its narration is still highly selective and is unashamedly biased towards Milk, Epstein is careful to ensure that Harvey Milk is not simply a significant gay figure but more of a democratic Pied Piper with a more universal charisma.

The film starts with a news flash announcing the deaths of Harvey Milk, the first 'out' gay man to be voted into public office in California, and Mayor George Moscone; the narration is soon brought in (over news stills) telling us that Milk 'had already come to represent something far greater than his office'. This observation is subsequently underlined as the film soundtrack cuts to the voice of Milk himself (thinking he could be the target of assassins) taping his will and commenting that he saw himself as 'part of a movement'. Harvey Milk is portrayed as a figure who represents, in the true Lukácsian sense, social forces and attitudes far greater than himself, his is an individual destiny that gives '*direct* expression to general destinies' (Lukács 1937: 152), and this idealisation of him would seem to stem directly from the coercive voice-over. This could undoubtedly also be said of *The World at War*'s treatment of Himmler, that he too was a representative figure who could function as an assimilation of Nazi ideology and action towards the Jews. But whereas *The World at War* maintains a superficial impartiality towards its material, *The Times of Harvey Milk* deftly insinuates that the film's central ethos is not grafted on but innate, that the visuals corroborate the narration but are not subservient to it. There are, for example, moments when the interviewees (all friends and supporters of Milk) substantiate the notion of him as an idealised representative figure: Sally Gearheart, an academic, saying, about her attitude the night of Harvey's murder, 'don't you realise the course of history has been changed', or Tony Anniano, a gay schoolteacher, commenting about the violence that followed White's conviction for manslaughter that 'you can replace a glass door ... but you can't replace Harvey' or Tory Hartmann confirming the idea of Milk as a symbolic figure when she recounts how 'it took his death' to make people see how important it was to 'come out'. The role allotted Fierstein's narration is confirmatory as opposed to purely instructional, so the 'voice' of *The Times of Harvey Milk* ostensibly comes from the active collusion between filmmakers, form, subjects and archive.

The Times of Harvey Milk is using the conventionalised voice-over-led documentary structure not to pseudo-objective ends, but as a tool in a subjective enterprise – the film's 'voice'. The image of Harvey Milk proffered by the documentary is wholly complimentary (there is one mention of Milk's short temper but little else that is negative), but the information is imparted so as to seem that this is the only accurate portrayal. *The Times of Harvey Milk* maintains its right to be selective and to emphasise what it chooses, and, as Bill Nichols posits, 'our attention is not on how the filmmaker uses witnesses to make the point but on the effectiveness of the argument itself' (Nichols 1991: 37). At times it does this in a flagrantly manipulative manner; this is not a clinical analysis of a series of events but an emotional eulogy, and as such it wants to bring its audience round, to make us feel as well as think the same way it does. To achieve this, Epstein deploys a variety of narrative devices, one of which is to construct a conflict around which the rest of the action revolves between Milk and White. As the film's central axis, this confrontation is personal, political and ideological. That Milk and White were such starkly different people, antagonists on the San Francisco board and representatives of vastly different values and beliefs, goes towards setting up the final confrontation: White's murder of Milk. Several strands running through the film can be traced back to this symbolic duel and the collisions that result from it. *Harvey Milk* is clearly an 'authored' film, and yet it also abides by the formal unity associated with expository documentaries; not only is it driven by a strong narration, but its narrative is structured around a series of collisions that emanate from the central Milk vs White opposition that heighten, explicate and crystallise the debates enacted therein such as gays and lesbians vs evangelical bigots, minority communities vs the white, middle-class, heterosexual majority.[5] It does not, however, put Dan White's case, which is more complex and troubled than the film makes it appear.[6]

About 50 minutes into the subsequently chronological documentary, the opening sequence is repeated (from a slightly different camera angle), thus signalling that the dominant narrative (Milk's significant if brief political career) is reaching its conclusion. The film's first 'ending' is thus the spontaneous candlelight march that occurred on the night of Milk's death. The manner in which the film builds up to this tragic, celebratory climax is deeply reminiscent of the funeral sequence that crowns Douglas Sirk's *Imitation of Life*: it is simply willing one to cry, and in so doing uses every technique of manipulation at its disposal. After the Feinstein news flash, the film cuts to a protracted sequence of interviews with the same friends and colleagues that have proffered choric opinions of Milk throughout, each talking about their immediate responses to hearing the news that morning and what they did afterwards. This section concludes with Billy Kraus waiting to join the march towards City Hall, and wondering why there were so few people there ('is this all that anybody cared?'). Having reached this moment of extreme pathos and Billy Kraus reporting how he was assured that the march had not reached him yet, there is then a cut to footage of the actual march: a wide street filled, as far as the eye can see, with people holding candles (this is not unlike the similarly delayed revelation of quite how many people are in attendance at the funeral in *Imitation of Life*). After the intensity of the build up to the march, these archive images work as an emotional release, a cinematic outpouring of grief, replete with Mark Isham's correspondingly poignant trumpet music. The cathartic spell this sequence casts is really only broken when Tory Hartmann says over the continuing footage of the march, 'Harvey would have loved this' – a brief respite before she too (in front of the camera) succumbs to tears. This false ending culminates in the respective funerals of Milk and Moscone, the former taking precedence over the latter. In many ways, *Harvey Milk* is a consummate melodrama and this build up to a moment of crisis, triumph or extreme emotion is a formal technique repeated several times.

It may come as a shock to some viewers that the funeral march is not the end of the film. After a fade to black the final section commences, dedicated to the trial and sentencing of Dan White and the street violence that greeted the verdict. There is something anticlimactic, un-Aristotelian about this transition, abruptly reminding those watching that this is more documentary than melodrama. Again, however, the underlying aim of this final stage appears to be to link the history of Milk's fatal conflict with White to wider issues, in particular justice and retribution. Clearly everyone involved in the film, both in front of and behind the camera, considered White's sentence lenient (there is even a strong hint of disappointment on television news reporter Jeannine Yeoman's face as she says 'I thought he might get the chair'). What the film achieves is a mimicking in those watching of the paradoxical emotions felt by the liberals in the film: that whilst they might be politically opposed to capital punishment and violence, they emotionally could not come to terms with the injustice, as they perceived it, of White's conviction for voluntary manslaughter.[7] Just as Epstein's film manifests both stylistically and formally its solidarity with Milk, so it also barely masks his and his fellows' antipathy towards White. For one, there are no specially shot interviews of Dan White's friends and family, so the film continues to make use of interviews with the same collection of Milk's friends. This has the effect of imposing an emotional continuum on the film that compels the audience to react to the last section through the feelings engendered by what has preceded it. We are automatically distanced from Dan White: we see him, his wife and friends only in news archive; even his tearful confession (played on tape to the courtroom) is not given to us 'unadulterated' but comes after a pre-emptive piece of voice-over has warned that the prosecution's gamble of using this to prove White's guilt backfired, as jurors found themselves feeling sorry for him. As an explanation of the violence that followed the verdict, there is a montage of interviews voicing cynical speculations on the reasons for White's 'light' sentence: that had he killed only the heterosexual Moscone, or had he been black, then White would have been convicted of murder. Ultimately, there is a strong sense (as the surety and calm of Milk's ethos is restored by the pre-credits sequence) that all violence and ugliness in *The Times of Harvey Milk* stems directly from White.

The World at War and *The Times of Harvey Milk* offer two examples of traditional voice-over as an explanatory and persuasive tool. They use expository narration, however, in different ways; whereas *The World at War* maintains a semblance of instructional objectivity, the degree of bias in *Harvey Milk* is evident throughout. The tonal differences between the two make definitions of the expository mode difficult. In their persuasiveness, both films could be termed 'propaganda', in that they set out to win the audience round to the validity of their points of view. The 'problem' with this is that documentary theory has been too eager to collapse the notions of 'persuasion' and 'falsification'; a slippage which stems from an adherence to the belief that to display bias is tantamount to creating a fiction out of facts, as the outspoken opinions of Robert Drew attest. As Noël Carroll argues, 'A film may be successfully persuasive without bending the facts' (Carroll 1996a: 235); a documentary may present the filmmakers' point of view through such overt means as a biased voice-over without forfeiting the claim to be a documentary. The extent to which material has been assimilated, concentrated and selected in traditional expository documentaries makes theorists uneasy, as does the domination of commentary and of a single perspective. This is not, however, to say that *The World at War* or *Harvey Milk* are pedalling 'lies'. Even when Carr is attacking an individualist, determinist approach to history, he is not maintaining that history does not include individuals, merely that they 'act in context, and under the impulse of a past society' (Carr 1961: 35). *The World at War* has, out of necessity, been selective in its use of material. Carroll again argues against assuming that selectivity and bias are interchangeable, commenting that whilst selectivity may 'make bias possible' or may even 'in some contexts invite bias ... it does not *guarantee* bias' (Carroll 1996b: 284). The questionable belief behind the theorisation of the narration-led documentary is that the voice-over automatically becomes the dominant and therefore subjectifying force behind every film in which it is substantially used, that its didacticism stems from its inevitable pre-eminence in the hierarchy of documentary devices. Instead, it should be acknowledged that a strong voice-over rarely renders the truth contained within the image invisible, that in effect these narration-led documentaries are films – even the least radical amongst them – that suggest that documentaries, far from being able to represent the truth in an unadulterated way, can only do so through interpretation, which in the case of narration is of the most overt and blatant kind.

   This interpretative function is not, however, necessarily at the expense of independent thought; it is not invariably the case that to 'tell' rather than to 'show' the facts is to immobilise the audience, to render them incapable of seeing the material before them in any way which might contradict the perspective of the film. The truth, therefore, does not only become apparent when the overt intervention of the filmmaker is minimised. This is why another common ellipsis in documentary theory – that form and ideology are corollaries – is likewise questionable. The inflexibility detected in the 'expository mode' has itself been a consistent characteristic of the theoretical writing that discusses it. Orthodox attitudes towards narration-led documentaries are thereby generally dependent upon the shaky assumption that films that share a formal device (the voice-over) also share an attitude and an ideological aim, that narration is a form of 'preaching' and the voice-over a device 'authoritarian by nature, elitist and paternalistic' (Youdelman 1982: 464). In 'Cinema/Ideology/Criticism', Comolli and Narboni recognise a category of political filmmaking into which both *The World at War* and *The Times of Harvey Milk* would fit: Category (d), which comprises

> those films ... which have an explicitly political content ... but which do not effectively criticise the ideological system in which they are embedded because they unquestioningly adopt its language and its imagery.
> (Comolli and Narboni 1969: 26–7)

Whilst this *Cahiers du cinéma* editorial is willing to positively acknowledge the ambivalence of, for example, the films of Costa-Gavras, when a comparable duality between content and form is approached within a documentary context, formal conservatism is presumed to override any other political or ideological position. Narration is assumed to be undemocratic and inherently distortive. There is therefore the suspicion that a voice-over has the capacity to violate the 'truth' revealed in the image. Pascal Bonitzer (1976: 326) asserts that a film's commentary 'should not do violence to the image', and yet the traditional opinion of voice-over is predicated upon the belief that it cannot but help violate, distort or compromise the image. The voice-over thereby prevents the event being represented from 'speaking', as if a film can possess only one point of view which will inevitably be that of the voice-over if there is one of any substance. If synch sound and the reproduction of the voice was 'the 'truth' which was lacking in the silent film' (Jean-Louis Comolli in Silverman 1988: 44), then why has the voice-over been so vilified? The traditional explanation lies in the disembodiment of the classic documentary narrator. Bonitzer (1976: 322) emphasises the voice-over's Otherness when he refers to it as:

… that voice of knowledge *par excellence* in all films, since it resounds from offscreen, in other words from the field of the Other. In this system the concern is to reduce, insofar as possible, not the informative capacity of commentary but its assertive character and, if one likes, its *authoritative* character – that arbitration and arbitrariness of the voice-off which, to the extent that it cannot be localised, can be criticised by nothing and no one.

Important here is not merely the identification of the voice-over's Otherness, but that such a voice achieves a certain authority through being both an arbitrator and arbitrary; capable of being both reasonable and logical as well as irrationally selective. That this dubious power is so often invested in a white, male, middle-class and anonymous voice necessarily cements the voice-over form as repressive and anti-radical. Kaja Silverman posits that, in Hollywood films, 'male subjectivity is most fully realised (or perhaps it would be more accurate to say most fully "idealised") when it is least visible' (Silverman 1988: 164). A case can be found for arguing something comparable in relation to the nonfiction film: that the 'voice of God' is a composite of various different manifestations of universality and power that include masculinity and anonymity. However, the reductivism that has plagued discussions of documentary's implementation of voice-over lies in the persistent refusal to either acknowledge any differences between *actual* voices or to distinguish between very different uses of the voice within the documentary context. The use of a female voice-over offers the most overt challenge to the narrowness of such criticism, but one can also point to the deliberately ironic and distanced narration in films such as *Land Without Bread*, *The Battle of San Pietro* and *Hôtel des invalides*.

Ironic narration: *Hôtel des invalides; The Battle of San Pietro*

In 1966 Scholes and Kellogg stated that 'a narrator who is not in some way suspect, who is not in some way open to ironic scrutiny, is what the modern temper finds least bearable' (quoted in Kozloff 1988: 102). This use of 'ironic scrutiny' has been evident in the use of commentary in documentaries since well before the 1960s (see the use of intertitles in Shub's *Fall of the Romanov Dynasty*), but forms part of an alternative tradition (of which Buñuel, Huston and Franju are notable exponents) whose idiosyncrasies have too frequently been subsumed with uncritical alacrity into the mainstream. As there is an alternative practical tradition, so there is an alternative (if stunted) critical tradition which prioritises the potential rather than the deficiencies of the expository mode. Alberto Cavalcanti is one such dissenting voice who, in the 1930s, writes of how he regrets the relegation of the voice-over to the 'comparatively minor role of providing continuity and "story" in travelogues, newsreels and documentary' since the advent of 'talkies' (Cavalcanti 1939: 29). What interests Cavalcanti are just the ironic possibilities of narration that modern critical orthodoxy have marginalised; that, for instance, the 'effect … which no audience can resist' of Joris Ivens' *The Spanish Earth* 'arises from the contrast between the cool, tragic dignity of Hemingway's prose on the one hand, and the terrors of the images on the other' (p. 29). To Cavalcanti, a film's 'poetic effect' results from the juxtaposition of 'rational', interpretative narration and emotive images; that 'while the picture is the medium of statement, the sound is the medium of suggestion' (pp. 37–8).

Although one might not necessarily want to categorise all such films as 'poetic', what Cavalcanti highlights is the challenging, radical effect of electing not to correlate image and sound. Similarly Bonitzer debates the use or otherwise of the 'free confrontation' between different narrative elements in documentary when challenging the 'seductiveness' of the dictum '*let the event speak*', commenting that, 'This is an interesting formula not only because in it can be read the elision of (the author's) point of view toward the event in question, but also because it displaces this "question of point of view" – which is so important for "politics" – to a problem of *speech*' (Bonitzer 1976: 320). The corollary of this, Bonitzer finds, is that the 'eye is carried by the voice' but a voice which remains '*without subject*' (p. 320). The analyses of Cavalcanti and Bonitzer offer pertinent insights into the paradox of the narration-led documentary form: that although the voice is considered 'dominant' over the images and thus to serve a didactic function, it may be powerless in comparison with that image. Films such as *Hôtel des invalides* and *The Battle of San Pietro* break the documentary's version of the cinematic illusion on which this contradiction is formulated, namely the creation of a 'classic' style that elides differences or tensions.

The traditional voice-over form emphasises the unity, and imaginary cohesion of its various elements; so the dominance of the narration covertly serves to emphasise the incontrovertibility of the images by refusing to dispute and doubt what they depict. Narration could thereby be viewed as a mechanism deployed to mask the realisation that this mode of representation, and indeed its inherent belief in a consistent and unproblematic truth, are perpetually on the verge of collapse, that commentary, far from being a sign of omniscience and control, is the hysterical barrier erected against the spectre of ambivalence and uncertainty. Indeed, many of the unconventional voice-overs signal their doubt that such a neat collusion between voice and image can ever be sustained, that even narration is not invariably allied to determinism, but has the potential to be a destabilising component of a dialectical structure that intentionally brings cracks and inconsistencies to the surface. In certain documentary films – when voice-over becomes a truly subversive tool, and one not bound by the conservatism of the expository form – the narration becomes a component capable of engendering such a dialectical distance, one that both draws the audience into sympathising for the image and sets them critically back from it.

In *Hôtel des invalides*, a documentary about Paris's military museum and allegedly Franju's personal favourite among his short films (Durgnat 1967: 47), the distance between official subject and critical tone is both consistent and pronounced. Unlike a more explicitly political voice-over film such as Ivens' *The*

Spanish Earth in which Hemingway's committed voice-over directly interprets the images (as when he says over shots of soldiers going to battle: 'This is the true face of men going into action. It is a little different from any other face you'll ever see') *Hôtel des invalides* is dialectical in that its narration does not provide explicit commentary and criticism, but rather creates the space in which such interpretations can occur. This is not to say that Franju's pacifism is hard to detect, but merely that it is only insinuated and never laid bare, notably through the increasingly absurd and strained relationship between the patter emitted by the guide escorting us and visitors around the armoury museum and the images and juxtapositions that comprise the tour (the 'misguided tour' as Durgnat defines it (p. 47)). Noël Burch's contention that *Hôtel des invalides* is so ambiguous that 'it can be read either as an attack on war, or (on a level that is perhaps less sophisticated but still perfectly cogent and perfectly 'natural' to a good many people) as a flag-waving patriotic film' (Burch 1969: 159) is both ingenuous and naïve. Yes, the film was commissioned by the French Ministry of the Army, but they were not entirely satisfied with the result, and their discontent no doubt resulted from detecting the thinly veiled tensions between thesis and antithesis. There is, for example, the sequence which cuts from a low angle shot of Napoleon over which the voice-over comments 'legend has its heroes' to the image of a wheelchair-bound veteran being wheeled to the foot of the statue by a nurse, to which the narrator adds 'war has its victims'. As Franju cuts between the petrified monument and the still living soldier, it remains unclear whether the soldier is looking at Napoleon, or indeed whether he can see or understand the objects his eyes happen to have alighted upon; as a result of this uncertainty, the issue of difference and tension between myth and the present is left for the spectator to ponder. The point of synthesis is the moment of viewing.[8] The constant, nagging demotion of the trappings and icons of past glory is a characteristic of *Hôtel des invalides*, but its 'openness' as a text stems from the lack of Hemingway-esque directional commentary. Take the juxtaposition between yet another shot of Napoleon (to which the guide simply adds, 'the Emperor') and his stuffed horse and dog, two of the more bizarre objects by which the museum remembers him; or the narrator introducing 'The bronzed head of General Mangin's statue' as the camera rather sumptuously pans around the head to reveal that half of it has been blown away. In both these examples what is signalled is the discrepancy between the brutality of war and the safety of its remembering, the one necessarily impinging on the other, so the mummification of experience witnessed in the army museum itself becomes an act of violence. Like the iconic wheelchair, the bland voice-over and the smiling, oblivious couple whose guided tour we are ostensibly following, trundle blithely on, so the swelling anger is ours and not the text's. *Hôtel des invalides* reaches no conclusion as such, although it suggests plenty. As the war orphans march crocodile fashion out of the gates and a flock of birds swings through the air (a reprise of an earlier sequence) the film appears to have made little definite progress. The 'progress', however, has been made by those making sense of the film's elisions and complex juxtapositions – primarily between voice and image, in which the confrontation between official thesis and subversive antithesis is encapsulated.

There are similar moments of disjuncture in John Huston's *The Battle of San Pietro*, the second film in Huston's wartime documentary trilogy – although built into this documentary's use of irony and detachment is a more involved debate around the limitations of narration itself. *San Pietro* and *Hôtel des invalides* elicited similarly negative responses from the bodies that funded them, and Huston's US Army superiors excised certain material from *San Pietro* when shown the completed version in 1944. *The Battle of San Pietro* is usually noted for being a 'classic direct-address documentary' (the narration is by Huston himself) as well as for its use of ironic commentary (Nichols 1981: 185ff). The film's use of irony links it to the tradition of intellectual, anti-establishment documentaries exemplified by *Land Without Bread* and, of course, *Hôtel des invalides*. Huston, for example, contradicts General Mark Clark's opening piece to camera declaring the cost of the hostilities in the Italian campaign not to have been 'excessive' by cutting from Clark to images of dead soldiers being stretchered onto a truck. Huston's voice-over is inconsistent; the laboured irony of the film's early sequences, for instance, gives way to a purely descriptive narration during the battle scenes (8–15 December, 1943). Some of the censorship problems Huston encountered were indirectly related to these tonal shifts. US Army records reveal several memos calling for the removal of footage showing identifiable dead American soldiers being hauled onto a truck, overlaid with excerpts from interviews they recorded whilst still alive.[9]

The army also requested further cuts to be made to the final, post-liberation reel, a section of *San Pietro* that raises further questions about the limitations and use of documentary narration. The reasons for the Chiefs' dissatisfaction with this final section seems to have been that it is tedious and detracts from the ostensible purpose of the film, one memo from Charles Stodter, Assistant Chief, Army Pictorial Service, remarking that 'the ending is somewhat long, particularly the sequence showing the children', and another from Curtis Mitchell, Chief, Pictorial Branch, suggesting that the same images be cut as they have 'little to do with the American soldier and [convey] little information about him to the public' (Culbert 1990). To return to the distinction between the overt, official subject of *The Battle of San Pietro* – namely, the American 1944 Italian campaign and the more universal, emotional subtext of human loss – this is the film's primary dialectic and, to borrow Eisenstein's terminology, the former is the documentary's 'tonal' register (its definite rhythms and movements) whilst the latter is its 'overtonal' or subliminal undercurrents. Huston, having interwoven with clarity and precision image, commentary, irony and passion, dispenses with such rationality when it comes to the conclusion of *San Pietro*, a sequence that is almost abstract in its dependency on raw emotion and an absence of intellectual and historical interpretation. It is as if all the astute counterpointing that precedes the entry into the devastated town was surface, the recognisable ploys of propaganda which fail wholeheartedly to prepare us for Huston's elegiac finale, arguably the heart of the film in which the dialogue between text and spectator is reduced (or rather refined) to the transference of unmediated feeling. This scene, in which the inhabitants of San Pietro re-emerge from their hiding places in the mountains, stands apart from the rest of the film by its lack of narration except of the most minimal, functional kind. The passage where this lack is most pronounced follows the information about there still being German booby traps in the town and the explosion of a building. A body is spied in the rubble; a man, beside himself with grief, is comforted by friends; a piece of choral music is laid over the images; the man hugs the dead, dust-covered body of what is probably his wife; he turns to look at the camera with an expression of pleading and anger; after which there is a sharp edit (as if the camera cannot bear this burden and has to look away) to two mothers sitting together, both simultaneously breastfeeding and crying. In the man's desperate gaze out to the spectator there is at once contained the desolation of what is captured in the image, the impotency of being the one doing the watching, and the intention in Huston to convey both this fractured relationship and his underpinning theme that the defining truth of war is loss. The man's gaze functions as metaphoric shorthand for the complexity of emotions and intellectual responses encompassed by this untraditional and thereby 'inadequate' propaganda film. Huston, by the end, conveys rather than explains the battle for San Pietro and what it meant to witness it. It is apposite, therefore, that the film brings us back from such an acute moment of despair through images rather than narration. Again this entails looking out to camera, but this time it is the laughing, inquisitive, trusting and self-conscious children whose gazes we meet. These ironically recall General Clark's awkwardness at the beginning of the film – his reluctance at first to address the camera as if avoiding it.

The loss of voice at the end of *San Pietro* is, paradoxically, as eloquent as the previous scenes packed with loquacious commentary. In Alain Resnais' *Nuit et brouillard* there is a sequence detailing the uses to which the Nazis put the remains (the hair, bones, fat) of the millions they exterminated. At one point Cayrol's otherwise calm and poetic narration falters: 'With the bones … they made fertiliser, or tried to. With the bodies … but words fail', the ensuing shots being of a bucket piled high with severed heads intercut with the headless bodies they once belonged to packed into boxes like sardines. The commentary then resumes: 'With the bodies, they tried to make soap', describing the horrors of the image they accompany. *Nuit et brouillard* here reflexively signposts the inadequacy of words, whilst ironically emphasising the descriptive powers of the film's otherwise lyrical commentary, the necessity of words to the power of the overall film.[10] Conversely, Huston's unremarked descent into silence in *San Pietro* creates a tension between images and words as it conveys the actual insufficiency of words to offer comfort or make images manageable. Voice-over is no longer a controlling mechanism.

The classical fictional model of the voice-over is as the revelation of a person's inner thoughts or the use of the internal monologue to 'turn the body "inside out"' (Silverman 1988: 53). As Silverman (p. 53) continues:

The voice in question functions almost like a searchlight suddenly turned upon the character's thoughts; it makes audible what is ostensibly inaudible, transforming the private into the public.

In direct contrast to this, the words delivered by a documentary voice-over are, traditionally, public or collective utterances, and, to return to Cavalcanti's distinction between the 'rationality' of sound and voice as opposed to the 'emotional stimulus' provided by images (Cavalcanti 1939: 30), the words introduce, interpret or explain images that might otherwise, in a multitude of ways, remain incoherent. The ostensible purpose of the 'voice of God' model is to absent personality and any notion of the internal monologue, to generalise, to offer an omniscient and detached judgement, to guide the spectator through events whilst remaining aloof from them. As Mary Ann Doane (1980: 43) elaborates, 'it is precisely because the voice [in a documentary] is not localisable, because it cannot be yoked to a body, that it is capable of interpreting the image, producing the truth'. What consequently occurs when a documentary narration falters, stops or acknowledges its inadequacy, as occurs in both *Nuit et brouillard* and *San Pietro*, is that the personal, subjective potential of that voice-over is unexpectedly permitted to surface, a rupturing of convention that forces a reassessment of the text/narration relationship and how that relationship impinges on the effect a film has on the spectator. Addressing the issue of words' insufficiency and by literally ceasing to speak, as Huston does in *San Pietro*, paradoxically brings to the documentary voice-over the intimacy associated with its fictional counterpart; the diminution of the voice, the acknowledgement of its failure, is in this instance the powerful expression of the 'inner voice', the subjective presence within the documentary. With *San Pietro* the tacit documentary 'pact' that the voice-over will remain objective, 'rigorously extradiegetic' and '[assume] autonomy as a discourse' (Guynn 1990: 157) inevitably disintegrates. Guynn later posits that the spectator of a documentary cannot 'identify with the voice of the commentary as he does with the camera, because the voice addresses him [sic]' (p. 159). Not only is the contention that we cannot identify with a voice that addresses us hugely problematic, but the relationship between a documentary's voice-over and its audience can be far more complex than Guynn believes. By the very revelation of tensions and cracks on the surface of the non-fictional (and in this case propagandistic) film, *San Pietro* constructs a richly ambiguous relationship between narration and audience which can encompass both the moments of intimacy and emotional revelation (when the words 'fail') and the more conventional public and direct mode of address (when the words can respond to the images). The unease with which Huston adopts the traditional expository form also creates an openness that allows for a far more active, interventionist spectatorship.

In *San Pietro* and *Hôtel des invalides*, the documentary's inherent instability (the act of faithful documentation) is signalled through the tension between official and unofficial message or intention and the emphasised inability of the voice-overs to convey the essence of what is being represented. What is in need of being dismantled, is the conventionalised understanding of what a commentary's role is within the documentary, and to achieve this the actual voice – its audibility, its tone and gender, its effect – must likewise be re-examined. Increased personalisation is the most consistently used means of altering the role of a documentary's narrator; Hemingway's informal, conversational tone in *The Spanish Earth*, by breaking down the rigid formality of the traditional narration (telling us, for example: 'I can't read German either') makes us seriously question the 'voice of God' mode and thus the validity of the critical orthodoxy upon which traditional analyses of narration are predicated. Alternative means of address have included the use of silence (*San Pietro, Nuit et brouillard*), the use of openly political narration (*Land Without Bread, The Spanish Earth, The Last Bolshevik*), the use of multiple voices (*Dear America*) and the use of women's voice (*Sunless, Are We Winning, Mommy?, Handsworth Songs*). The last of these options is the most recognisably confrontational, as it challenges, from several angles, the conceptualisation of the documentary voice-over as a repressive ideological, patriarchal tool.

The woman's voice: *Sunless*

In 'The Photographic Message' Barthes, when discussing the relationship of text to photographic image, argues that 'the closer the text is to the image, the less it seems to connote it' (Barthes 1977: 26), that an image's connotative function ('the imposition of second meaning on the photographic message proper' (p. 20)), is reduced by the literalness of any accompanying text. There is a parallel to be drawn here with the use of voice-over in documentaries. The traditional expository mode of direct address relies on proximity between text and image: the words explicate the visuals, telling the spectator how he or she should interpret them; the potential for secondary, connotative meaning is limited. A crucial component of such an 'unproblematic' narration has traditionally been held to be the masculinity of the 'voice of God', the traditional tones of authority and universality. In less recent documentaries, the mere presence of a female voice-over would tamper with this unity, as deviance from the single, male voice could be argued to subvert that surety, engender doubt and divest the disembodied male voice of its 'discursive power' (Silverman 1988: 164). As French feminist Annie Leclerc observes:

> Man has always decided what can be talked about, and what cannot … How can female thought of any substance come into being if we are constrained to think along lines laid down by man … As yet, I am only really able to think one thing: that female thought can exist, must exist so as to put an end at last, not to male thought itself, but to its ridiculous – or tragic – soliloquy.
>
> (quoted in Moi 1987: 78–9)

Leclerc's suggestion is that the very presence of a female voice in a traditionally male environment is a means of creating a critical distance, of making one think about the use and adequacy of 'man-made' words.[11] Although the use of women's voices in non-fiction filmmaking has greatly increased over the past decade, the manner in which the expository mode has been theorised has not taken such historical changes into account. There are two ways in which, in the UK for example, the woman's voice has started to be heard: as a detached, omniscient narrator in the 'voice of God' mould and as the voice of the woman filmmaker from behind the camera. Differences are emerging between the two categories in terms of actual quality of voice. The female narrator is more often than not authoritative, relatively deep voiced; popular actresses and personalities used in the UK include Jancis Robinson, Zoë Wanamaker, Lindsay Duncan and Juliet Stevenson. This differs greatly from earlier notable uses of the woman as narrator in documentaries such as *Are We Winning, Mommy?* or *Handsworth Songs* in which the female voices heard in voice-over are less definite, more idiosyncratic, personal and probing. Both these documentaries are indicative of documentary's realisation in the 1970s and 1980s that a woman's voice embodied protest because women had traditionally been sidelined by documentary and history. This more personal, individual woman's voice is now frequently to be found in documentaries in which a female director can be heard (narrating, asking questions) from behind the camera. It is intriguing that filmmakers such as Molly Dineen, Jane Treays or Lucy Blakstad, who all interject their own voices into their films, have very similar voices and styles of delivery: wispy, middle-class and rather self-consciously unauthoritative. Whereas women narrators conform more readily to the masculine voice-over model, the director–narrators fall more into the category of woman's voice as other.

The equation that seems perpetually to have been made is between the woman's voice as physical utterance and the 'voice' as the metaphoric accessing of women's inner selves, their thoughts and identities. This attitude assumes that gender is an issue, principally because the gender of the 'universal' male voice is hardly remarked upon, whereas the specificity of the female voice too frequently is. The extreme examples of feminists conflating the 'voice' (in both its actual and metaphoric guises) with sex and gender are to be found in the writings of Luce Irigaray and Hélène Cixous, who, responding to patriarchy's over-reliance on seeing and looking, link a woman's 'voice' directly with her body and thoughts, so the adoption of a feminine voice necessarily offers the potential for anti-patriarchal radicalism. Echoing this idea that to 'let women speak' is a political act, both Doane and Silverman in their respective discussions of the female voice in (largely fictional) cinema, identify as the reason for the critical importance granted women's voices film's ready correlation (supported by the twinned mechanisms of fetishism and voyeurism) between the visual domain and the feminine. As Silverman comments, Freudian psychoanalysis (to which most analyses of cinema as vision-centred are indebted) stipulates that 'vision provides the agency whereby the female subject is established as being different and inferior' (Silverman 1988: 17), so an active voice can be mobilised to counter the passive position thereby allocated to women. The female voice-over offers another instance of drawing attention to the frailty of the documentary endeavour to represent reality in the most seamless way possible. It is not the voice of universality but of specificity, and signals the impossibility and the lack that the single male voice-over frequently masks. The 'lack' at the heart of documentary filmmaking and, more importantly, how it has been interpreted, is its inability to accomplish its purported aim to give as authentic a representation of reality as possible. The traditional voice-over can be construed as one of the symbolic substitutes for this loss of control and omniscience. A female commentary is thus an overt tool for exposing the untenability of documentary's belief in its capacity for imparting 'generalised truths' faithfully and unproblematically. This breaking down of tradition and expectation is particularly pronounced in documentaries such as *Sunless* that use the gender of the woman's voice-over in a significant way, a politicisation of the voice that is not evident in the use of women as narrators of conventional expository documentaries.

The relationship between image and female commentary in Chris Marker's *Sunless* is complex: the voice-over is spoken by a woman (in the English-language version, Alexandra Stewart), who in turn states that she is relaying not her own thoughts and observations but those contained within a series of letters from the fictional Sandor Krasna, the contents of which find parallels in the film images themselves. The boundaries between these various personae are far from rigid and thus the central relationship between image and words, traditionally so logical, becomes, in *Sunless*, fluid and mutable. The illogicality of this relationship, rather than functioning as a release from conventional constraints, has continued to trouble critics who, in turn, have constructed various means of imposing order on the film's central dynamic. Terrence Rafferty, for example, suggests that,

> The far-flung documentary images of *Sunless* are assembled as an *autobiography* – the film has no subject except the consciousness, the memory of the man who shot it – yet Marker attributes this consciousness to the invented 'Sandor Krasna', removes it from himself to a yet more spectral entity.
>
> (My italics; Rafferty 1984: 286)

Jan-Christopher Horak and Edward Branigan likewise conflate Marker and the female commentary, Horak saying about the films up to and including *Sunless*:

> While rejecting the ever-present but invisible commentators of traditional documentary films, Marker's films are inscribed by the presence of their invisible narrators. However, it is not the 'voice of God' of classical newsreels and documentaries that is heard, *but rather the personal and highly recognisable voice of the author, Chris Marker*, who speaks to his audience directly from offscreen.
>
> (My italics; Horak 1997: 50)

Branigan collapses the differences between 'voices' still further when referring throughout his discussion of *Sunless* to the spoken words of the
'cameraman' [sic], for example:

> During the prologue, the cameraman states that one-day he will juxtapose
> the image of the three children with black leader at the beginning of a film.
> ... I would like to suggest that the film *Sunless* is a cautionary tale. The
> cameraman is aware that in remembering images he has filmed, he may be
> too late in recognising their significance and emotional value.
>
> (Branigan 1992: 212, 215)

All of these (male) critics prove themselves overly eager to rid *Sunless* of its
complexity, favouring the reimposition of the hierarchical structure dominating
the majority of voice-over documentaries predicated upon the assumption that
the (usually male) commentary is the automatic corollary of the 'author' behind
it, and that the images are purely illustrative of that amalgamated point of view.
Sunless is thus perceived to be 'autobiographical', to contain the 'highly recognisable' voice of Chris Marker, and its narration is interpreted as nothing more
than the collected statements of the 'cameraman', although the film itself
consistently problematises such notions of centralisation. Branigan's conclusions
are particularly crude (and offensive if one considers that a female narrator
becomes a camera*man*). In needing to create a locus for the film's meaning, he
fabricates a composite persona of the 'cameraman', who, apart from indicating
once again that the image is to be prioritised over the words (a dubious
contention when considering *Sunless*), even fails to take into account the roles
Marker acknowledges for himself when, in the final credits, he claims responsibility for 'conception and editing'.[12] Clearly all these discussion of *Sunless* come
from an unerringly *auteur*-ist position, the reductivism of which fails to recognise the effects – on the spectator as well as the text – of the film's deliberate
dissipation of point of view.

By means of comparison, one could cite the very different use Marker makes
of voice-over and letters in *The Last Bolshevik*. In this later (1993) documentary
about the forgotten Russian filmmaker Alexander Medvedkin, who died on the
eve of Perestroika in 1989, the narrator (in the English version, Michael
Pennington) straightforwardly operates as the verbalisation of Marker's
thoughts, the film taking the form of six letters from him to Medvedkin. In the
pre-title sequence an exchange between Medvedkin and Marker is documented,
the former berating the latter for never writing even a few lines, and the latter
replying (via the narrator) 'Dear Alexander Ivanovich, now I will write to you
...'. The voice-over in this instance is readily identified as the 'I' of the film and
as the mouthpiece for Chris Marker; conversely, the narration of *Sunless* functions to create rather than collapse critical distance, the essential schism between
the gender of the actual voice and that of either the fictional writer of letters
(Krasna) or the director (Marker) being a differentiation that is emphasised
throughout the film. What characterises the female voice-over is the inconsis-

tency of its reported relationship with Krasna. At times it indicates a disturbing lack of independent thought, as if content to be simply a vehicle for translating pearls of wisdom from the venerable traveller; a feeling that is most pronounced when sentences are prefaced by one of the catalogue of servile utterances such as 'he wrote me …', 'he told me …', 'he described to me …' which lend the female voice-over a Desdemona-esque passivity as the receptacle for the Great Man's tales.[13] There are other moments, however, when the narrator comments upon what she is told, and there are quite protracted passages between the observations initiated by an explicit directive from Krasna during which it becomes unclear whether she is voicing independent thoughts perhaps triggered off by her dialogue with Krasna or whether she is merely continuing with the reading and relaying of the letters.

There is one particularly multi-layered series of sequences which exemplifies the confusions and contortions, beginning with the revisiting of the locations for *Vertigo*. The reverential *Vertigo* sequence ('in San Francisco I made a pilgrimage to a film I've seen 19 times') is the closest *Sunless* gets to being openly personal and autobiographical: an imaginary dialogue between a film-maker and one of his favourite films which in turn leads to the reflexive consideration of 'his' own (as it turns out imaginary) film. With childish obses-siveness, *Sunless* relives *Vertigo*, visiting the San Francisco flower shop where 'James Stewart spies on Kim Novak – he the hunter, she the prey?', following the same city streets down which Scottie trailed Madeleine, 'he' (Krasna?) had followed all the film's trails even to the cemetery at the Mission and the art gallery in which Madeleine contemplates Carlotta Valdes' portrait with its spiralled hair – 'the spiral of time'. This is not just a replica journey but a new, interpretative one, responding to, analysing, reworking Hitchcock's film, perhaps as we are being asked to do whilst watching *Sunless*. As the *Vertigo* sequence draws to a close by referring back to *Sunless* and the shot of the children in Iceland with which Marker's film had opened, the relationship of Marker to the film he has ostensibly created is once more complicated, as the voice-over refers to that first image as the 'first stone of an imaginary film' which 'he' will 'never make' but which nevertheless bears the name 'Sunless'. Thus *Sunless*, the visual and aural material its audience is engaged in watching, is cast into the realm of the imaginary, coming to comprise little more than a tendentious collection of memories and travel footage held loosely together by a voice-over whose origins and authenticity remain obscured to the end.

This obscurity spills over into how the film approaches the issues of represen-tation and recollection, the main underlying questions raised by the image and the voice-over. Throughout *Sunless* there is a running analysis of the intercon-nection between film and memory, two things which the normative documentary model might prise apart but which here are perceived as equiva-lents. Memory is personal history, subjective recollection prone to the distortions of 'Chinese whispers', whilst documentary film is conventionally the representation and objective collation of a collective past, a generalised history that can legitimately assume its place within a factual context. *Sunless* works against such a simplistic dichotomy, proposing as analogous the acts of remembering and filming in a sequence where the erosion of the divisions between image, voice-over and letters are particularly pronounced:

> I remember that month of January in Tokyo – or rather I remember the images I filmed in that month of January in Tokyo. They have substituted themselves for my memory – they *are* my memory. I wonder how people remember things who don't film, don't photograph, don't tape? How has mankind managed to remember? I know – the Bible. The new bible will be an eternal magnetic tape of a time that will have to reread itself constantly just to know it existed.

Unlike the classic expository documentary, this rumination does not suggest a finite or definite correspondence between image and narration; whilst the voice-over discusses means of remembering, of how memories are constructed, the images show people praying at temples in Japan for the beginning of the Year of the Dog. In the place of an analysis of these images is an analysis of the event–film relationship that necessarily preoccupies much theorisation of documentary: does memory exist independently of being filmed, or is memory constructed through being recorded? The act of remembering thus becomes synonymous with the act of recording, and although the means by which this is achieved may have changed (hence the cursory reference to the Bible), the equivocal outcome remains consistent. To return to the initial issue of how the voice-over in *Sunless* functions: as some writers seek to clarify the identity of the narrator and her place within the Krasna/Marker/voice-over triangle, so they likewise wish to replace the intellectual elasticity exemplified by the above passage of commentary with a controllable and contained series of gestures and ideas. Edward Branigan begins, rather implausibly, by suggesting that *Sunless* be categorised as a travelogue (which is to impose one kind of 'order' on it), before going onto suggest that the film is 'an instance of postmodernism rather than travelogue', and so constructing another 'logic' by which it can become manageable (Branigan 1992: 207–8). Whilst this search for coherence is understandable, it seems more appropriate with a film such as *Sunless* to take it on its own terms, to accept that there are three sources for the narration, and that the relationship between them remains oblique. This discordance is more interesting than striving to 'discover' in the film a unity of purpose; take the mention of Sei Shonagon's lists. In *The Pillow Book* Sei Shonagon, as the narrator of *Sunless* states, notes down things that, in her everyday life, attract, displease and fascinate her, in no particular order and with no particular end in sight. One of the categories cited by the *Sunless* narrator is that of 'Things which quicken the heart', which in *The Pillow Book* are as follows:

> Sparrows feeding their young. To pass a place where babies are playing. To sleep in a room where some fine incense has been burnt. To notice that one's elegant Chinese mirror has becomes a little cloudy. To see a

gentleman stop his carriage before one's gate and instruct his attendants to announce his arrival. To wash one's hair, make one's toilet, and put on scented robes; even if not a soul sees one, these preparations still produce an inner pleasure.

It is night and one is expecting a visitor. Suddenly one is startled by the sound of rain-drops, which the wind blows against the shutters.

(Sei Shonagon 1971: 51)

This list of 'Things that quicken the heart' is personal, idiosyncratic and, one suspects, ephemeral in that, on another day, Sei Shonagon might have compiled a totally different list. This is not a definitive list of 'things that quicken the heart' nor one that will necessarily be recognisable to those who read it; instead, what the list makes one do is to think, however fleetingly, of what would be in one's own list of 'things that quicken the heart'. *Sunless* works in a not dissimilar way on its audience: it offers up images that fluctuate between the domains of the personal or the mundane (the essence as well of *The Pillow Book*) and the historical or generally recognisable (the essence of the classic documentary), which are in turn juxtaposed against a transgressive and ambiguous voice-over that only sporadically coincides with them. The film's dominant thesis becomes: beyond the moment, beyond the collision of image and sound in front of one at any one time, there is no grander meaning, tomorrow's list of 'things that quicken the heart' is not constrained by today's, one image or piece of voice-over is not conditioned by that which preceded it.

Whereas traditional voice-over documentaries are about closure, *Sunless* remains intentionally open, and within this openness the female narration (in its distance from both Marker and Krasna) provides a space for the interpretations of the 'data' or 'files' to take place, files which are usually linked by a random association rather than causality. Likewise the narrator/Marker/Krasna triangle. It is not sufficient to identify the female voice as being Marker's or the 'cameraman's' (Rafferty, draws a parallel between 'the unseen protagonist of *Sunless* [and] the man with the movie camera' (Rafferty 1984: 286)), for this fails to assist the act of watching *Sunless* or aid us in our understanding of its lack of narrative or closure and its emphasis on the mundane, the inconsequential and the ephemeral. Instead, the film is inviting us to enjoy its randomness, and in this it is playing with the notion of what constitutes a documentary. As Marker (1984: 197) has noted, 'the word "documentary" leaves a trail of sanctimonious boredom behind it. But the idea of making files ... suits me well'. It is pertinent that Marker usually works within more conventional forms of documentary, and that all his films (whether the more overtly political ones or the more personal and subjective ones)[14] then go on to participate in a dialogue about the nature of filmmaking rather than blithely accept the harsh parameters and make do. *Sunless* can only be made to conform to the traditional expository model it nominally belongs to if, as has been attempted, one unproblematically correlates the voice-over with Marker; then, quite conventionally, the images and the narration in the film would explicate and consolidate each other. By not definitively establishing mutuality, however, Marker refuses to clarify or classify the film, as the voice-over (if it is not Marker's 'voice') is a fictional construct within a documentary framework.

Conclusion

Sunless raises several problems and questions about narration in documentary and the way it has been interpreted. It is not possible to say about Marker's film that, 'The authoring presence of the filmmaker is represented by the commentary and sometimes the (usually unseen) voice of authority will be that of the filmmaker him- or herself' (Nichols 1991: 37). Even in *The Battle of San Pietro* (which Nichols cites as an example of the actual voice of the narrator being that of the filmmaker and thus a direct verbalisation of Huston's point of view) is not so easily compartmentalised, as the narrator's words do not consistently coincide with what one infers to be Huston's opinions and feelings. The voice-over in *San Pietro* literally disintegrates, disappears at times and signals more clearly the collapse of this presumed symbiosis between voice and argument. The false opposition set up by most theoretical discussions is between the 'raw' visual material (which, if it could be left unadulterated, would provide us with a 'truer' representation of the events being recorded) and the forces of subjectivity such as the voice-over that endlessly thwart its objective nobility. Thus, narration (endlessly subsumed into the far more specific category of the 'voice of God') has come to signify documentaries at their most distortive and fictionalising because of the connotations of individualism, instruction and so on that the actual presence of a *voice* conjures up. Many voice-over documentaries, however, do not conform to the 'voice of God' model, and yet their diversity has been underplayed. Films such as *San Pietro* or *Sunless* engender in their audiences doubt about the hierarchical binary oppositions that dominate thinking about documentary: that to show is more real than to tell, that the image contains a truth that a narration actively interferes with, that any subjective presence destroys the possibility of objectivity completely. By the time we get to *Sunless* and its multiple confusions of 'voices' the standard theories become untenable. Brian Winston notes that breaking norms can in itself be 'positioned as a deliberate blow against hegemonic practice. For instance, it can be argued that *A propos de Nice* and *Land Without Bread* depart from the norms exactly to critique them' (Winston 1995: 86); one could extend this and suggest that not only are such films critiquing the norms but they are permitting a concomitant diversity of reaction and thought from their audiences. For the films that adopt the non-'voice of God' narration model, the actual documentary comes out of an acknowledgement, refinement and rejection of how commentary and its supposedly inherent didacticism is conventionally perceived. In addition to this, narration becomes a dialectical tool; even when it is most conventionally used as in *The World at War* or *The Times of Harvey Milk*, the limitations of the voice-over do not preclude the possibility of an alternative interpretation being left open and accessible to the audience. Once again, therefore, documentary becomes a negotiation between the film and its subject, of which the narration is a constituent part. Voice-over does not signal the obliteration of the 'purity' of the factual image, although it may offer an alternative and even contradictory view of it.

Part II

The legacy of direct cinema

In the Introduction to this book, American documentary filmmaker Errol Morris was quoted as saying that '*cinéma vérité* set back documentary film-making twenty or thirty years' (quoted in Arthur 1993: 127). Morris is here referring to direct cinema, popularly but erroneously known by its French name. Direct cinema is often viewed as the single most significant intervention into documentary filmmaking history, so what is wrong with it? Morris takes issue with various direct cinema beliefs: American *cinéma vérité* filmmakers (such as Donn Pennebaker and Richard Leacock) approached documentary filmmaking as merely a means of recording events; their attempt to deny and absent their own personal perspective (that is, their belief in film's ability simply to relay faithfully that which it records); the belief that through their observational methods they could get to the truth in a way that other forms of documentary filmmaking could not. Similarly, Emile de Antonio, whose polemical, personal films also directly challenge direct cinema's belief in observation, has said

> *Cinéma vérité* is first of all a lie, and secondly a childish assumption about the nature of film. *Cinéma vérité* is a joke. Only people without feelings or convictions could even think of making *cinéma vérité*. I happen to have strong feelings and some dreams and my prejudice is under and in every-thing I do.
>
> (Rosenthal 1978: 7)

What is wrong with direct cinema is essentially what its exponents said about what the films did, not necessarily what the films themselves achieved. De Antonio's prime target here is the belief of American *cinéma vérité* that any film could or should be objective. Because Robert Drew and those who followed him were fond of saying what their films were about and how they should be interpreted, theorists and practitioners alike have tackled direct cinema in accordance with how it has defined itself. This has remained the crucial problem and the reason for the observational form – ostensibly so liberating – setting back documentary for twenty or thirty years.

The observational mode, despite the vigorous arguments mounted against it, remains extremely influential, for it freed both the style and content of documentary. The films of Drew, Leacock, Pennebaker, the Maysles brothers and Wiseman focused on the individual, the everyday, the contemporary; they attempted to keep authorial intervention to a minimum by adopting a more casual, observational style that had as its premise the desire to follow action rather than dictate it, to see and record what happened to evolve in front of the cameras. Of course, these aims, as Morris and de Antonio point out, were unrealistic, but nevertheless, an understanding of direct cinema is seminal to any study of documentary. Although this section of the book will not rehash the same old discussions of the 1960s pioneers, but will instead look at the important influence that American observational documentary has had on more modern work, this Introduction will tackle the issue of why direct cinema's legacy has proved so problematic to the evolution of documentary practice and theory alike. Most practitioners recognise, by now, that documentary film can never offer a representation of real events indistinguishable from the events themselves, although theory has not yet come to terms with the value of such a realisation.

The resigned and stale understanding of documentary film and its history stems largely from two factors (and consequently from their intersection). The theoretical problem – discussed earlier – is that documentary history has too easily been circumscribed and confined by the imposition of a 'family tree' structure, an understanding of its evolution that assumes that one style of film-making begets and is rendered obsolete by the mode that replaces it. The practical problem posed by documentary – which will be examined here – relates directly to the practice and critical evaluation of direct cinema. Direct cinema is a 'problem' because its exponents believed (although not all – and one of the failings of documentary theory has been to sideline the dissenting or questioning voices of Fred Wiseman, for example, or at times the Maysles brothers) that, with the advent of portable equipment and with the movement's more informal style, they could indeed show things as they are and thus collapse, better than any other form of documentary, the boundary between subject and representation. This is the established and conventionalised mission of observational documentary: to offer a real possibility of showing events and people in as unadulterated a state as possible. It seems inconceivable that a current documentary filmmaker would utter naively, as Richard Leacock did about his relationship with John Kennedy during the making of *Primary*, that the then presidential candidate forgot at times that he was even being filmed. Cameras were not that small and Kennedy was an astute politician. The direct cinema 'problem' is that most of its great American exponents stood by the authenticity of their filming methods and the end results they achieved, and by and large the copious theoretical discussions of these films have sought merely to dismantle, dismiss and reject this truth claim by scavenging for sequences, edits and shots that contradict the direct cinema mantra. *Vérité* is a sticking place because it successfully 'proves' two mutually exclusive things: that documentary's driving ambition is to find a way of reproducing reality without bias or manipulation, and that such a pursuit towards unadulterated actuality is futile.

Practitioners and theorists alike have assumed that direct cinema's ethos is objectivity, and that, in turn, 'objectivity' and 'observation' are synonymous. This elision has proved highly detrimental to the conventionalised perception of direct cinema. Bill Nichols comments of observational documentary that it 'appears to leave the driving to us' (Nichols 1983: 52), that the filmmakers' paramount desire is to absent themselves (and, by this, Nichols and they mean their subjective influence) from the filmmaking process and the resulting films, so that 'in pure *cinéma vérité* films, the style seeks to become "transparent" in the same mode as the classical Hollywood style' (Nichols 1983: 49). For Nichols and others the observational style is problematic because it implies the filmmakers' loss of voice, thereby insinuating that 'pure' observation comes at the expense of commitment, interventionism and authorship. This is an inadequate conflation, and to question Nichols' strident pronouncements one can pluck any number of examples from the observational 'canon'. To suggest that the voice of Drew Associates is absent from *Crisis* is to downplay the socio-political potential of the observational style, which in this instance clearly suggests a preference for Robert Kennedy over George Wallace (see Chapter 5). It is the critical possibilities of the observational mode that have been historically downplayed, but which have been taken up in the modern era.

The disparity between the observational ideal and much observational directing practice hinges on the troublesome notion of 'purity', evoked by Nichols and others in relation to observational documentary. Brian Winston, when talking about Roger Graef's work in the 1970s, says that he 'uses the *purest* of direct cinema modes. However complex the topic, he eschews interviews and narration. In the hands of his long-time collaborator and cinematographer Charles Stewart, the style of these films is *minimally interventionist*' (Winston 1995: 208; my italics). What is clearly being held up for approval here is the grail of pure documentation, a piece of 'pure' observation being thought of as necessarily superior to and 'better' at doing what it has set out to do (that is, represent a series of non-fictional events) than its more mendacious cousins deploying such 'false' mechanisms as voice-over, interview and the actual presence of the filmmaker. Not only are observation and objectivity being wrongly conflated, but also assumptions are being made about style and the use of technology. The technological innovations that paved the way for direct cinema in America and *cinéma vérité* in France in the early 1960s – lightweight cameras, portable sound equipment, stock that could be used in lower light conditions – led to a less formal, more passive and responsive style of filmmaking and a concomitant adherence to an ideological belief in the possibility of accurate representation. One critic who immediately subsumes all these different elements into one is Stephen Mamber when arguing

> At its very simplest, *cinéma-vérité* can be described as a method of filming employing hand-held camera and live, synchronous sound. This is a base description, however, for *cinéma-vérité* should imply a way of looking at

the world as much as a means of recording. ... The essential element of *cinéma-vérité* ... is the use of real people in undirected situations.

(Mamber 1972a: 79)

Thus technology, style and attitude become one.

In examining the zealous pronouncements of the 1960s observational film-makers themselves, it becomes instantly apparent how this misjudgement occurred, for it was they who cemented the view that the belief in purity and objectivity was sustainable. There is a certain evangelical quality about many of the comments, such as Al Maysles' statement 'I regard our films as the purest form of cinema' or his brother David's belief that 'we don't impose anything on the people we film. We are the servants of our subjects rather than the other way round' (Kolker 1971: 185). Absent entirely from this description of their methods is any fundamental acknowledgement of the filmmaking process itself being the intervention that invariably makes all the difference, and this is how American *cinéma vérité* has been accepted and defined: as naïve, simplistic and misguidedly idealistic. But as a result of such fervent utterances – to which one could add many others such as Robert Drew's assertion that 'the film maker's personality is in no way directly involved in directing the action' (quoted in Winston 1993: 43) – this perception of direct cinema has stuck.

Why this poses such a problem is that 'purity' in this context is unobtainable, there are always too many other issues spoiling the communion between subject and viewer across a transparent screen, and so the majority of the criticism levelled at *vérité* in America has focused on moments which show the films to have failed in their messianic endeavour. The films are easy targets in this respect, precisely because of the impossibility of their designated aims. Having eschewed the ostensibly authoritarian devices of previous documentary modes (narration, archive, thesis-led structures) observational documentary rather rashly proclaimed itself not to need any methods beyond observation (a defini-tively passive activity), and this included authorial intervention. By a process of osmosis, it seemed, the subject matter was to be conveyed to the audience. As Noël Carroll (1996a: 225) suggests, no sooner had 'the cinema of truth' arrived as an idea, 'than critics and viewers turned the polemics of direct cinema against direct cinema': Carroll perhaps fails to go far enough with this assertion, because it is the very quality of the *vérité* statement of intent, its alleged purity, that provokes critics and viewers to turn against it. As Carroll continues, 'Direct cinema opened a can of worms and then got eaten by them' (p. 225).

Comparing the statements by the Maysles brothers and one of their films (*Salesman*, 1969) illustrates the discrepancy between execution and ideal. The film is guilty of several violations of direct cinema's code: it uses non-diegetic music on two occasions; it edits (for effect) sequences out of chronological order; it is highly selective in what and who it chooses to focus upon. These are all elements that, to some degree, are the impositions of the filmmakers; they are tools of interpretation. Such manifestations of a subjective presence are only problematic because of the way in which direct cinema defined its own aims, to many other documentary filmmakers the cutting together, for example, of two sequences temporally separate but thematically related (as occurs in the juxtaposition of Paul, the focal salesman, travelling by train and the bible selling convention he participates in) would not be an issue. The Maysles in interview have felt compelled to dismiss or qualify this sequence as uncharacteristic, as 'dictated' by content. As a technique, such parallel editing makes them both 'a little nervous' (Levin 1971: 278); later in this interview they stipulate that the purpose of observational film editing was merely to compress material, not to manipulate it. There are other instances of 'impurity' in *Salesman*: the superimposition of the Beatles' *Yesterday* over the conclusion of another unsuccessful selling attempt by Paul; the ironic use of the similarly extra-diegetic *If I Was a Rich Man* overlaid onto a sequence of Paul driving from one failed sale to another. Perhaps the Maysles' justification for these impositions would be that both tracks initially had a diegetic source – a gramophone in the first instance, a car radio in the second. One of the more troubling examples of manipulation in *Salesman*, because it suggests more than a deployment of supportive narrative methods, is the very end of the film. The Maysles brothers have referred to their decision to prolong the final shot of Paul looking, apparently despairingly, out of a hotel window, calling this, rather coyly, a 'fictionalisation' (Levin 1971: 276), but they have not explained the whole manner in which this final sequence is edited. One of the things the sequence strongly evokes is the growing alienation of Paul, a markedly less successful bible salesman than his colleagues, culminating in the final shot. *Salesman* concludes with an end of the day discussion between the salesmen the film has been following, cutting between what seem to be two sides of the same room. What the viewer does not expect, however, is that the sequence comprises material from two different sources: a hotel room from much earlier in the film (offcuts from sequences already seen) and a hotel room from later on, after the salesmen have reached Florida. This falsification potentially alters the sequence's whole meaning. Because of where it is presumed to come in the overall sequence of events, Paul's vacant gaze out of the window conveys resignation, defeat, despair, the imminent loss of his job; when, however, it is realised that this shot comes from earlier in the film – from before Paul's plight was fully realised – it begins to take on alternative and less bleak meanings: Paul might just have been getting hungry waiting for the other three to get ready. The Maysles brothers have simply applied the most basic of Kuleshov's discoveries: that what matters above all else is that a sequence of shots *appears* to be logical, not necessarily that it *is*; the issue is whether or not this is appropriate to a piece of direct cinema, to which the answer has to be no.

No, that is, until one comes across statements by direct cinema filmmakers that contradict (or at least admit the shortcomings of) the ideal of the pure image. In another interview from the one quoted above, Albert Maysles says something quite different about the nature of the truth observational documentary can discover:

> We can see two types of truth here. One is the raw material, which is the footage, the kind of truth that you get in literature in the diary form – it's immediate, no one has tampered with it. Then there's the other kind of truth that comes in extracting and juxtaposing the raw material into a more meaningful and coherent storytelling form, which finally can be said to be more than just raw data.
>
> (Levin 1971: 277)

Here, Albert Maysles is admitting the difference between rushes and a film when he draws a distinction between the truth of the 'raw data' and that of the finished, edited product. In creating the final sequence of *Salesman* out of disparate images and unchronological bits of film, the Maysles brothers are thus constructing the underlying truth of the film: that Paul is not just the narrative core of the film, but its emotional core as well; a tragic, failed figure with whom the filmmakers and the audience alike sympathise and empathise. The end of *Salesman* is a subjective manipulation of events to suggest a character and story that the Maysles brothers, presumably, felt was implicit in the material they had acquired. This, however, is a far cry from the professed ideals of direct cinema, and highlights the issues underlying the 'problem' of purist observational film. With virtually every step, *Salesman* (like many of its contemporaries) denies the validity of the notion of filming 'undirected situations'; besides the anomalies cited above, there are other instances which suggest that sequences were more than likely set up (shots of subjects just happening to enter hotel rooms whilst the camera's running; one bible selling sequence in which a neighbour enters and fails to look in any way surprised at the presence of the Maysles brothers at their friends' dining table).

The key issue is that observational cinema has been mis-defined, and has mis-defined itself. Any documentary, including observational ones, testifies to the absence rather than the presence of purity at its heart. Having presented itself as the mode most capable of collapsing the difference between image and reality, of best representing an unadulterated truth, direct cinema suffers particularly harshly from such a realisation. If one strips the films of the theoretical baggage they come burdened down by, they offer less stifling, more exciting possibilities. *Salesman* and *Meet Marlon Brando*, or the political films *Primary* and *Crisis* which are discussed in Chapter 5, show the notion of documentary purity to be deeply flawed, but this is not what makes them significant and interesting. Rather, it is the suggestion that the dynamism of the documentary text is predicated upon and created by the central dialectical relationship between content or unadulterated truth and representation, not destroyed by it.

The core of direct cinema films is the encounter before the camera, the moment when the filmmaking process disrupts and intrudes upon the reality of the world it is documenting. This neither invalidates it as a means of recording and conveying that reality, nor does it mean that documentary is simply an elaborate fiction. In the case of Paul Brennan, *Salesman* suggests that he was a struggling bible salesman before the filming began, this is his establishing truth.

He is also created afresh during filming with the Maysles brothers; particularly in sequences in which he is flagrantly playing to the camera (singing in the car and talking directly to camera, delivering a monologue in his wavering Irish brogue), Paul is quintessentially offering a performance of himself in a comparable manner to Brando in *Meet Marlon Brando*. The final composite 'Paul', whom the film evokes and the audience goes away with, comprises both these facets, the shown and the implied. In both the contemporary forms of observational documentary to be discussed here, the same juxtaposition is paramount.

Docusoaps and other recent evolutions in British observational documentary indicate that the puritanism of early direct cinema has been replaced by more realistic expectations that permit the correlation within one film of observational practice and more obtrusive filmic elements. Likewise, the journey film is entirely the result of capturing an encounter – capturing, therefore, the collision between the off-screen, establishing truth that was there before the cameras turned up, and the truth that emerges from the dialogue that intrusion elicits. In journey documentaries such as *Shoah* or *London*, the search for a subject is prioritised over any straightforward conclusion, and the films concomitantly emphasise that a documentary and its thesis can only evolve at the point of film-making, and that the encounter is the most tenable reality a film offers. This premise, ironically, has its origins in American *cinéma vérité*, in statements such as Albert Maysles' 'I've always been interested to see what happens when two strangers meet' (Levin 1971: 282). The difference between Albert Maysles' perception of the accidental encounter and that enacted in the more recent films cited above is that the significance for Maysles lies in the new-found ability to observe the meeting between strangers in as discreet a way as possible; to filmmakers such as Lanzmann and Keiller, the accidental encounter directly involves them and is much more overtly reminiscent of the interactive strain of *cinéma vérité* found in the films of Jean Rouch. The origins of both journey films and docusoaps, however, lie in the work of early observational documentary: the overriding interest in people as subjects over theses; the prioritisation of the mundane occurrence over the monumental event; a predilection for following subjects and actions as opposed to leading and constructing them.

The remainder of this book will, from a variety of angles, examine the legacy of direct cinema and the manner in which subsequent filmmakers have largely ignored the pronouncements of the observational filmmakers themselves in favour of engaging with and developing the techniques they pioneered. The chapters immediately following this Introduction will focus on two documentary forms (the docusoap and its position within the British observational tradition; the modern journey film) that inherently display the impossibility of collapsing the boundary between the event and its representation. Both genres or modes emphasise the moment of encounter – between filmmakers and subjects – around which a documentary is constructed and which no documentary can totally mask, whether this is Jane McDonald in *The Cruise* beckoning Chris Terrill and his camera, Claude Lanzmann pressing a Holocaust survivor to speak or the fictional Robinson and the Narrator in *London* being diverted from their intended journey by an accidental occurrence. Both forms thereby realise and illustrate the deficiencies of how direct cinema defined itself, questioning the foundations of observational cinema whilst still indicating and incorporating its practical strengths – namely, that, unlike more historical or thesis-led forms of documentary, it can capture unpremeditated, surprising and potentially destabilising moments on camera. Unlike their direct cinema predecessors, however, the filmmakers to be discussed in the following chapters understand these accidental moments as made by, rather than independent from the filmmakers' intrusion into the subjects' world; that the important truth any documentary captures is the performance in front of the camera.

3   New British observational documentary

'Docusoaps'

Bill Nichols, in his attachment to documentary's genealogical development, implies that observational documentary as it is commonly understood 'dies' and is rendered obsolete by the advent of more interactive and reflexive modes of non-fiction filmmaking. Instead what has occurred is an evolution from within the parameters of observational documentary, so that the form, in all its permutations, remains recognisably 'observational', whilst incorporating many of the tactics and devices of its so-called interactive, reflexive and performative successors. Firstly, it is wrong to imply that observational documentary ceased to be popular once de Antonio and colleagues introduced more interventionist forms of filmmaking; within the observational mode's continuing popularity, especially in America and the UK (where it is popularly known as 'fly-on-the-wall'), there has emerged a desire both to address the mode's shortcomings and to incorporate into the traditional observational framework other elements of documentary filmmaking. Since direct cinema, the Anglo-American observational tradition has gone through several stages: the later one-off films of Pennebaker, the Maysles brothers, Wiseman brothers *et al.* (*Grey Gardens, The War Room, Hospital*) have stayed faithful to the cause, modifications were introduced by such television series *An American Family* (Craig Gilbert, 1972), *The Family* (Paul Watson, BBC, 1974) and *Police* (Roger Graef, BBC, 1982) and the genre has since been more radically altered by the interventions of specific filmmakers such as Nick Broomfield, Molly Dineen and Michael Moore and popular series such as the stream of docusoaps to have appeared on British television in the late 1990s.

Docusoaps have brought a new set of issues to the question of observational documentary. *The Family* is generally credited as being the significant antecedent of the docusoap, although Watson's later *Sylvania Waters* (BBC, 1993) is a more plausible direct source with its focus upon entertainment and the larger than life 'star' Noeline and the controversy that raged over Watson's alleged manipulation of her and her husband Laurie into vicious stereotypes. The recent proliferation of the 'docusoap' started specifically with the long-running series *Vet School* and *Airport*, which began in the mid-1990s, and with the two 1995 series *HMS Brilliant* and *The House* (although this discussion will argue that these two series should not be subsumed into the docusoap category). The characteristics that have come to represent the docusoap subgenre of observational documentary are its emphasis on the entertainment as opposed to serious or instructive value of documentary, the importance of personalities who enjoy performing for the camera, soap-like fast editing, a prominent, guiding voice-over, a focus on everyday lives rather than underlying social issues. Although, by the end of the 1990s, the docusoap started to go out of favour with channel controllers, the series, with very few exceptions, have been phenomenally successful with viewers and have helped to redefine the observational documentary mode. The emergence of the docusoap signals very clearly the growing unhappiness with classic observational transparency and passivity, the absenting of an authorial voice and the abstention from any overt means of demonstrating the filmmakers' presence. The need to modify the observational mode has been a driving force behind British documentary film-making in particular. British 'fly-on-the-wall' has tended to include elements such as voice-over and interviews that would have been anathema to Drew Associates and the direct cinema films that followed in their wake; the British tradition has also, though, been keen to preserve the most fundamental elements of observational documentary such as the importance of people and the detail of their lives. What the docusoap has responded to, however, is the pervasive modern concern with the notion that documentary's most significant 'truth' is that which emerges through the interaction between filmmaker and subject in front of the camera (classic direct cinema being predicated upon the different idea that documentary was simply the recording of events that would occur whether or not the cameras were present).

Docusoaps form part of this developing trend towards a greater interest in the active interaction between film, filmmaker and spectator; they also relax some of the boundaries between documentary and fiction (as the term 'docu-soap' attests), a factor that has raised awkward questions about falsification and reconstruction. Docusoaps pose interesting and, at times problematic, questions about degrees of acceptable intervention by the filmmakers into his or her subject material; they continue in the tradition of John Grierson more than that of Robert Drew and exemplify the 'creative treatment of actuality' (Rotha 1952: 70) he espoused. The fundamental preoccupation is with 'creativity' being ascribed to 'documentary', but only because creativity is taken, very rigidly, to denote anything that detracts from the document, the truth, the evidence at the heart of a non-fiction film. The intention of this discussion is to highlight the shifts that have occurred within the modern British observational documentary tradition towards this more relaxed position, reflecting back to the perceived shortcomings of direct cinema in the 1960s before examining the series *HMS Brilliant* and *The House*, the rise of the fully fledged docusoap with series such as *Driving School, Hotel, The Cruise* and concluding with a considera-tion of the work of Chris Terrill, whose presence as an *auteur* problematises further the pursuit of a purely observational style.

As in the case of *cinéma vérité* and direct cinema in the early 1960s, the evolution and current extension of the parameters of observational film and television is in large part due to specific technological advances. Although Annette Kuhn, for one, resists the assumption that technology was a determining factor where *vérité* and direct cinema were concerned, positing instead that the opposite might be true – that 'certain types of equipment were developed and marketed expressly to make a specific type of filmmaking possible' (Kuhn 1978: 75), the most commonly held view of the technology–form relationship is that advances in sound and camera equipment had a radical effect upon the type of film (documentary or fiction) that was conceived or could be envisaged. Just as the wave of observational films at the beginning of the 1960s was made possible, it is argued, by the appearance of lightweight cameras and portable sound equipment that could record live, synchronous sound (see Mamber 1972a: 79), so the current interest in similarly observational styles of programme making in Britain have been influenced by equivalent technological advances. The first significant factor has been the rise of non-linear editing systems such as Avid; these have enabled filmmakers to work on video in a way comparable to how they once worked on film, to edit quickly and to experiment with sequences and cutting styles. Traditional linear video editing was slow and inflexible. Any observational style documentary or series is, by being predicated upon observing action as opposed to dictating it, necessarily going to amass a higher than average shooting ratio, and immediately prior to the arrival of Digicam, 16-mm film was getting too expensive as the documentary's medium of choice. Coupled with the fact that such series are now invariably shot on video (thus producing an even greater amount of rushes than the 16-mm films of the 1960s), the development of an alternative to linear editing has been a crucial factor. The other important advance has been the introduction of digital video cameras (DVC), small 'handicams' increasingly operated by directors who, whether because of taste or financial restrictions, are willing to experiment with multiskilling. The first high-profile series to use 'digicams' was Chris Terrill's *Soho Stories* (BBC2, 1996), for which Terrill operated both camera and sound, subsequently followed by series such as *Relate* (BBC2, 1998) about marriage guidance counselling. Clearly there are financial benefits to working with DVC and non-linear editing equipment (as Paul Hamann has commented, docusoaps already cost on average only a third of the price of the equivalent in light entertainment or sitcoms and he has sought to reduce their average cost to the BBC from £80,000 to £65,000 (Hamann 1998: 6)), but there are also creative ones such as greater intimacy and immediacy. Again, therefore, technological changes have enabled documentary filmmaking to shift direction. Although filmmakers such as Molly Dineen (camera) or Nick Broomfield (sound) have been using 'multiskills' in their films to specific effect, now such techniques have become more readily available and the results more widely accepted.

A discussion of contemporary British observational filmmaking is necessarily going to focus upon the docusoap subgenre that has most comprehensively made familiar and popularised the styles made possible by such technological advancements. The distinctions, however, between old-fashioned observational documentaries and docusoaps are not always easily identifiable. Paul Hamann, while head of BBC documentary and history department, has defined docu-soaps quite loosely as series 'constructed around a small group of charismatic characters in a common endeavour' (Hamann 1998: 6). This definition is too broad perhaps to be of substantial theoretical use, but nevertheless highlights two areas that are key to the subgenre, namely the emphasis on 'characters' grouped together by work, pleasure or place/institution. Both of these features have clear antecedents in the wider observational tradition. The seeking out and prioritisation of 'characters' or subjects who stand out has been a consistent ploy of the observational mode since direct cinema and *cinéma vérité* emerged. *Salesman*, with its focus upon Paul, testifies to this, and to the realisation that an entertaining and different 'character' is a facilitating narrative structuring device. The concentration on a fixed place (or shared experience) has been another tactic deployed by traditional observational cinema, most notably in the institution-based films of Fred Wiseman, and has functioned as an additional means of lending coherence to a sequence of otherwise unplanned events.

What, though, distinguishes docusoaps from other forms of observational documentary? One factor is the marginalisation of issues (socio-political, histor-ical, etc.); another is production values. Series – still shot on film – such as *HMS Brilliant* (Chris Terrill, BBC1, 1995), *Nurse* (Jenny Abbott, BBC2, 1998) and even *The House* (Andrew Bethell, BBC2, 1995) all incorporate, either explicitly or implicitly, certain issues (women in the front line, the state of the nursing profession, grandiose over-spending at Covent Garden, etc.) that transcend the boundaries of their form and give the films a significance or direction beyond their entertainment value. Whether docusoaps ever possess such weight or substance is debatable; some, like *Vets' School* and *Vets in Practice* or *Children's Hospital* proffer information in addition to character and plot, whilst others such as *Driving School, Pleasure Beach, Clampers* or *The Cruise* more consciously elevate personalities over situation. Another, now conventionalised, feature of the docusoap is the imposition of fast editing and overt structuring devices more akin to those of soap operas (hence the coined term 'docusoap'). Docusoaps tend to comprise short sequences and to intercut different narrative strands, not necessarily to create a point through such juxtapositions, but rather to move the story along; they also frequently have opening sequences that introduce the audience to the 'characters' each episode will focus upon, closing sequences that anticipate the next episode and function as hooks to maintain audience interest, and often give each episode a title. Within this observational/soap framework, docusoaps also include elements such as narration, interviews and music conven-tionally excluded from traditional observational documentaries.

Opinions of the value and quality of the docusoap vogue differ, especially among old school observational documentarists. Whereas Roger Graef has vociferously defended docusoaps, commenting 'I am pleased to see television recognises that ordinary lives are worth watching' (Graef 1998), Paul Watson argues that 'there is no analysis, no insight, no unexpected side to the story, no light shed ... their only function seems to have been to turn the rest of us into peeping toms' (McCann 1998). Graef, however, conflates docusoaps (somewhat erroneously) with the traditions of classic observational filmmaking, namely 'filming events as they happen, without lights, staging or interviews' and 'editing in chronological order' (Graef 1998), whilst Watson differentiates between that tradition (into which he places his own pioneering series *The Family*) and the new wave of 'cheap series' that merely '[point] a camera at someone wanting self-promotion' (Watson 1998). Watson comments, 'when I created *The Family*, I had an agenda, my own voice, a point of view ... I made the films with a clear idea of the story I wanted to tell and in the hope of providing genuine insights into the human condition'; to him docusoaps are 'just dross' that 'inspire no controversies and enrich nobody'. Watson's charge is that docusoaps have trivialised the documentary form and, concomitantly, have prioritised entertainment value over seriousness of intent.

Ex-BBC producer Mark Fielder (series producer of *Driving School*) argues that the essential distinction between a docusoap and an observational documentary is 'down to the weight and substance of the material', and compares 'a serious piece of social comment' such as *Nurse* with *Driving School* which he characterises as 'a series about how a bunch of drivers do in their driving test'. To Fielder, 'soap (including the non-fiction variety) implies a soft, bubbly, somewhat content-free approach to television. That's not to say it's bad, it's just lightweight and probably very entertaining' (Fielder 1998). In a similar vein, journalist Adam Sweeting remarks, when discussing *Hotel*, that

> the word 'documentary' used to carry connotations of authority, gravity, and probity. ... Today, the word has shed its original meaning. Much of the material being paraded as 'documentary' has only the most tenuous link with the factual events it claims to examine or reappraise.
>
> (Sweeting 1998)

The evident preoccupation behind these comments touches upon the basis for the very definition of 'documentary' as a discourse of sobriety, as Nichols terms it, as if there is a natural affinity between factual representation and earnestness of endeavour. Docusoaps, for one, question this affiliation in a manner that differentiates them from their observational counterparts, despite the common lineage, and it is the mounting of this challenge to traditional definitions that provokes Channel 4 commissioning editor Peter Dale when he rather censoriously comments

> Documentaries were once cherished by broadcasters because they fascinated us and contributed to our understanding of the world. ... Today, documentaries are cherished because they entertain.
>
> ... It would be ironic if, at this time of greatest popularity, the documentary genre was dying for want of genuine curiosity and passion.
>
> (Dale 1998: 17)

In contrast to Dale and others, Nick Shearman, who initiated several of the key popular observational series to have come out of Bristol BBC – *Vets' School, Vets in Practice, Holiday Reps* – argues fundamentally that docusoaps (a term he dislikes) have substantially broadened the appeal of documentary. The primary tool, according to Shearman, in achieving this has been the prioritisation of people over issues, the elevation of the emotional response and personality. Shearman is an advocate of 'people-based' documentaries that possess a universality enabling them to 'appeal to a broad range of people and to touch on common experiences' (Shearman 1998); he believes in the validity of this intention and its legitimacy as a documentary form. The manner in which docusoaps are here being described is somewhat akin to how one might expect mainstream drama to be referred to: as a text that mobilises in the spectator patterns of identification, empathy and emotional fulfilment. In this, docusoaps also appear illustrative of the observational preoccupation with masking the author and focusing the experience of viewing a documentary on the interaction between subjects and audience. In accordance with this, many current observational series are directed by relatively inexperienced producers/assistant producers. Not only are the people prioritised over potential issues, they are also (as in any formulaic genre) prioritised over the *auteur*-ist identity of the filmmaker.

Antecedents: *HMS Brilliant; The House*

HMS Brilliant (Chris Terrill, BBC, 1995) and *The House* (Andrew Bethell, Double Exposure/BBC, 1995) were unexpectedly successful observational series that proved the catalysts for the recent resurgence of interest in observational documentary on British television. *HMS Brilliant* follows the crew of the first British Navy vessel to take Wrens as it patrols the coast of the ex-Yugoslavia; *The House* infiltrated the Royal Opera House, Covent Garden, during the period before its recent closure for renovations (it re-opened 1999). The two series exemplify the main routes observational documentary could take: Terrill's work is more classically observational in that his films are largely examinations of institutions and the issues they illustrate (although *The Cruise* is a notable exception), whilst *The House* had a more direct stylistic influence upon docusoaps with its use of ironic, pointed narration, its confrontational editing and its pursuit of crises and star performers. Terrill has outlined how working within the docusoap framework on *The Cruise* gave him 'much more room for creativity and personal interpretation and bias' because here 'you are looking at a world and interpreting it your way' (Terrill 1998). Terrill's approach to observational filmmaking has been to tread a balance between acknowledged bias, creative interpretation and fairness to the subjects under scrutiny. The technical and formal choices are thus subjective and personal, although the actual filming methods are perhaps not; as Terrill (1998) says

> To make observational films you've got to be a fairly thick-skinned chameleon, you've got to change, to go with the flow. I enjoy being taken

into communities and new ways of thinking, and find I can't always disassociate myself. Part of my way of seeing is to tap into other people's ways of
seeing, to see things through their eyes. ... The other key point is never to
be judgmental. One does have one's own moral code, one's ethical stance,
but you've got to be broad minded and mustn't try and distort the way
those in the films see things.

This stance of consciously working at absenting his own point of view whilst
remaining aware that he still possesses one, Terrill relates to his own anthropo-
logical background, and is especially relevant to some of the issues raised by
HMS Brilliant, a six-part (50-minute each) series about a Royal Navy vessel.
This was the first time the Navy had permitted filming on a ship on active
deployment in a war zone, and Terrill and his crew spent twelve weeks filming
the series, living alongside and in similar circumstances to the crew of the ship.
Terrill's immersion in navy life (he is a former cadet and his parents served in
the Navy during World War Two) and his non-interventionist attitude to
filming are acutely scrutinised in episode three of *HMS Brilliant*, 'Rocking the
Boat'. The episode revolves around preparations for and the performance of
'The Sod's Opera', a revue show which resembles a traditional twelfth night
entertainment during which the junior classes exchange places with their superiors and can say what they want. The episode is structured not just around this
event, but around the concomitant issue of Wrens on active duty, and culminates in a group of Wrens performing a version of 'I Will Survive' that is
drowned out by the jeers from the largely male audience.[1] Towards the beginning of the episode, Lieutenant Commander Bob Hawkins, who throughout
the series espouses a variety of patriotic and intensely traditional views, gives an
interview in which he intimates his unease with women on active duty,
commenting that they are 'the fairer sex and we [men] are the people who
should protect them'. He indicates how much he, 'a masculine guy', appreciates
the ship's exclusively male environment, saying 'I enjoy the camaraderie, the
aggression of a warship'. Hawkins' conflation of 'camaraderie' and 'aggression'
is interesting as it illustrates very clearly, from within a non-fictional context, the
violent exclusivity of Eve Sedgwick's notion of 'homosocialism'; it also predicts
the confrontational irony of Hawkins' own contribution to 'The Sod's Opera':
a drag act.[2] Following on from Hawkins' interview are a series of sequences that
further the debate surrounding women on active duty: a brief montage of principally negative comments by other male crew members about the presence of
the Wrens on board *HMS Brilliant*; an interview with Lieutenant Tracey
Lovegrove during which she observes that the ship is 'very much a man's world'
and how women are excluded from the 'male bonding'; an interview with
Captain James Rapp in which he articulates the differences he perceives between
the men and the 'girls' aboard his ship. This initial issue-prioritising sequence
concludes with Hawkins suggesting that a country that chooses to send its
women to the frontline is 'morally bankrupt'.

During these ten minutes, there is no intervening commentary from Terrill (voice-over is entirely absent from *HMS Brilliant*); the intercutting between the various elements is to set up the revue – the illustrative proof of the ideological argument – without direct manipulation. Rehearsals for 'The Sod's Opera' are juxtaposed with further interviews and discussions about the women at war issue, most notably the Wren's run through of 'I Will Survive' being sandwiched between one male crew member suggesting that Wrens on board are a temptation to married men and another saying that women lack the stamina of their male counterparts and are forever complaining. The final preparations and the revue proper take up the final section of the episode. The men's contributions are: Leading Seaman Micky Goble telling crude jokes that are bleeped out, a close harmony quintet, a parody gay act and Hawkins in drag; the women's contribution comprises a mock thank you speech to the men and 'I Will Survive', which closes the film. As a woman, viewing the Wrens struggling defiantly through their rendition of Gloria Gaynor's feminist anthem is deeply moving, in part because the women sing quite badly; the booing from their male colleagues hardly comes as a surprise to them or us, and what the sequence cements is an implicit counter-bonding between the women on the screen and those watching. As Terrill himself observes, this climactic confrontation was 'sort of a stand off'.

With regard to his adherence to the belief that, as a filmmaker, he does not want to impose his views on his films but rather take on and understand those of his subjects, Terrill comments about this specific episode of *HMS Brilliant*, 'I was obviously trying to show that there are many attitudes to women and to women in the front line. All these people were also my friends, and its wasn't for me to agree or disagree with Bob Hawkins, who had a very particular line that women should not go to sea'. What comes as a surprise, perhaps, is Terrill's own attitude to the question of women in the armed forces, which is that he has 'difficulty relating to the idea of women in the front line', a view that he qualifies by saying, 'but that's a personal thing that has no part in a Chris Terrill film' (Terrill 1998). Arguably it is even quite plausible to think, whilst watching, that the opposite is true – that Terrill's ideological sympathies are with the Wrens. Terrill acknowledges that he has to fight his own judgement and cannot 'paintbrush myself out completely, because I have to make decisions about what goes into the film', establishing the principle that, even if a subject is highly emotive, 'it's not for me to be emotive about it' whatever the responses of the audience watching. In his discussion of non-fiction and objectivity, Noël Carroll examines the relationship between subjectivity, bias and selection. Carroll refutes Balazs' assumption that 'a personal point of view in every shot is unavoidable' (Carroll 1996a: 227), arguing instead that not only is this dubious, but that the premise upon which such a view is founded is flawed. The crux of Carroll's argument is that the brandishing of the term 'subjectivity' to signify 'everything that doesn't suit the criteria of the objective' (p. 230) is to misinterpret the 'objectivity' itself. Just as scientific research can be classified 'objective', Carroll maintains, despite its selectivity, so can documentary. It is just such a relaxation of the twin notions of 'subjectivity' and 'objectivity' that one discerns in the later documentaries of Chris Terrill, whose way of manoeuvring himself into an environment through what he calls 'a passive sort of exploitation' (Terrill 1998), exemplifies one way in which observational documentaries can still articulate issues through editing and the words of the interviewees rather than through overt authorial intervention.

The House is a comparable series, but also markedly different in its attitude towards subjectivity and the treatment of issues and people. Its style is to implicate the filmmaking itself in the confrontations and issues raised by its content, most concretely through Jancis Robinson's pointed, ironic and intrusive voice-over. *The House* is not passively observational, but actively so; the filmmakers (though falling short of directly engineering crises) were, for example, fore-warned of conflicts that were looming, such as the imminent sacking of the Box Office manager, which subsequently features in Episode 1, 'Star Struck'. The whole nature of the series is to pursue crises and to structure episodes around them, and in so doing the significance of the institution is marginalised in favour of the individuals involved, as is the presence – however implicit – of issues. As Andrew Bethell has commented, *The House* is not really about the arts, but about 'fear and loathing in the work place' (Bishop 1996: 13); it is not institution-specific but universal in its appeal. Much about the style of *The House*, such as the hand-held camera's furtive pursuit of people and its presence at crucial moments of tension, conforms to the ideals of modern observational film; the series, however, is also generally credited as being the immediate precursor to subsequent factual soaps, a shift of emphasis indicated by its demotion of seriousness in favour of 'character'-based entertainment. The major distinction to be made between *HMS Brilliant* and *The House* in terms of technique is that the latter uses mechanisms such as voice-over as critical devices to guide spectatorial responses to the programmes' content; whereas *HMS Brilliant* adopts a relatively fluid narrative and is only occasionally structured around crises, *The House* prioritises conflict over every other element. In the first episode, the emphasis on entertainment, crisis and ironic tone are immediately evident as American singer Denyce Graves loses her voice during the first performance of *Carmen*. There is, to begin with, a clearly cynical inflection to the narration and the direction, depicting Graves as a prima donna, but, by the end, the over-dramatisation has become a genuine crisis.

A discernible pattern emerges through the series, so that each episode comprises one major and several minor crises, some of which are resolved by the end of the episode, with others remaining open, to be resumed in later weeks. In Episode 2, 'Horse Trading', for example, the major crisis is the phenomenal overspend caused by last minute alterations to the designs for both the Royal Ballet's production of *Sleeping Beauty* and the Royal Opera's *Katya Kabanova* (in excess of £60,000 on each and overtime expenses of £117,000). Linked to this central structuring device are various subsidiary arguments, problems and rivalries: a horse slipping on the shiny *Kabanova* set (necessitating yet more modifications); the rivalry between Royal Ballet ballerina Darcy Bussell and guest star Sylvie Guillem for the most prestigious dates of the forthcoming

American tour of *Beauty*; another slippery floor, this time causing Bussell to slip several times during the ballet's final London rehearsal. The significant aspect of *The House*'s crisis structure is the lack of discrimination or hierarchical placement; all major and minor crises are valued according to their narrative as opposed to their political, social or ideological importance. Thus the laying off in the final episode of established older Royal Ballet dancers in order to save money, or the protracted pay discussions between personnel and unions in Episode 4, are given comparable weight to the dispute between traditionalists and modernists over the Opera House's revival of Harrison Birtwhistle's *Gawain*. This uniformity clearly anticipates docusoaps' underpinning desire to entertain; likewise the very use of (mini)crisis structure narrative patterns is a characteristic that will feature heavily, as is the fast editing between different but interlinked strands of a single episode. What substantially sets *The House* apart from the series it is said to have influenced is its production values. At a cost of £150,000 per episode, a nine-month shooting period and twelve-week editing time per each one-hour episode (from a shooting ratio of 1:28), *The House* – like *HMS Brilliant* – proved a costly venture.

It is interesting that both Terrill and Bethell followed up *HMS Brilliant* and *The House* respectively with series that can straightforwardly be classified as docusoaps: *The Cruise* and *Pleasure Beach* (1998, Bethell's BBC1 series about Blackpool pleasure beach). What makes this classification uncomplicated is, above all, the emphasis upon relatively inconsequential subject material, with which inevitably comes the subjugation of events to personalities such as Jane McDonald, the singer on the Caribbean cruise liner. Terrill experimented on *The Cruise* with seeing if he could 'make films that were much more about positive aspects of the human condition: endeavour, effort, triumph over adversity, dealing with emotions and coming through, comradeship, teamwork' (Terrill 1998), universal qualities common to most docusoaps. Other generic features that became naturally affiliated with the emerging subgenre of docusoaps are also evident in *The Cruise*, namely the featuring of characters (usually introduced by first names only) in upbeat title sequences,[3] music, fast cutting and the use of voice-over (although *The Cruise* only inserts narration at the end of each episode to tell the viewer what to expect in the subsequent instalment). Most of these contravene the 'rules' of traditional observational documentary as they signal overt intervention on the part of the filmmakers (although some other features – such as the use of direct interviews with the subjects – have already become conventionalised). These mechanisms can also be viewed as an extension, an evolution of the observational mode, as they address directly some of the deficiencies or inaccessibilities of more earnest predecessors.

Within this evolutionary process, the crucial element is the parallel with soap operas, and more particularly the development of an increasingly soap-like narrative structure. A 'crisis structure' peculiar to or characteristic of the current wave of popular British observational documentary was evident in *The House*, as well as in early docusoaps such as *Airport* and *Vets' School*. The pursuit of events with an in-built narrative structure rapidly became one of the mainstays of early direct cinema, as this circumvented the problem of feeling compelled to impose a narrative on events to render a documentary comprehensible. The aim of Robert Drew and others was also, however, to find and film events that were monumental; events that were so significant in themselves (such as a closely contested presidential primary election or the integration of the University of Alabama) that their filming seemed, to the participants in the crisis, unimportant by comparison. The docusoap's 'crisis structure' is more to do with creating narrative tension than capturing a significant moment. Michael Waldman, series director on *The House*, commented at the time of making the series that, 'getting narrative from observational documentary is hard. We had to impose a structure [during editing] and that is what took the time' (Bishop 1996: 13). Waldman then explains how this need came to affect the shooting process, that, for the early weeks of filming, they cast their net wide and filmed what material they could, whilst by the last two months the direction in which the series was going had emerged, so they 'had a shopping list' (ibid.).

Blithely perhaps, Waldman has re-opened one of the most contested areas of documentary practice – the right and need of the filmmaker to intervene in the direction of material he or she is filming. Many subsequent docusoaps have depended upon moments of crisis (*Clampers, Driving School, Airline, Airport, Hotel*) and they insert such confrontations in varying degrees. *Hotel*, in fact, is concerned with the structuring of tension almost to the exclusion of any other tangential matters. In one episode (which even begins mid-crisis), one confrontation – the Duty Manager on the telephone to the wife of the hotel dishwasher who has failed to turn up for work – gives way immediately to another crisis – two guests complaining about the rudeness of one of the waitresses at breakfast – which, in turn, gives way to the fractious preparations for two major functions. Editing is here used for the accumulation of a *Fawlty Towers*-like farcical tension. Chris Terrill considers series such as *Hotel* to conform to the current shift towards 'making television about confrontation and aggression because it's sexy watching'. Conversely, in *The Cruise*, as Terrill (1998) remarks, 'there's very little confrontation, very little happens and there are very few events'; the determining structuring device remains the personalities of the subjects followed so that 'there's a narrative coming out of who they are and what they're doing'. Creating a crisis as many series do is to falsify, to an extent, narrative events.

Docusoaps: the documentary as entertainment

The exemplary docusoap is structured and edited to maximise entertainment value. Unlike direct cinema 'crisis structure' films, docusoap crises are primarily concerned with the mundane and the non-monumental, and so the creation of a structure performs the very different function of making everyday events coherent and entertaining. Mark Fielder's opinion is that the fast editing, short sequences style of docusoaps serves to divert attention away from their lightweight material: 'It's like running on lilies floating on a pond, you can't spend too long on each [scene] because the story will sink ... so what you have to do is keep moving, keep offering flashes of excitement, a bit of colour, a bit of a joke, an emotional moment – nothing too heavy' (Fielder 1998). This entails editing the documentary material along the lines of popular fiction, in particular the soap. Whereas the media derogatorily coined the term 'docu-soap', there are real parallels to be drawn between the fictional and non-fictional soaps that in part serve to explicate the latter's appeal to audiences. Nick Shearman recounts how, whilst his series *Vets* and *Holiday Reps* were running, he counted the number of sequences in an average soap opera and compared that with an average *Vets in Practice*. He found that the two 'were vaguely similar, and that the length of a scene was never more than two minutes and generally around a minute and a half in length. They [soap operas] were also using intercutting in precisely the same way' (Shearman 1998). Traditional soaps cut between a pool of relatively stable characters, focusing on a limited group within each individual episode. Likewise, Shearman describes how *Vets* tended, from very early on, to juxtapose three stories per episode, frequently intercutting two (because parallel editing usually works better) and inserting a third half-way through. This is, broadly speaking, the structuring format still used on recent series of *Vets in Practice*, although Rachel Bell, the 1998–9 series producer, elaborates that there are, in addition, usually four animal stories per programme and between 18 and 21 scenes, which actually suggests that the scenes have become progressively shorter over the series' long run (Bell 1998). The prevalent tendency in later docusoaps is towards accentuating the soap parallels; *Lakesiders* (Hart Ryan for BBC1, 1998) series producer Guy Davies maintains that on average his 28-minute episodes contained 130 sequences (Dams 1998: 17), in addition to which the series was transmitted immediately after *EastEnders* and directly mimicked the BBC soap opera in its title sequence and music.[4] This fast editing is a feature that categorically differentiates the docusoap from both traditional observational documentaries (more likely to be renowned for their long takes and minimal editing) and from contemporary observational documentaries such as *HMS Brilliant* or *Nurse* that seldom adopt the same soap structure. Editing has two primary functions: to forward narrative and to create argument; in a docusoap the former is dominant. Unlike a comparable theme at the centre of a Fred Wiseman film or an institution-based observational series, any 'big theme' around which a docusoap could be structured tends to be preoccupied with forwarding the narrative or offering factual background material than with ideological or political issues.

The overriding factor that differentiates docusoaps from other forms of observational documentary is thus entertainment; they are more popular with viewers than other forms of documentary programming (*The Cruise* achieved approximately 11 million viewers, *Driving School* peaked at 12.45 million and even long-running series such as *Vets' School* and *Vets in Practice* have remained stable at 8 million) and whether or not they are broadcast pre- or post-watershed (9 p.m.) is a crucial issue. The docusoap, on the whole, is thought to appeal to a mass, family audience, and there are relatively few subject areas that naturally fit post-watershed, although with *Estate Agents* (Shearman Productions for ITV, 1998), *Jailbirds* (Chris Terrill, BBC, 1999) and *Paddington Green* (Lion Television for BBC, 1999), docusoaps have also infiltrated the post-9 p.m. slots. The target audiences and the concomitant emphasis on entertainment are the most plausible reasons for the nature of docusoap subjects – animals, hospitals, the police and related jobs, shopping – and for the rapid, short concentration span editing. The programmes' universality is thereby an essential component of their success, although what they might also lack is critical distance. Albert Maysles remarked that 'our films very much proceed from particulars to generalities' (Levin 1971: 280–1), ostensibly functioning, therefore, in much the same way: manoeuvring universal points from individualised situations, creating an identificatory bond between spectator and subject. The important distinction between old and new methodologies, though, resides in how this 'universality' is effected. *Salesman* possesses a grandiloquence beyond its superficial mundanity and functions as a 'tragedy of the common man' comparable to Arthur Miller's *Death of a Salesman* to which it was, at the time, readily compared, whereas contemporary docusoaps aspire merely to represent a life more ordinary. Maureen in *Driving School*, for instance, is not made into a tragic figure but a likeably average one, a difference that perhaps stems from divergences in style. *Salesman* permits characters to develop slowly, without much outside commentary or intrusive guidance and to have a subliminal existence only partially represented by their conscious actions on film, whilst *Driving School* hints at very few 'human condition' issues beyond what is there on the screen. A spectator of direct cinema is invited to extrapolate significance from the action as represented; the substantive quality of docusoaps is their paramount desire to entertain, to replicate in some way the narrative lines of popular drama, to appeal to a mass audience, and to divert rather than just interest and instruct.

Underlying this issue of entertainment, however, is the spectre of falsification, briefly alluded to during the discussion about editing and structuring. However much the argument is that soaps (and, by extension, docusoaps) are popular because they are ordinary, because they replicate or represent the everyday; as Chris Terrill intimates, 'life is never lived at that pace' (Terrill 1998) so even the documentaries are inevitably interpretative. The question of 'honesty' has been paramount to docusoaps. Some of the considerations are factual, others more aesthetic. For example, in 1998 several allegations were made in the press that Ray Brown, the 'star' clamper of *Clampers*, was not, except in emergencies, a clamper at all but a desk-bound supervisor who had last been a regular on the beat at least two years before the series was transmitted. These rumours were confirmed by Southwark council. *Driving School* was likewise challenged by the press. The sequence most frequently cited is that in which Maureen Rees, on the eve of another attempt at her theory exam, wakes in the middle of the night and asks her husband Dave to test her on the Highway Code. The sequence is a reconstruction, and Jeremy Gibson (head of BBC Television Features, Bristol) and others have gone on record exonerating themselves from blame, commenting that, having gleaned that Maureen *did* get up at night through panic, it was perfectly legitimate to recreate such a sequence without the film crew having to camp out in her bedroom for an entire night. Another such instance of reconstruction occurs in *Pleasure Beach*, during a bomb alert. The alert is real and filmed as it happened, as are the telephone calls concerning it; these scenes are then juxtaposed with shots of security staff searching Blackpool pleasure beach. The bomb alert is an authentic individual action, but the subsequent search is, like Maureen's night-time panic, a representative typical one (although the search in *Pleasure Beach* is not a reconstruction, but the filming of a subsequent bomb alert). Andrew Bethell maintains that taking such a liberty is, once more, legitimate. One of the problems with such a presumption is that the audience's awareness of this kind of conduct is likewise presumed. Jeremy Gibson and Grant Mansfield (Executive Producer, *Driving School*) have both argued that the audience will be able to pick up the signs that a sequence such as Maureen waking up and revising her Highway Code is reconstructed, but is this sufficient?

Mark Fielder problematises the issue when he recounts two other sequences from *Driving School* which were, in different ways, set up. The first is a sequence in which Dave gives Maureen a driving lesson in a multi-storey car park, which Francesca Joseph, the series director, specifically suggested, realising in advance that such a situation, for a nervous driver, would produce a crisis.[5] Fielder comments that 'it was no accident that they [the Reeses] were asked to do that scene' because the producers 'realised pretty quickly through filming the series that certain situations would provoke them to have rows' (Fielder 1998), which is indeed what occurs at the end of the multi-storey car park scene when Dave forces Maureen out of the driver's seat to complete the manoeuvre.[6] The second 'fabrication' is more contentious as it involves actually altering the course of the series' narrative. The producers on *Driving School* were concerned that Maureen, the series' 'star' subject, would not pass her manual driving test, an event they felt would be the series' natural and desired conclusion, and so suggested that she learn instead in an automatic car. Maureen agreed, having indicated that this was an option she had already considered. As Maureen's instructor in Cardiff did not have an automatic vehicle, the producers intervened to effect this switch, putting Linda (the instructor in Cardiff) in touch with Pam (one of the Bristol instructors featured in the series) and having them enact a scene on Clifton Downs in Episode 2 in which the two women discuss Maureen's case, the result of which is that Pam agrees to pass her on to her colleague Paul. As Fielder asks, 'How do you tell that story in reality? You can tell it in voice-over and no one would quite believe it. ... The ... reality is that Linda and Pam didn't know each other, so we had to make the introduction. That was our intervention into the story' (Fielder 1998). Clearly the actions of the producers in this case directly altered the course of events as they would have, in all probability, unfolded (although Maureen has subsequently passed her manual test as well), yet Fielder's justification for this is that he personally did not think 'it was critically important, because in the end what was important about Maureen's story was how she dealt with driving, the pressures on her, her relationship with her husband, which we didn't alter, and finally whether or not she was going to pass which is what people really cared about' (Fielder 1998).

This is an interesting defence of manipulation within a documentary, but one which many would find deeply problematic. On 8 December 1998 the BBC held an editorial policy meeting at which new guidelines were issued concerning 'Staging and re-staging in factual programmes'. Having acknowledged that 'there are few factual films which do not involve some intervention from the director, even those which are commonly described as "fly on the wall" or observational documentaries' (BBC 1998: 2), the guidelines proceed to similarly identify certain 'production methods' (specifically single camera set ups) that 'make it impossible to record all events exactly as they happen' and to then single out the accepted techniques (such as cut-aways) commonly deployed to combat this (BBC 1998: 2). This section of the document concludes with a series of bullet points itemising 'acceptable and unacceptable practice in factual programmes', many of which pertain directly to instances of overt intervention on the part of the producers:

- Programmes should truthfully and fairly depict what has happened.
- Programmes should never do anything to mislead audiences.
- While it may, on occasions, be legitimate to re-shoot something that is a routine or insignificant action, it is not legitimate to state or re-stage action which is *significant to the development of the action or narrative, without clearly signalling this to the audience.*
- Contributors should *not* be asked to re-enact *significant* events, without this being made clear in the film. ...
- If significant events have been arranged for the cameras that would not have taken place *at all* without the intervention of the programme-makers, then this must be made clear to the audience.
- Shots and sequences should never be intercut to suggest that they were happening at the same time if the resulting juxtaposition of material leads to a distorted and misleading impression of events.

(BBC 1998: 3)

These prescriptive guidelines highlight two key areas: informing the audience of any staging or re-staging procedure, and gauging the significance of the intervention to the film overall. *Driving School* was not covered by such guidelines and the decision to construct a sequence that would otherwise not have taken place would now be construed as a violation of such rules, despite arguments that the staging of the driving instructors scene does not alter what is 'critically important' to the series as a whole. The producers' intervention altered the subsequent path of the narrative; without the scene *Driving School* would have not followed the same story line, and in the absence of any categorical signals, the audience remained ignorant of the fact that this scene is staged specifically for the cameras. Arguably, the scene signals its intention via the stilted performances of the two driving instructors and through the implausibility of the set-up: that Pam and Linda, both featured in the same series but from different cities, happen to know each other. The sequence is too neat and uncomplicated: Linda says 'I'm glad I've seen you, Pam – I've got a pupil for you', Pam mentions Paul, Linda concludes 'he sounds ideal, Pam' and they exchange cards. As with Jeremy Gibson's assumption that the audience will read the signs in the night-time sequence, the honesty of this fabricated scene is dependent upon a similar discernment, but should this be presumed? The new guidelines suggest not, outlining instead the necessity for 'labelling' as opposed to subtle implication.

One issue to be addressed is thus whether or not the pull towards entertainment compromises the docusoaps' potential for honesty. The arguments that drive this book are: that documentaries inevitably fall short of being able to reproduce authentically the actuality they film; that the notional grail of the non-fiction tradition – that a mode of representation exists that can break down the barrier between reality and illusion – is a false utopian ideal. In recognition of this, many of the contemporary documentaries discussed start from the opposite premise that all documentary is circumscribed by its technical and theoretical limitations and can only present a mutable truth – the truth that comes into being as the documentary is being filmed. Chris Terrill (1998) articulates a new (arguably more realistic) approach to observational filmmaking than that adhered to by direct cinema when he says:

> Our stock in trade [in documentaries] has to be honesty; not necessarily truth, whatever truth is – truth is a construct. We deal in perceptual truth, personal truth, not absolute truth. Who deals in absolute truth? Nobody does. It's continually an interpretation, a relating of events as we see them to our audience.

This opinion is very similar to Emile de Antonio's observation that honesty and objectivity are not even closely related. It is also worth recalling Terrill's argument that docusoaps particularly offer 'much more room for creativity and bias', that, paradoxically, the subgenre's affiliation to dramatic methods ensures, in his estimation, its increased honesty, if indeed honesty is equated with the expression of a personal and perceptual truth. The flaw in this idea is that most docusoaps do not employ comparably overt methods as authorial intervention to signal their interpretative as opposed to categorical truth, except for standardised devices such as interview. Terrill, in series such as *Soho Stories*, *The Cruise* and *Jailbirds*, can be heard from behind his camera conversing with the subjects of his films – just as Molly Dineen or Lucy Blakstad can (this does seem to be a more female trait) – a device that necessarily identifies the specificity of the situation represented. For all the use of emotive music (sad for Maureen's test failure or the death of a pet, for example), fast editing, guiding narration and packaging, the docusoap retains one feature of the direct cinema legacy: the anonymous camera and filmmaker. In the absence of such a straightforward device as speaking in one's own film or appearing in it, as Nick Broomfield does, both the BBC guidelines and Chris Terrill, from differing perspectives, propose that additional measures should be enforced to ensure the mutability of the truth represented is understood by those watching. (Whether or not such direct forms of intervention are more 'honest' than their less visible counterparts is examined more extensively in Chapter 6.) Chris Terrill's fundamental premise is that documentary filmmakers are and should be 'constantly accountable', and this is not necessarily covered by simply assuming that the viewer recognises the artifice of the factual material.

The issue that highlights most clearly the question of artificiality within the context of observational documentary is that of performance – both the performance of the filmmaker and that of the subject in front of the camera. At times, performance, lying and documentary ethics are linked, as in the case of Carlton's documentary *The Connection* (Marc de Beaufort, 1997) in which several participants in a documentary reputedly about a drug run from Colombia to Britain assumed roles or faked actions. Likewise, in the pulled Channel 4 documentary *Fathers and Daughters* (1998), it was discovered, on the eve of transmission, that one of the father and daughter pairs interviewed for the series were, in real life, partners (the television company only realising this when the woman's actual father contacted them after seeing the programme's trailer). In both these cases, subjects of a documentary were deliberately pretending to be someone they were not – in *The Connection* with the full knowledge of the filmmakers, in the latter without. Performance in observational documentaries is normally a more nebulous issue. As they had actively pursued events with an in-built 'crisis structure', so the exponents of direct cinema also pursued subjects who were professional performers, thinking that this would once again reduce to a minimum the distortive effect of the camera on the subject's behaviour. In *Meet Marlon Brando* or *Don't Look Back*, neither Brando nor Dylan drops his guard for the camera or stops performing; the filming process becomes an extension of their public personae. Clearly, performance within an 'ordinary lives' observational film or a docusoap is a very different matter, as the 'characters' who become familiar through the programmes – with the exception of *The Cruise*'s Jane McDonald or the various performers in *The House* – do not have a history of professional performance and are thereby enacting themselves exclusively for the benefit of the cameras. In a tangible sense, Maureen Rees and others only come into being as performers through and at the point of filming, which is an artificiality that the direct cinema directors sought to avoid.

The immediate response to the notion of performance in documentary is to criticise it as a falsification – an element not to be trusted. The journalist Allison Pearson, for instance, has commented about performance in docusoap:

> In the hands of its most serious practitioners – directors such as Molly
> Dineen and Roger Graef – documentary aspires to tell us something about

the human condition. The docu-soap, by contrast, tells us something only about the condition of human beings who know they're on television.

(Pearson 1998)

Pearson's dismissiveness stems from her perception of performance as an obstacle to serious documentary endeavour; she fails to equate it, as Chris Terrill does when referring to his current interventionist approach which utilises the interaction between filmmaker and subject, with 'a new honesty' (Bishop 1998: 17). Terrill's opinion is compatible with Jean Rouch's suggestion that, in *cinéma vérité*, people's reactions are 'infinitely more sincere' on camera than off *because* 'they begin to play a role' (Levin, 1971: 288). Sincerity is thus equated with an acknowledgement of the filming process, so although 'a camera's a camera, an object which you can't not notice' (Fielder 1998), a documentary is inevitably built around its presence – and the concomitant presence of the crew. In a docusoap, however, there is very little engagement with the theoretical permutations of this awareness; they remain, by and large, programmes that circumvent the overt acknowledgement of performance.

The docusoap subgenre's dependence on the notion of the star performer is, in this context, problematic. The defining paradox of docusoaps is that they purport to be interested in the excessively ordinary, whilst at the same time having reached the level of success and notoriety they have done by the discovery and promotion of 'stars' – individuals who, more than those around them, transcend and achieve an identity beyond the series that created them. Such 'characters' are actively sought by filmmakers. Maureen in *Driving School* proved crucial to the series' popularity, so much so that without her it 'would have been virtually impossible' (Fielder 1998), and since it ended she has starred in a follow-up *Driving School* special, copious independent television appearances and has acquired an agent. Likewise, Trude from *Vets' School* and *Vets in Practice* now has an exclusive broadcasting contract with the BBC and only works as a vet part time. Newer docusoaps such as *Clampers* and *Lakesiders* arguably take the issue of stars a step further by not merely focusing on characters they think the public may like, but inviting subjects to perform exclusively with the camera in mind. In the *Clampers* Christmas Special (BBC1, 1998), Ray Brown, already known as a character who sings whilst on clamping duty, halts the narrative progress of the programme to perform festive numbers (at the end of his day, for example), with arms swaying and a decidedly embarrassed colleague by his side cajoled into joining in. This is no longer something Ray does whilst clamping, it is now an activity that has replaced it.

There are two separate issues here that, with the rise in the docusoap's popularity, have becomes blurred: the acknowledgement that the more engaging and likeable subjects should be prioritised, and the very tangible potential for an alternative and lucrative career on the back of a docusoap's success perhaps undermining the documentary intentions of the original series. Both Maureen and Trude are significant because they became stars as a result of the viewing public liking them, suggesting that one crucial element of the star/audience rapport is the potential for identification. According to Nick Shearman (1998), Trude had 'no concept of acting up' for the cameras; similarly, Mark Fielder stresses that Maureen and Dave Rees just happened to be less affected by the presence of the cameras than the others featured in *Driving School*. The accidental popularity of Trude and Maureen conforms to one ideal of documentary: that it 'has to feel slightly effortless and as if bits fall into place' (Shearman 1998) without too much manipulation. The comparable popularity of Ray Brown or the wannabe singer Emma in *Lakesiders* appears more manufactured, less an accident than an actively sought addition to the respective docusoap narratives. Despite Trude's success without resorting to 'acting up' for the cameras, Shearman comments that, particularly in a long running series such as *Vets*, the subjects 'start to give you what they think you want' (Shearman 1998) – that is, they produce performances with the end television product already in mind.

The series 'special' emerged directly from the docusoaps' success and its concomitant creation of successful stars. In addition to *Clampers at Christmas*, Jane McDonald's wedding to her long-term partner Henrik is the focus of *Jane Ties the Knot*, a 1998 *Cruise Christmas Special* was broadcast, Maureen from *Driving School* was featured in a follow-up programme and the wedding of vets Joe and Emma was likewise given a dedicated episode. Inherent within this is the reversal of the normative relationship within the observational mode between the subject matter and the individuals focused upon to represent it. This emphasis on the single performer, despite its possible derivation from direct cinema, runs counter to the establishing ethos of observational documentary; it does not merely observe even the moment at which the performance is produced, but rather invites the stars to exist as separate entities from the documentaries they are affiliated with. From this perspective, performance interferes with rather than enhances reality because the presence of the cameras has irrevocably altered what documentary subjects might be like if they were not being filmed. Most observational style documentaries retain a keen sense of off-screen space, an existence that will not be terminated when the cameras are switched off; *Nurse*, for instance, shows the trainee nurses to have altered substantially through the series without the audience having been party to the primary causes for those changes. With many of the docusoaps and particularly the later ones, there is, conversely, the feeling that the documentary set-up has created the situation, that the off-screen space is, if not empty, then not the predecessor or an adjunct of its on-screen counterpart.

Hotel is one of the first series to signal this severance, principally through its prioritisation of performance and conflict. If one briefly compares *Hotel* to *HMS Brilliant* a substantial discrepancy emerges between the two approaches. Whereas *HMS Brilliant* is about observing life on a Royal Navy vessel and offering as many viewpoints of this as possible, *Hotel* is not about the Adelphi, Liverpool, as much as it is about those who work there. In *Hotel*, the mundanity of working in a hotel is marginalised in favour of character development, unless the everyday detail supplies an argument, confrontation or crisis.

The majority of the series revolves around the protagonists (notably manageress Eileen Downey, chef Dave Smith and operations manager Brian Birchall) and their interaction with the camera and with each other. A familiar device of the series is a character turning to confide in the camera, to put his or her side of a story in the immediate aftermath of a quarrel or crisis point. In one episode – during which the kitchens are over-stretched, catering for two large Saturday night functions – there occurs a running argument (much of which is bleeped out, despite the post-watershed transmission slot) between the chef and the operations manager. The reasons for this confrontation are sidelined in favour of the protracted slanging match that ensues between the two men; we never do find out precisely how the chef coped with the catering problem, and instead are offered personal insights into how the men view each other. It is almost as if the fact that Dave and Brian work in a hotel is an incidental detail not a defining factor in how they are represented. Conversely, *HMS Brilliant* is overtly concerned with the workings of the ship and with the contextualisation within that environment of the personnel, a difference that is most clearly signalled by the series' identification of those featured by rank and full name, whereas *Hotel* (like other docusoaps before and since) identifies its 'characters' by their first names alone. *HMS Brilliant*, in the tradition of observational documentary, includes incidental and mundane detail such as cooking and cleaning that is only in part significant because of what it reveals about the people engaged in it. A series such as *Vets in Practice* offers a compromise position: the vets function as the consistent, long-standing 'characters' with whom the audience become familiar, whilst their personalities rarely obstruct the audience's access to the animal stories that make up their work.

Chris Terrill

An emphasis on personalities again signals the impossibility of the traditional observational documentary's adherence to the faithful recording of people 'being themselves', for the presence of stars immediately suggests that individuals change in front of the camera, that the person that emerges in a filming situation is not necessarily interchangeable with the person off camera. Chris Terrill's belief in the 'new honesty' that is now available to filmmakers impinges directly upon the issue of how subjects perform for the cameras. Dai Vaughan, writing in the 1970s, makes a distinction that is still pertinent today, when he comments, 'for those who bewail its absence, honesty is a moral problem. For those who try to achieve it, it is a technical one' (Vaughan 1974: 73). Technical equipment is at the heart of the debate surrounding honesty and documentary, for it is specifically equipment and its use that remains at the heart of contemporary forms of observational documentary. Technology and technique are invariably correlated in an era of documentary filmmaking that has spawned not only the docusoap but, earlier, the *Video Diaries* style of self-filming and self-examination, a use of the apparatus as confessional that has persisted in much British television documentary (for example, the cameras placed in the individual bedrooms in *The 1900 House* (Channel 4, 1999) to which the various members of the family recorded their daily experiences). The emergence of lightweight DVC cameras was an expedient inevitability.

The progression within Chris Terrill's work, from a broadly classical style of observational filmmaking in *HMS Brilliant* to one of greater intimacy, immediacy and authorial intervention from *Soho Stories* to the present, suggests the relationship between technology and form is equivocal. At the time of making *Soho Stories*, the technology was available for Terrill to alter his filmmaking style; the series was shot and recorded by him alone using a small DVC camera. He continued in this mode for his subsequent project *The Cruise*, which he similarly photographed and directed, but he shot the material on a large Beta camera and had an independent sound recordist who, radio linked to Terrill, remained 'always around the corner' (Terrill 1998). Technology, therefore, ultimately enables Terrill to develop a distinctive authorial style of documentary filmmaking, a style that he is keen to foster; as he comments, 'The number one of observational documentary filmmaking is not narrative or equipment, it's relationships'. Non-linear editing methods initially made it possible to develop a different way of working, which, in turn, led to the use, in a similar context, of more traditional equipment.

The manner in which Chris Terrill talks about his change of approach strongly implies that technology and style are interrelated. One feature that remains consistent through his recent observational work (including *HMS Brilliant*) is Terrill's desire to 'become very much part of the community I'm filming' and to live among his subjects for a considerable stretch of time, thereby building relationships that are necessarily predicated upon intimacy and trust. This way of filming also becomes apparent on a technical, filmic level. In *Soho Stories*, a prostitute offers Terrill some 'poppers', as if forgetting he has a camera and she is being filmed; likewise in *The Cruise*, Jane McDonald looks out for Terrill – joking that it must be hard for him walking backwards all the time, warning him that he is about to be hit by a coach (for which he thanks her), raising a glass to him as New Year sounds. Of this mutuality Terrill (1998) says: 'I find that if I've lived in a place long enough I get to know people well and there's a mutual trust established, so the camera all but disappears off my shoulder. So it's just me, my camera and the situation.' This conflation of director/photographer and camera engenders a potentially contradictory response to the broadcast material, emphasising the casualness and immediacy of the represented situation and acknowledging the reflexive referencing of the filmmaking process and apparatus. As the former is conventionally considered to be the result of having forgotten the latter, this indicates the development of a new and complex aesthetic.

Terrill does not regard the inclusion of his own voice or the gesturing towards his own presence as an obstacle to the audience's involvement in observational documentary; this is a major departure from the mode's classic antecedents as documentary credibility is no longer presumed to be found in the camera's transparency or objectivity. In fact, Terrill's argument is with the

fly-on-the-wall premise behind such an assumption, saying about his relationship with Jane McDonald, the singer in *The Cruise*:

> The camera might well not have been there in the end. And again, the shift
> occurs on a technical level – she's talking to me, so I – or rather the camera
> – becomes a presence, much more than in the conventional way of making
> observational films where there's a pretend invisible wall. ... I now interact
> in a much more up-front way. I've never understood the fly-on-the-wall
> label. ... I'm making a film about a community – a cruise ship, whatever –
> having a film made about it. I'm part of a new dynamic; let's admit that.
>
> (Terrill 1998)

This 'new dynamic' is the result of a relaxation of the divisions between observation and interaction, hence the crucial recognition that the medium's
artificiality is a means of achieving intimacy rather than distance. With this,
Terrill has fused two underpinning ideals of observational documentary: the
prioritisation of the personal and the everyday and the much more recently
prevalent acknowledgement of the filmmaker's presence as a means of accessing
the personal and the everyday.

This duality is significant when it comes to the treatment of *The Cruise*'s
obvious star, Jane McDonald. Terrill's point that Jane's subsequent success is, at
least in part, due to her already being in show business,[7] suggests that, like
Brando or Dylan in the 1960s, she is already a performer so her performance
within the documentary is a logical extension of an innate characteristic. Unlike
the 1960s examples, McDonald does not use the camera/Terrill to create
another barrier, instead she treats both him and the apparatus as friends –
confiding in them; letting the camera into her bedroom on Christmas Day
morning when, with no make-up on and a hang-over, she looks at her least
glamorous; allowing Terrill to film her tearful telephone conversations with her
mother. The significance of the camera can be gauged in an early sequence (in
Episode 1, 'Let the Dream Begin') showing McDonald preparing to go on
stage for the first time as a 'head-liner'. The preparations for performing take
precedence over the performances themselves, for the obvious reason that this
will grant the audience greater insight into character, show McDonald at her
most vulnerable (she talks at considerable length about how nervous she is) and
also show the transition from non-performer (or rather, performer only in the
context of the documentary) to professional performer on stage. Of greatest
interest in *The Cruise* is thus the documentary performance, the realisation of
Terrill's observational/interventionist aesthetic centred on the interaction
between subject and camera. In moments such as the minutes immediately prior
to walking out on stage, McDonald, much as Jean Rouch intimates, is more
revelatory, more intimate than perhaps would have been the case had she
merely been observed; she, in effect, talks to us, the audience, about her fears
and aspirations, her belief on the one hand that 'if I don't make it to the top it
wasn't meant to be', which is instantly qualified with 'I *will* make it'. The audi-

ence, Terrill insists, recognise that *The Cruise* is a film about a community having a film made about it; that, in other words, the series is a reflexive exercise that readily acknowledges its divergence from that same community when the camera is absent. Within this 'new dynamic', the camera thus 'almost becomes representative of the audience' (Terrill 1998), so, quite neatly, interventionist filmmaker and passive viewer have been merged.

Once again, Terrill furnishes a technical explanation for the effect of this critical observation, commenting that 'in purely technical terms, your subject will probably be looking at me down the lens, which means looking at the viewer – eye to eye contact – giving a film intimacy ... I want the audience to feel they were, to all intents and purposes, with Jane in the wings before she went on.' Significantly, Terrill also realises how he can sever this closeness simply by opening the eye he usually keeps shut whilst shooting, because 'if I open it people will probably look at my left eye rather than down the lens. I can draw a gaze slightly off-camera.' The look slightly off-camera, as occurs throughout a more traditional series such as *HMS Brilliant*, is automatically more formal and less intimate than the one through the lens; it is also conventionally believed to be less disruptive. It is this affinity between director, camera, subject and audience that distinguishes Terrill's docusoap output from that of others, the fact that there is both an *auteur*-ist and a reflexive role that can sit comfortably within the more conventionally passive aesthetic of observational documentary. The point at which these elements meet is the performance for the camera. It is not only Jane McDonald who forms an affiliation with the audience through the lens; many of the other passengers and crew likewise look out for, respond to and confide in Terrill, the camera and, by extension, us.

It is the measure of control over the filming process, as well as Terrill's presence as a voice off-camera and his role as camera operator, that makes his films qualitatively different to other docusoaps, despite superficial similarities of subject matter and packaging. The sense of control suggested by the acts of filming his own material, and increasingly using his own voice, sets Terrill's within a different *auteur*-ist tradition of documentary filmmaking, one that is in part about defining his own identity, and not merely emphasising the significance of the subjects pursued. Perhaps the resultant hybrid – observational reflexivity – is equally ambivalent in terms of its relation to the problematic term 'honesty'; it might be more 'honest' to admit that each documentary is about a set of people reacting to being filmed, it also sets up more of a barrier for viewers bred on observational films that maintain a certain distance.

Conclusion

Overall, the evolution of the observational mode into docusoaps has necessarily opened up the definition of the genre and posed questions about its aesthetic and its ethos. In this respect the role of performance is key: in Terrill's films we see the intersection with another prominent subgenre of the 1990s, the documentary characterised by the performance of the filmmaker; in the docusoaps as a whole we also see the inclusion of elements and techniques that previously would not have found such a prominent place in observational films, such as voice-over, reconstruction, music, fast, fictional-style editing. Gone in substantial part is the passivity of observational film, the sense that neither filmmaker nor audience has the right to interfere, that such intervention would inevitably and irrevocably taint the reality of what is on screen. Contemporary observational films assume, in their very fabric, that such a reality, unaffected by the filming process, is an impossibility, concluding that what they are able to achieve is the negotiation of a different understanding of truth – one that accepts the filmmaking process and one that acknowledges the essential artificiality of any filming set-up. Many docusoaps are so much about entertainment that, arguably, the producers are far from overly concerned with the theoretical issues this raises, and maybe such issues are raised more by those watching than those making the programmes. The more interventionist role of the documentary author and the significance of that performance, however, have increasingly become both theoretical and practical concerns.

The impact of the docusoap has been great, but the subgenre has relatively quickly lost its appeal. The circle has come full circle, as the Channel controllers and executives, by the end of 1999, had started to request fewer fully fledged docusoaps and more serious, committed documentary series instead. Terrill's *Jailbirds*, about a woman's prison, is effectively a compromise series: part old-fashioned observational documentary, part personality-rich docusoap. What docusoaps achieved, from a theoretical perspective, was extended proof that modern documentary has, for the most part, left traditional observational practices behind, and has evolved styles that prioritise performance, the filmmaker's presence, entertainment. The subsequent chapter on 'Journeys' in contemporary documentary will examine another way in which the traditions of direct cinema have been modified and modernised, one in which the filmmaker is more dominant and in which the reflexive nature of much documentary is brought out.

4 Documentary journeys
Shoah, London

The influence of direct cinema has been widespread. The preceding chapter discussed the problems of this legacy with reference largely to popular film practice, whereas the new journey documentaries, to be examined here, signal the influence of direct cinema upon more intellectual and relatively elitist documentary filmmaking. *Shoah* and *London* are illustrative of the growing tendency to offer a critique within the films themselves of the issues surrounding documentary representation, issues that direct cinema, with its unflinching faith in observation, naively took for granted. This reflexivity has further advanced the practice and theory of observational documentary. Journey films are structured around encounters and meetings – often accidental or unplanned, they are about not necessarily knowing where they will end up. These characteristics recall direct cinema's interest in the moment when people meet; they also very clearly recall direct cinema's French counterpart, *cinéma vérité*, exemplified by Jean Rouch and Edgar Morin's *Chronique d'un été* (*Chronicle of a Summer*) which opens with the filmmakers (who, like several later observational filmmakers, trained as anthropologists)[1] discussing embarking upon a film study of happiness, followed by two women collaborators going out onto the streets of Paris to collate material for the film, Nagra and microphone in hand. The essential difference between this *cinéma vérité* approach and that of Robert Drew and his followers is the ostentatious forefronting of the filmmaking process; the crew of *Chronique d'un été* do not hide behind the supposed transparency of film, they do not remain anonymous *auteurs*. Many journey documentaries borrow from both observational traditions: the close attention to detail and personality of direct cinema and the focus upon the moment of encounter with the filmmaker of *cinéma vérité*. The presence of the author is a significant intervention in journey films such as *Shoah* and *London*: the visibly intrusive presence of Lanzmann in the former, and the invisible but equally clear imposition of Keiller onto the latter. Although both films are concerned with the inherently unpredictable meeting or encounter, they are very obviously guided by the presence of their respective authors.

Direct cinema was founded upon an uncomfortable paradox, that whilst the films were putatively concerned with the unpredictable action not dictated by the filmmakers, they also desired and sought ways of imposing closure on their ostensibly undetermined action. Nichols and others have thereby drawn parallels between direct cinema documentaries and the classical Hollywood style, intimating that both modes of filmmaking emphasise transparency (the disguise of the cinematic apparatus); it could be added that both modes also demonstrate a desire for certainty or the desire for narrative closure. Robert Drew's quest for subjects with an in-built 'crisis structure' (a series of events that are predestined to follow a logical, closed path) or the imposition of a clear ending onto *Salesman*, for example, are illustrative of direct cinema's tendency to give coherence and logic to the potentially incoherent and illogical material observational films could easily unearth. Both *Shoah* and *London*, with their adoption of actual and metaphorical journey structures, challenge these notions of certainty, predictability and transparency, although they approach their subject material very differently. *Shoah* is Claude Lanzmann's nine-hour film about the Holocaust; Lanzmann goes in search of camp survivors, ex-SS guards, collaborators and bystanders to piece together a documentary – entirely comprising specially shot footage – about the Nazi extermination of European Jews. Patrick Keiller's *London* is a film that charts a journey through various parts of London by two figures we never see: the Narrator, recently returned to England, and his ex-lover and academic, Robinson. Whereas *Shoah* stresses the moment of encounter between Lanzmann and his subjects, *London* is more concerned with the reflexive potential of film; both films offer personal visions, but whilst Lanzmann's journey is tangible and real, the travelling at the centre of *London* is left ambiguous.

The term 'journey', applied to documentary, is either a very concrete term or a deeply nebulous one. In his chapter entitled 'Chrono-logic' Brian Winston argues that 'journey films solved actuality's big narrative problem – closure. How should films finish? Obviously, a journey film ends with the end of the journey' (Winston 1995: 104). Winston links journeys exclusively to time, observing that the journey through time has commonly been used as a means of creating logic ('chrono-logic') out of potentially shambolic or unrelated events; thus he categorises city films such as *Berlin: Symphony of a City* and *Man with a Movie Camera*, as journeys because they construct a narrative around the passage of time, usually the passing of a single day. This 'became documentary's preferred way of capturing the urban experience' (Winston 1995: 104), a means of making potentially incoherent images and events cohere within the panoply of the 'city film'. Winston then similarly ascribes 'chrono-logic' to non-city documentaries such as Jennings' *Listen to Britain* whose 'strongly inscribed diurnal pattern' compensates for the film's otherwise weak narrative (Winston 1995: 105). There are various types of documentaries that do, though, feature literal journeys, the most obvious example being the travelogue, the documentary equivalent of the road movie. Contemporary television still possesses an interest in the documentary as exploration: great train journeys, travel shows, individuals – usually a celebrity – going in search of a place or a person or even an idea, following a trail or arriving at a special destination. Series such as Michael Palin's *Around the World in 80 Days* or his homage to Hemingway are simply structured around a journey focusing on Palin's actual travels in pursuit of a particular experience and a specified knowledge. Winston's point is essentially that documentary journeys are about passing through and ordering time, that journeys give coherence to an otherwise fragmentary series of events and images. Journeys, therefore, impose logic. The travel film, however, contradicts this: it is more of an actual journey, a journey through time and space, but it is also fundamentally not structured around an argument or indeed around a desire to impose narrative cohesion; it is simply a chronicle of events linked by location, personality or theme.

The quest, whether or not it is related to an actual journey, is a pervasive documentary impulse; the dilemma, though, has been how to give structure to that dangerously unstructured instinct. The twin impulse, amongst theorists in particular, has been to push random events into a narrative, a structure, a logical form. What is intriguing about *Shoah* and *London* is that, like the sequential but not necessarily developmental travelogue, they do not have a hard and fast logic imposed on them: both possess narratives that are only superficially closed by their concluding images and words; both are more preoccupied with charting moments of encounter and examining the act of journeying than of reaching a fixed destination. Winston, however, focuses on the enthusiasm for completeness and linearity – as if the very act of embarking upon a journey is determined by its end – and quotes Roland Barthes on 'Completeness' in the process. Barthes, under the subheading 'To depart/to travel/to stay', states that completeness is the 'basic requirement of the readerly', later adding that a narrative without its requisite constituent parts (a departure and an arrival) 'would be a scandal' (Barthes 1973: 105). Is Barthes maintaining that only completeness can make the process of reading (or watching) pleasurable? Barthes' implied answer in the affirmative is not unlike Hayden White's assumption that history, in order to be meaningful, must be cogent and complete. In making a distinction between history and more rudimentary information-structuring forms such as annals and chronicles, White presumes that narrative is needed not only to give the events structure beyond the chronological (that is, to transform them into history), but to give them meaning, which 'they do not possess as mere sequence' (White 1987: 5). In White's estimation, the annals and the chronicle are merely components of a sophisticated history, insufficient in themselves. As proof of this, he lists the entries into the *Annals of Saint Gall* for the years 709–34, in which many years are left blank (years in which, one is left to deduce, nothing happened) and which appear to give equal weight to quite disparate events: in 722 'Great crops' is entered; in 731 'Blessed Bede, the presbyter, died' (White 1987: 6–7).

Such recording methods exasperate White because there is no causal logic and no hierarchy or prioritisation of information; accordingly, the 'importance' of the events recorded 'consists in nothing other than their having been recorded' (p. 7). Such non-narrative forms abound in documentary journey films. Many journey films – like a chronicle – are structured around what Edward Branigan (1992: 20) would term a 'focused chain':

a series of cause and effects with a continuing centre. For example, the continuing adventures of a character, the events surrounding an object or place, or the elaboration of a theme.

Unlike more random categories such as the 'heap' or the 'unfocused chain', the 'focused chain' possesses an internal logic and cogency, whilst still failing to abide by the causal regularity of the conventional narrative in which the sequence of events is all-important and in which 'the ending situation can be traced back to the beginning' (p. 20). The two films to be discussed here are focused chains: *Shoah* focuses on a shared theme, the events in *London* are grouped around a common location.

Although much documentary practice and theory demonstrates this over-riding need for total narrative cohesion, many journey films, ironically, do not. The city films cited by Winston possess a central location – the city – and frequently abide by a diurnal structure. The action therein contained, however, is almost invariably non-narrative; in both Dziga Vertov's *Man With a Movie Camera* or Alberto Cavalcanti's *Rien que les heures*, image association and not causal logic often determines the order of shots (Vertov's juxtaposition of eye lids closing and window shutters, Cavalcanti's compilation of kisses). Likewise the travelogue has a beginning and an end, but there is little sense that its participants have progressed in anything other than a physical way. Many documentaries are effectively chronicles or chains; it is not the case, therefore, that all potentially open documentaries seek to impose a narrative that will render them retrievable and comprehensible. An increasingly common observational documentary form is the diary form exemplified by *Video Diaries*, made possible, as docusoaps have been, by the emergence of smaller video cameras that untrained people can use, and cheaper, quicker editing facilities. Diaries are journeys in the broadest sense of the term, they chart a progression through time of an individual to whom something happens which, in turn, gives the diary a focal point beyond the details of daily existence. An illness, a crisis, a moment of change, the witnessing of an extraordinary event have all been regularly featured on *Video Diaries*; its 90-second offshoot *Video Nation* often simply focused on the mundane.

Films or series such as *Hoop Dreams* and *7-Up* are film diaries, they are constructed around a sequence of events, the conclusion of which is not known at the outset. *Hoop Dreams* follows, through school and college over a number of years, two teenage black boys who want to become professional basketball players; *7-Up* is a television series that interviews a social cross-section of people every seven years to see how their lives have changed and what they have done. The series started in 1963 when the subjects were seven years of age; the last programmes were *42-Up* (1998), and although some of the interviewees have dropped out, most of them still agree to be interviewed every seven years. The pleasure of these journeys derives from observing people change over time, getting to know them, observing their growing familiarity with the filmmakers, predicting the future and frequently having those predictions overturned. Both start off inherently speculative and *7-Up* will remain so until Michael Apted, its originator, decides to conclude the project (although *Hoop Dreams* is a complete film, there have been suggestions that the filmmakers are interested in doing a follow-up film). The premise, in these instances, is to follow subjects with no definite end in mind, as no one can know exactly how the lives of the individuals featured will turn out; the films are poised between certainty (surety of intention and motivation) and uncertainty (the unpredictability inevitably caused by the individual subjects), and the trajectory or conclusion of either is the result of a combination of imposed formal structure and unexpected changes in direction. Although the exponents of direct cinema preferred and sought finality and closure as do Winston, Barthes, White and Branigan, in documentary there has been a more consistent realisation that structural fluidity can be liberating and positive, an acknowledgement, perhaps, that the relative formlessness of a genre such as the city documentary is preferable to a rigidly enforced completeness.

Bill Nichols suggests that there has been a pervasive shift in our understanding of the very word 'documentary':

> Traditionally, the word *documentary* has suggested fullness, and completion, knowledge and fact, explanations of the social world and its motivating mechanisms. More recently, though, documentary has come to suggest incompleteness and uncertainty, recollection and impression, images of personal worlds and their subjective construction.
>
> (Nichols 1994: 1)

Perhaps Nichols gets a bit carried away here, but he is correct to suggest that documentary no longer needs to seek out ways of controlling its own unpredictable elements and that, on the contrary, non-fiction films are now more likely to be constructed around such instabilities as memory, subjectivity and uncertainty. The new journey film is indicative of this trend, taking the traditional documentary concerns of enquiry (itself a type of journey) and travel to create a loose subgenre of the observational mode, borrowing from direct cinema the key notion that a documentary and its thesis is dictated by events as they unfold in the present and in front of the camera. The action the films represent is the result of a dynamic, dialectical relationship between fact, filmmaker and apparatus. The journey has now become a more abstract, intellectual concept than it was previously. In a film such as Wim Wenders' *Notebook on Cities and Clothes*, the act of following and making a documentary about the Japanese fashion designer Yohji Yamamoto becomes the basis for a reflexive, ruminative examination of filmmaking itself. *Shoah* exemplifies a more passionate and emotional sort of journey, but the distant intellectualisation is again prevalent in Patrick Keiller's two mock travelogues, *London* and *Robinson in Space*, in which continues the travels (this time through the Home Counties) of the Narrator and Robinson. The characteristics that differentiate such journeys from their literal counterparts (the travelogue, the celebrity journey, the road movie) are their prioritisation of the personal and the incomplete; like the 'focused chain', the films are comprehensible without abiding by a monolithic narrative determinism. Both films superficially conform to Winston's journey structure (both emphasise the act of travelling and seeking out destinations); they also demonstrate a lack of closure or finality, and are far more concerned with the emotional and intellectual possibilities of the open journey or the journey constructed out of accidental encounters, subjective memory and curiosity. Neither conveys a clear sense, at the outset, of a conclusion; they are quests. Their starting point is the accidental meeting of so many direct cinema films – the chance encounter, the unexpected revelation, the ongoing dialogue with a set of events that are still in the process of unfolding. Both films, however, treat this legacy ironically, as they strongly suggest that Lanzmann and Keiller have, conversely, planned their films meticulously.

Although the films will be examined separately, there are thus several parallels between *Shoah* and *London*. Both are intellectual, academic and elitist (if compared to popular genres such as docusoaps), and both resemble the essay form. They both assume, it is fair to say, a certain amount of knowledge on the part of their spectators, and they both get immersed in the details of their respective journeys. Both documentaries play on the idea of the traditional travel film, Keiller's film much more definitely. They both use the journey form as a metaphor for discovery, on the part of *Shoah* more overtly, as Lanzmann is a constant presence through the film, asking questions of witnesses, and probing and forcing them to speak about the Jewish extermination programme. Both films also, despite being directed by men who are not primarily filmmakers, integrate a very distinctive style into their films' arguments: Keiller's film is characterised by an ironic visual stasis – the film comprises a series of tripod-mounted shots intercut with each other or with black leader – Lanzmann, on the other hand, synchronises his obsessive delving into the details of the Final Solution (the deportations, the trains, the daily experiences of the camps) with endless, slow tracking shots and pans. Both are masochistic viewing experiences that promise, on one level, a conclusion and knowledge but ultimately give us nothing of the sort; both are intensely personal films but they deny voyeuristic or sensuous gratification – *Shoah* in part by not including any archive of the Holocaust, *London* by suppressing the passion Keiller evidently feels for the subject under the static images and authoritative, cool voice-over. They both further suggest great momentum (*London* through words, *Shoah* mainly through images) but are fragmentarily structured and are unable to supply a definite route towards a resolution.

Claude Lanzmann's *Shoah*

As Nichols suggests in his discussion of the epistemological shift away from documentary connoting completeness, fact or explanation, non-fiction films have become more intrigued by forms and subjects that challenge these certainties, so that 'History and memory intertwine; meaning and action, past and present, hinge on one another distinctively' (Nichols 1994:1). In this (although Nichols then sees a blurring of fact and fiction as a modern trait, which is not appropriate to *Shoah*) Lanzmann's documentary epitomises this change. He finished *Shoah* in 1985, and in many ways it is the antidote to the conventional, authoritative documentary representation of the Holocaust that preceded it and – if one then considers Marcel Ophuls' hunting of Klaus Barbie in *Hotel Terminus*, made in 1988 – instigated an alternative, investigative and person-alised way of tackling the Nazi past. Whereas previous films such as *Nuit et brouillard* or *The World at War* were dependent upon the power of archival images of Nazi atrocities (and much later Steven Spielberg commented that he chose to make *Schindler's List* in black and white because that is how we recall the Holocaust), Lanzmann excluded such images, preferring personal testi-mony. His account is further personalised by being selective and only focusing on the extermination of the Jews. Lanzmann himself, on screen for most of the film, is the focus of *Shoah*'s journey, compelling survivors to speak, following in the tracks of the trains to the camps, reliving the Holocaust. Lanzmann's inter-action with the people he meets forms the basis for the film and its argument, as he explains:

> The concept was built during the work. If I had had a concept at the beginning, the film would be very bad. It would be too abstract. No, I had an obsession. ... I have made the film and the film has made me.
>
> (Lanzmann, 1985a: 322)

This obsessional quality is demonstrated by the sheer volume of material Lanzmann collated and the time *Shoah* took to make: he shot 350 hours of film over 11 years and in 14 different countries; he then spent four years editing this down. Lanzmann further describes the editing as a journey, a search for the right way of presenting the material; when he got stuck he 'would stop until I could find the proper way. And there were not several ways, there was only one' (Lanzmann 1990: 83). In miniature, the viewing experience mirrors the epic scale of this journey; it is rewarding but difficult to watch *Shoah* at one sitting and it unfolds before us slowly.

The film's power stems in part from the central journey being both metaphorical and actual, both concerned with the emotional and intellectual comprehension of the Holocaust and with its physical organisation and execu-tion (a quality mimicked by the arduous experience of making or watching it). The clearest symbol of the film's journey is the train and its concomitant para-phernalia of tracks, stations and steam. Trains, however, can only function symbolically as elucidations of less concrete journeys: the personal journeys of the interviewees compelled by Lanzmann to summon past memories into the present, descriptive domain; the identificatory and often equally personal jour-neys undertaken vicariously by Lanzmann and the spectator; the journey to the camps and to extermination; the journey towards a cumulative knowledge of the detail of the Holocaust assimilated through a meticulous amassing of facts, numbers and evidence; the journey encircling absent archival images. Lanzmann identifies the paradox of *Shoah* – that it is both intensely concrete and, despite his fears, abstract – when he comments, 'I precisely started with the impossibility to tell this story. I put this impossibility at the very beginning' (quoted in Colombat 1993: 305). Colombat's interpretation of Lanzmann's words and film – that 'At the end of the film, the Shoah remains unspeakable and unnamed. The film, however, "evokes" it' (p. 305) – proves insufficient, as the Shoah is far from 'unnamed' or 'unspoken'; in fact, Lanzmann's entire film enacts the process of naming and speaking – what Colombat means, perhaps, is that it does not show it. The effect of the multiple journeys in *Shoah* is to bring into the present a series of events that, principally through archive, have been contained within the past.

The multiple journeys *Shoah* undertakes are, in part, the expression of this struggle between the possibility and the impossibility of representation. *Shoah* is not linearly structured; it functions as a collage of interconnecting words and images; it does not definitively conclude; its journey is not about getting to a destination, although the ultimate destinations of the gas chambers and crematoria are repeatedly evoked. Many critics have been troubled by *Shoah*'s fragmentary overall structure, and have manifested a need to impose order on it. Colombat comments, for example:

> the general structure of the film describes first the progressive implementation of the extermination process, from life in the Polish *shtetlehs* to the deportations, the first selections, the arrival, the discovery of the camps and of the Final Solution; the systematic process from the implementation of the first exterminations to the annihilation of a complete people; the discovery that no escape or survival is possible and the importance of saving at least one Jew that could testify and in doing so would defeat the Nazi plan of total annihilation.
>
> (Colombat 1993: 308)[2]

Much of Colombat's formulation makes sense, but at times it appears that quite disparate narrative elements are, for the sake of convenience, yoked by violence together. That Colombat is straining a point is particularly evident in a section such as 'V: No escape possible – the role of memory' into which Colombat groups extracts from several testimonies that have arguably no more to do with memory than many others in the film. The point, perhaps, is that *Shoah* just does not conform to notions of linearity and closure. Adopting this as her premise, de Beauvoir finds in *Shoah* a far more fluid structure:

> The fact that many times they [the witnesses] speak about the same events does not tire you. To the contrary. You think of the intentional repetition of a musical phrase or leitmotiv. For, with its moments of intense horror, peaceful landscapes, laments and resting places, what *Shoah*'s subtle construction calls to mind is a musical composition. And the whole work is

punctuated by the almost intolerable din of trains rushing towards the camps.

(de Beauvoir, 1985: iv)

De Beauvoir suggests links between words and images that better capture the experience of watching the film, indicating the extent to which the journey *Shoah* undertakes is inconsistent and fractured. To return to Winston's assumption that a journey necessarily implies finality and a coherent trajectory: *Shoah* both affirms and denies this. Intellectually, Lanzmann's mammoth exploration possesses an inherent coherence that is the source, perhaps, of Colombat's summary of the film's structure. The argument running through *Shoah* echoes historian Raul Hilberg's proposition (voiced in *Shoah*) that the Final Solution, though a radical 'turning point' or a moment of 'closure', remains a continuation rather than a break with the past. As Lanzmann himself comments, 'the film is not made of memories. ... The film is the abolition of all distances between past and present; I have relived the whole story in the present' (Colombat 1993: 302).

The process of 'reliving' the Holocaust (and it is significant that Lanzmann uses 'I' here, identifying himself with this), and of eliminating the distance between past and present, centres on the interaction between Lanzmann and the interviewees he pursues. These encounters are (as befits a film preoccupied with bringing past events into the present) intensely physical: Claude Lanzmann travels to them, walks with them, asks them to re-enact as opposed to merely relate events and gestures from the past, sometimes in locations that directly recall them. It is the concreteness of these encounters that ostensibly belies Lanzmann's contention that the story is impossible to show. Two interviews that illustrate the physicality and presentness of Lanzmann's pursuit of personal recollection are those he conducts with Jan Karski and Abraham Bomba.

The interview with Karski, a Professor in America, is characterised by tension and vividness. He is extremely reluctant to re-summon the memories of being a courier for the Polish government, of visiting the Warsaw ghetto and of being asked, by his Jewish guides, to tell the Allies what he had seen, with the intention of precipitating an official denunciation of the confinement and extermination of the Jews. Initially he terminates the interview. Karski has repressed his Holocaust memories for 35 years, so when he eventually agrees to 'go back' and relive the events, he is doing so publicly for the first time. In Lanzmann's words, 'one must know and see, and one must see and know. Indissolubly' (Colombat 1993: 301); Karski's 'testimony' is unusually compelling in its ability to do this because of its frequent use of the present tense ('every day counts'; 'perhaps it will shake their [the Allies'] conscience'). [3]

Abraham Bomba's 'reliving' of the past is more literal than Karski's. When in Treblinka, he cut the hair of women and children just before they were taken into the gas chamber; after the war he continued to be a barber in the basement of New York's Pennsylvania station, but was retired by the time Lanzmann found him. Bomba is interviewed whilst cutting hair in an Israeli barber shop Lanzmann hired specially, because

> I knew that this particular moment – the cutting of the hair in the gas chamber – was extremely important to me. It was the reason why I looked for this man specifically. He was the only reason.
> (Lanzmann 1990: 95).[4]

Bomba's interview is illustrative of the dual journeys underpinning *Shoah*'s recollection of the past: its desire to use testimony to collapse the difference between past and present through the process of 'reliving', and its concomitant emphasis upon evoking the final destination of the journey the majority of Jews made – to their deaths in the gas chambers. Bomba is thus crucial, for he is describing the moment just prior to death. The significance of this is paralleled by Lanzmann's insistent urging of witnesses to talk against their will; with Bomba, for instance, he compels his crying witness to continue speaking.

Conducting the interview as Bomba is in the act of cutting a man's hair is a brutal example of the film's use of testimony. The sequence is not mimesis, but re-enactment, enough of a trigger to transport Bomba (before our eyes) back to the horrific scene he is describing, but detached enough from the details of that scene to remain bearable. Bomba refers only to cutting the hair of naked women and children inside the gas chamber, not men (as he is in *Shoah*), and of trying to make them 'believe they were getting a nice haircut' as well as cutting 'as fast as we could' because there were 60–70 women in the chamber at any one time (Lanzmann 1985b: 115). This vacillation between care and efficiency is echoed in the manner in which Bomba cuts the hair of the man whilst being filmed: his client's hair is dry and the cuts are small – delicate but ineffectual. Inherent, therefore, in this repetitive action is the distance Lanzmann feels his witness requires (Lanzmann 1990: 98). On this issue of gender difference Lanzmann comments:

> *Lanzmann*: I think he [Bomba] would not have agreed to do this with women, and I think that I would not have agreed. I think that would have been unbearable. It would not have been transmitted, I am sure. It would have been obscene.
> *Felman*: It confirms the fact that what you're doing in the staging is not representational.
> *Lanzmann*: Absolutely. The film is not at all representational.
> (Lanzmann 1985b: 97)

As with the rest of the film, this interview with Bomba is a gruelling journey; we experience the tensions, the pauses, the tears. The sequence is an evocation, but actually an evocation of events that are not merely absent from *Shoah* because it eschews archive footage, but which will never be evoked. Lanzmann concludes the Yale seminar on *Shoah* by raising the hypothetical question of the most graphic archive of all – a film of 'three thousand people dying together in a gas chamber' (Lanzmann 1985b: 99). From this hypothetical Lanzmann extracts a correlation with Bomba's testimony:

> no one human being would have been able to look at this. Anyhow, I would have never included this in my film. I would have preferred to destroy it. It is not visible. You cannot look at this. And if the customers of Bomba in the barbershop had been women, it would have been, for me, of the same kind of impossibility as that of the gas chamber. (p. 99)

Underlying Lanzmann's physical quest, the fragmentary journey he does undertake, is the complete and linear journey the majority of Jews took – and which the interviewees' words relive – to the gas chambers and crematoria of the camps. This is why *Shoah*'s journey is impossible: the conclusion of Lanzmann's encounters, all the film's tracks and trains will inevitably stop short of their historical destination, the moment of extermination.

There is a certainty about this ultimate absent journey that problematises the concept of *Shoah* as a film predicated upon the moment of encounter, of not being predetermined and guided by Lanzmann. Todorov reproaches Lanzmann for denying the individuality and personal will of his witnesses in favour of his desire to have them bear witness on behalf of those who died (see Colombat 1993: 303), and there is a sense running through *Shoah* that, for all its non-linearity, there is a definite journey, a definite narrative, but not one that can ever be transmitted (or indeed that is borne out by history). Although the conclusion to *Shoah* is ostensibly open (a final, lengthy shot of a train of wagons rumbling slowly by), the final words are Simha Rottem's as he remembers re-entering a deserted Warsaw Ghetto and thinking to himself 'I'm the last Jew. I'll wait for morning, and for the Germans'. The paradox contained within *Shoah* is that, despite the finality of this journey evoked repeatedly by the witnesses, the film inhabits a perpetual present. Marcel Ophuls identifies this tendency against the far easier acceptance of the inevitability of time passing when suggesting

> This constant blending of the past and present, rather than a mere juxtaposition, this constant effort to erase time in order to re-create a continuous reality, is, as far as I can see, the basic principle on which the whole film is constructed.
>
> (Ophuls 1985: 19)

Such an intention is facilitated by *Shoah* being a film, for, as Bill Nichols says

> Images, as we know, are always present tense. Their referent, what they represent, may be elsewhere, but this absent referent seems to be brought to life in the present moment of apprehension, over and over.
>
> (Nichols 1994: 117)

Both the journey Lanzmann physically undertakes in *Shoah* and the way in which that journey is filmed enact the entrapment within a perpetual present. This stasis is heavily ironic in a film visually dominated by moving trains and a permanently restless camera. The cinematic apparatus is probing, questioning, it leaves nothing alone. In this, the presentness of the film image incessantly relives the experiences evoked through the witnesses' testimonies. Complementing this and often graphically demonstrated is Lanzmann's own physical journey through this perpetual present, wanting to relive it himself. He recalls, for instance, whilst walking, during filming, from the gates to crematorium of Auschwitz-Birkenau, how he asked himself 'At which moment did it start to be too late? … How to transmit these questions? How to transmit these feelings to the spectators, to the viewers?' (Lanzmann 1990: 89). Within *Shoah* Lanzmann actually marks out the journeys the Jews took, as he enquires where the boundary of Sobibor stretched to, proceeding then to step over that by now invisible mark (thereby rescoring it again). Lanzmann's aim here is, to 'relive all of it, to retrace the steps', to thus cross the 'imaginary line' so that the experience as well as the boundary 'becomes real' (quoted in Insdorf 1989: 252). It is thereby logical that Lanzmann's own involvement extended to pushing the dolly for the tracking shot into Auschwitz; he needed to cross and redraw these lines himself. The camera – the apparatus through which the questions Lanzmann raises concerning how the present effect of such actions and images can be transmuted – becomes the focal point of his filmic quest, the juncture between emotional or intellectual intention and practicality. *Shoah*'s visual style is dominated by tracking shots or 'travelling shots' as Lanzmann refers to them (Lanzmann 1990: 91–2). Many of these shots tautologically track the tracks that carried millions to their deaths, creating an inevitable correlation between style and subject. Lanzmann's camera mimics the actual journey by bringing the filmic representation and the spectator closer to the events it relives: for instance hiring a horse and cart on which to mount the camera to pass through Chelmno at roughly walking pace, or the repeated use of the moving (tracking or hand-held) camera to simulate or parallel a personal account of a particular passage of events. *Shoah*'s camera, whether hand-held or mounted, is thus its tool of re-enactment: its steady pace, the frequent use of 'excruciatingly long takes' (Kellman 1988: 24); except in rare instances, such as the zoom into the Treblinka station sign which Lanzmann refers to as 'a violent act' (Insdorf 1989: 252) the eschewal of disruptive cinematic techniques for denoting elisions of time and thought such as jump cuts, montage, rapid zooms or pans.

The camera is insistent, as if learning, assimilating, committing to memory the scars that the grass and forests weakly camouflage; its steady journeys are the film's physical ballast; its slow, purposefulness is the single element of *Shoah* that most forcefully recalls *Nuit et brouillard*. There exists a consistent juxtaposition between the factual quest that characterises the journey through the individual testimonies (Lanzmann's pursuit of his witnesses, his cross-examinations, his repeated desire for clarification and amplification) and the camera's complementary probing of the landscapes. *Shoah*'s use of perpetual motion suggests an incomplete action, a lack of finality that is clearly a feature of both *Shoah*'s intellectual and emotional journey (focused on Lanzmann) and its actual journey (as exemplified by the travelling camera and the trains, the actual mode of transportation to the camps). The probing camera is linked to the film's personal journeys by conveying the sense of bearing witness. Because of the regularity of *Shoah*'s camera movement, there is also a sense in which, for all the differences between the individual stories, there is a shared journey that all of them undertook and are still undertaking as they participate in the film; a journey back to the site of their collective memory. Lanzmann compels all his interviewees, whether Jews or those implicated in their extermination, to lay down a testimony for others; the restless camera is the acknowledgement, often, that this is being done. Lanzmann too is bearing witness by visiting the sites of atrocities, and the camera is most closely affiliated to him. During Filip Müller's testimony, the two types of journey – the physical/technical journey and the personal – coalesce.

Müller, a Czech Jew and survivor of five liquidations of the Auschwitz 'special detail', recounts (significantly) the first time he entered the Auschwitz 1 crematorium. His words emphasise his incomprehension at what he saw:

> I couldn't understand any of it. It was like a blow to the head, as if I'd been stunned. I didn't even know where I was. Above all, I couldn't understand how they managed to kill so many people.
>
> (Lanzmann 1985b: 59)

Müller's look (on his face in interview as he recounts this sequence as well as the look of the camera) is, as he says, one of incomprehension. The accompanying visuals function as ways of explicating, making real Müller's responses. This is, in large part, due to the characteristic slowness, persistence and length of the 'travelling shots' that start with a slow track out from Auschwitz 1's Black Wall (against which prisoners were rounded up and shot) before progressing to hand-held shots for Block 11, the new chimney, and finally the ovens. This sequence has the camera mimic the movements of the individual describing the scene, travelling at walking pace to the crematorium and inserting rare whip pans as if looking around the dark oven chambers. Another journey is the sequence's mirroring of the evolution of the Nazis' methods of extermination. Underscoring the images again is the mutuality of knowledge and seeing; we are being offered a rendition of what Müller first saw. This degree of personalisation is unusual in *Shoah*, in which the camera's movement (representative as it is of the intensely physical presence of Lanzmann and his crew) more frequently retains an abstract quality, a pervasive, dogged momentum taking us through the film but not making the ultimate, precise link between location and testimony. However contextualised, the look of the camera in *Shoah* is linked to the film's lack of archive, to Lanzmann's argument that we no longer look meaningfully at archive images of the Holocaust because we have become inured to their effect and meaning. The camera mimics the eye looking, as Müller's did, for the first time before this desensitisation occurred, it transports us, along with the witnesses and Lanzmann, into the film's ever-presentness.

The movement of the camera mimics and is an extension of the trains transporting the Jews to the camps whose incessant, regular journeys scarred the landscape of Europe; the actual modes of transportation are thus instrumental in conveying to the spectator the arduousness of the film's journeys. *Shoah* emphasises both trains and rail tracks. The repetition of image and event is significant, but so is the realisation (that only comes with such repetition) that the Final Solution necessitated quite so much hardware and covered quite so much ground. Most documentaries focus on the rounding up of the Jews and on the camps – that is, the trains' departures and destinations; their journeys are frequently cut. *Shoah* correlates the individual stories/journeys and the repetitive, communalised journeys of the trains along existing or now eroded tracks. Lanzmann comments, 'I built a structure, a gestalt! I didn't tell one personal story – the subject of the film is the extermination of the Jews, not the handful of survivors' (Lanzmann 1985a: 324). The trains are emblematic of the Jewish journey across Europe, cumulative journeys criss-crossing Europe's landscape in both space and time; they – like the camera's tracking shots and pans – convey a collective experience, bringing together the individual voices populating the film. The individual train shots in *Shoah* are not often in themselves significant (apart from on the odd occasion, Lanzmann does not draw attention to any particular train, which may be construed as reflecting the anonymity imposed on the Jews – and others – who travelled on them to the camps), they are generic, emotionally rather than specifically meaningful.

One train journey in *Shoah* that is meaningful in itself is that of the steam locomotive driven by Henrik Gawkowski which re-enacts the transportation of Jews to Treblinka. Coming only 48 minutes into *Shoah*, this sequence is the first to give the spectator a point of view parallel to that of the victims. The camera looks forward at Gawkowski, the steam and the tracks ahead; as the train slows and pulls into the station, it holds a shot of the sign stating the destination: Treblinka (Figure 4.1). This is a case of re-enactment as precise as Bomba's. Again, proximity to the original events is important, and Lanzmann hired an engine (though no wagons) comparable to the one Gawkowski would have driven.[5] Consolidating this, Gawkowski, unsolicited by Lanzmann, makes a gesture of cutting his throat – the final greeting he gave the Jews as they filed off the train; a gesture that is later repeated by other Poles in Chelmno.[6] Gawkowski craning out of his window, the track behind him obscured by smoke, looking back in the direction of the imaginary wagons has become emblematic of *Shoah*, a 'pillar of the film' in Lanzmann's words (Lanzmann 1990: 88). The trains, treated as both specific and generic, are symbolic of *Shoah*'s oscillating journey between past and present; they and the tracks on which they travel, whilst anonymous, are linked to particular journeys, notably those to the camps. The incompleteness of the trains' journeys is conveyed by repetition: trundling along the tracks and coming to a halt at the camps' loading ranks. Their journeys are stuttering, fragmented; there is an incon-

Figure 4.1   Shoah

Source: Courtesy of BFI Stills, Posters and Designs

gruous lack of finality about each terminated voyage, denoting the impossibility again of Lanzmann's endeavour to tell this story, and the juxtaposition of steady fluidity of movement (the camera, the moving trains) with the act of grinding to a halt characterises the film.

Despite the endless repetitions of gesture, image and sound, Simone de Beauvoir's view that the spectator does not tire of watching the film is true; she also says of *Shoah*, 'I should add that I would never have imagined such a combination of beauty and horror. True, the one does not help to conceal the other' (de Beauvoir 1985: vi). De Beauvoir sees *Shoah*'s ambivalent beauty as resulting from its greatness, but her description of the film also conveys a sense of pleasure (of 'magic' as de Beauvoir says) which is harder to define and nego-tiate. *Shoah*'s pleasure, I'd posit, stems from its identification of and play upon a quite specific form of masochism, deriving from the multitude of journeys that Lanzmann, the witnesses and the spectator undertake. Firstly, there is the effect of nine hours of repetition not being dull but totally absorbing, no doubt because of its content. But having said this poses a problem of its own; although I have not noted the amount of time given to interviews and words in *Shoah* relative to trains, tracking shots and pans, that the film's complete text is so short (200 small, not densely packed pages) suggests that the latter group predominate. The repetitiveness of *Shoah* as a visual, cinematic experience is masochistic, in that the length of our journey as spectators is so long and also so aesthetically minimalist. *Shoah* is not like *Nuit et brouillard*, which offers an at times uncomfortably aestheticised representation of the Holocaust with its juxtaposition of black and white archive and colour, its use of Cayrol's poetic voice-over and Eisner's contrapuntal music. Lanzmann's film centres on lack as opposed to gratification: the lack of archive images (themselves a conventional source of catharsis), the film's lack of satisfying closure despite the excessive searching, travelling, talking. To embark upon a journey that can never end (but which nevertheless takes us nine hours and Lanzmann several years) is inherently masochistic; the fact that this denial then gives us pleasure of sorts makes it indubitably so.

The journey becomes especially masochistic when the conflict between the implied, preferred resolution and the film's actual irresolution is considered. *Shoah* ends ambivalently: Simha Rottem's total extermination scenario followed by another procession of rumbling train carriages. *Shoah*, despite being populated only with the words of survivors and the living, is – as Lanzmann's sometimes brutal insistence that his witnesses must speak on behalf of the dead attests – about the Jews who died. The uncomfortable fact remains that the narrative's preferred ending is encapsulated within Rottem's fearful, but false conclusion that he is the last Jew left alive. This is, in turn, suppressed in favour of the film's actual inconclusiveness. There is both a linear journey running through *Shoah*, of which Rottem's words are the culmination, and a circular journey made up of a collage of repetitions. In direct contrast to the multitude of renditions of the Holocaust that could be termed 'survival myths' because they prioritise survival and escape such as *Playing for Time, Escape from Sobibor, Schindler's List* and *La vita è bella* (*Life is Beautiful*), *Shoah*'s suppressed logical ending would be total annihilation. The culmination of *Shoah*'s masochism as a viewing experience is that, having admitted that some Jews survived to bear witness, Lanzmann compels these witnesses to relive the events (as if in the present), a repetition that necessarily entails reliving the horrific fear of their own extermination. Lanzmann's aggression towards many of his witnesses suggests that they are being urged to re-stare into the abyss in just this way.

Shoah exemplifies the documentary as quest, as search, as the place for documenting and recording what many would want to remain hidden and others find too painful to recall. The film's multiple journeys centre on Lanzmann, whose personal quest is in keeping with many aspects of the documentary journey tradition: it is active, physical; it focuses on the moment of encounter with his witnesses and it conveys tangibly to us, the audience, the sense of travelling through time and space. It goes against, however, the notion that journeys can only be defined as such if they have a definite conclusion. *Shoah*'s ambivalence in this respect signals a tension that has become a characteristic of the modern documentary journey, namely that a belief in certainty and the desire to impose coherence on a potentially chaotic series of events are themselves being brought into question.

London and the reflexive journey documentary

Although Patrick Keiller's *London* could be argued to start from a similar premise, it undertakes a very different sort of journey. Keiller is a British avant-garde filmmaker, one of several filmmakers to have come to cinema from other professions (Keiller trained as an architect, Peter Greenaway as a painter) and to conform to the tendency of such directors to bring to documentaries certain qualities of the avant-garde and to take issue with and confuse the boundaries between fictional and non-fictional filmmaking. Many of the films of Keiller, Greenaway or Chris Petit, for example, do not differentiate clearly between such categories. Much of Keiller's work likewise treats conventional notions of narrative ironically. *London* is Keiller's first full-length film; it was funded largely by the BFI (whereas a substantial proportion of British documentary emanates exclusively from television) and was produced by Keith Griffiths, who also works with Petit. Many of Keiller's earlier films, such as *Stonebridge Park* (1981) or *Norwood* (1983), display, in miniature, the obsessions with place, history and architecture to be found in *London*. Like the work of many of his contemporaries, *London* is excessively stylised and self-conscious, amongst other things an intellectual rumination on the nature of audio-visual compilation and the act of representation. At first glance, it fits uneasily alongside docusoaps, for instance, as an example of how the values and conditions of direct cinema have been both cemented and developed; but there is another growing tradition, demonstrated also in the more recent work of another British documentary filmmaker, Nicholas Barker, that takes the attributes and ethos of observational cinema (its interest in contemporary life, detail, personalities, mannerisms) as the basis for reflexive films that simultaneously debate these observational foundations. Unlike *Shoah*, *London* is a detached film – one senses Keiller's passion in it, but viewing the film is not an emotional or passionate experience – and yet both documentaries dispute the notion of the linear, closed journey, and in this they imply an active, dynamic relationship with their respective spectators.

London shows the travels around the city of two middle-aged men whom we never see: the Narrator, who has just returned from serving as the photographer on a cruise ship, and his friend and ex-lover Robinson who lives in a flat in Kennington and teaches part time at the University of Barking. The film charts two interconnected journeys: the intended journey which is Robinson's 'pilgrimage to the sources of English Romanticism' as the Narrator states as they set out, and the journey made up of their unpredictable encounters that often send the men off course. Their journey is divided into three 'Expeditions', although further intertitles appear in between – some are explanatory ('Vauxhall' before a shot of the MI5 building next to Vauxhall Bridge), while others are cryptic or ironic ('Utopia' before a shot of the murky waters of the Thames). *London* juxtaposes a richly evocative, densely factual and cogitative voice-over (spoken by Paul Scofield) with a series of universally static, tripod-mounted shots of different images of London, not always in tandem with the narration. The identity of the Narrator and Robinson are perpetually in doubt because we never see them (is Robinson, the collator of images, really the Narrator – or is the Narrator, a ship's photographer, Robinson? Are either Keiller's alter ego?); in fact we see very few people at all, including those the Narrator says he and Robinson have encountered whilst on their travels. Although these travels have a definite chronological structure and show various important historical events, such as John Major's return to power in the 1992 General Election, the film's journey reaches no definite conclusion and the stated premise for Robinson's quest is fragmented and all but lost along the way. Indeed, there is a less successful sequel to *London* – that is, *Robinson in Space* – which embarks from Reading, so the journey of the two men is ongoing.

London falls within the category of the city documentary; like many such films, it conforms to a chronological structure as the action takes place over a year (January–December 1992) as specified in intertitles. This, however, is only spasmodically relevant, for much of the time *London* exhibits the more significant trait of the city film: a lack of interest in narrative cohesion and cogency except of the most perfunctory kind, and an interest, instead, in non-narrative forms such as lists, catalogues, chains – forms that link material in casual rather than causal ways. This highlights further parallels between Keiller and other British art cinema filmmakers; Greenaway has, since his early documentary days, been heavily preoccupied with lists and the collation of statistics (*Dear Phone, Act of God, Drowning by Numbers*), Barker is likewise concerned with compiling information and personal detail rather than imposing a definite argument or structure on his films (*Signs of the Times, Unmade Beds*). City films pursue a very characteristic type of journey: one that has a broad purpose (finding out about a city) but one which is prepared for the accidental encounters or events that will inevitably occur once the journey is underway. Concomitantly, they do not dwell on the most recognisable and familiar aspects of a city (the tourist board image) but tend to unearth its submerged and obscure outer reaches; as Iain Sinclair says about Keiller, he finds buildings that 'had no idea that they had been lost until Keiller nominated them' (Sinclair 1997: 300). As with many city films, *London* thus becomes identifiably personal and idiosyncratic, the view granted of England's capital is not the expected, popular one (although cliché, tourist snap shot elements remain) but the unofficial one. Like Lanzmann, Keiller is most intrigued by hidden, private history.

The expeditions around which *London* is structured are, throughout, problematic. The central journey is only ostensibly purposeful. Robinson has long held, the Narrator tells us, an ambition to undertake an academic study of London's crumbling cultural architectural history, so there is a motive and a purpose to the Expeditions, much as there is a meticulousness and a precision to Keiller's choice of images and words. There is a consistent tension between the intentions of Robinson and the Narrator and the inherent instabilities of the actual journey they undertake; their progress is continuously hampered or interrupted by events and journeys towards a specified destination frequently diverted or curtailed. Whilst the Expeditions enact this conflict between the cerebral, intellectual journey as planned and its reality, clearly evident is the film's lack of concern over its own 'incompleteness', owing much to Laurence Sterne's stream of consciousness novels such as *Tristram Shandy*, which enacts an endless struggle between its slim narrative line and the numerous exuberant digressions. As Sterne (who is referenced in *London*) mocks the novel, so Keiller parodies the non-fiction film's pursuit of developmental structure. *London* exhibits the potential for such coherence (the stabilising narrative strategy of 'character', for example, could said to be deployed, although the fact that we never see Robinson or the Narrator mitigates against this, and the film perfunctorily charts a circular structure, as views from Robinson's window top and tail the 'expeditions') but these elements lack earnestness.[7] The ambiguous characters in *London*, far from establishing a cause–effect logic, serve to expose the dependency of common narrative on such elements. The Narrator, however loquacious, is not given a 'character' as such, but is a site where ideas, observations and fact collation congregate. There are some similarities between him and Keiller (Barwell 1997b: 161), but to interpret him as autobiographical would be limiting. Similarly there is no motivation afforded Robinson, with whom we become acquainted in far more depth through the Narrator's words, but who may only be a fantasy figure fabricated by those words. Such strategies are generally undermining of narrative equilibrium.

The journeys Robinson and the Narrator undertake echo this fragmentary quality. The bomb on Wandsworth Common that prevents them from getting to Strawberry Hill where they are bound, or the discovery in Stoke Newington of a Daniel Defoe landmark when Robinson and the Narrator had set out to discover relics of Edgar Allen Poe, undermine the intended journey and, in turn, pose questions of the feasibility of their predetermined endeavour. The digressions, however, are invariably more interesting than the journey that is lost. This ironic treatment of the sensible, purposeful journey finds a parallel in *London*'s attachment to the false logic offered by a chronological structure. That the action takes place over a year may be the film's organising principle, but the suggestion that the passage of time necessarily means that the journey is pursuing a particular path or progressing towards a specific destination is illusory. Instead, *London*'s circumlocutory style and its preoccupation with the collation of images and experiences rather than their organisation into a linear structure, suggests more that the journey's destination is of little significance except as a frustratingly unreachable ideal. Despite these frustrations, rather like Vertov's man with his movie camera, the Narrator in particular gives the impression of not being unduly demoralised or deterred by the difficulties they encounter.

In tandem with this energy is the repressed but nevertheless evident passion of *London*'s subsidiary journeys through the city's cultural history (which is sorely missed by Robinson) and, more markedly, the political landscape of 1992. Patrick Keiller's particular engagement with the latter can be detected, amidst the witty commentary that endlessly complicates the spectator's understanding of the Expeditions:

I was beginning to understand Robinson's method which seemed to be based on a belief that English culture had been irretrievably diverted by the English reaction to the French Revolution. His interest in Sterne and other English writers of the 18th century, and in the French poets who followed Baudelaire, was an attempt to re-build the city in which he found himself as if the 19th century had never happened.

The whole journey in *London* is given a quaint and dynamic quality through the implication that it is being undertaken by two men who stubbornly refuse to rejoice in the modern city (although the film itself indubitably does), and who choose to continue their despairing rail at the replacement of a European cultural heritage by a grimy present in which Montaigne's name is given to a Soho school of English and an oppressively large, garish poster for the Chippendales now dominates the view from the window at the Savoy Hotel where Monet once stayed. It is ironic and bathetic that the film is obliged to dwell visually on the modern. This modern chronicle (which conceivably represents Keiller's alternative Expeditions) sheds a cynical light upon Robinson's lofty ambitions, exemplifying *London*'s fractious relationship between past and present. Particularly ignominious is the realisation by Robinson and the Narrator that the BT Tower (that 'monument to their tempestuous relationship', as the Narrator recounts) now resides on the site of Rimbaud and Verlaine's house; Rimbaud and Verlaine no doubt being the idealised Romantic prototypes that Robinson and the Narrator have sought to emulate.

In contrast to these historical amblings is *London*'s journey through the political events of 1992, the subtext that suggests Keiller's personal bias. Rather like the annals quoted from by Hayden White, *London* offers a selective as opposed to comprehensive skirt through the year's events. As befits a journey, it is as if by chance that Robinson and the Narrator are present at, for example, the Conservative's general election victory celebrations in Smith Square and John Major's return to Downing Street, the Queen Mother's unveiling of the statue to 'Bomber' Harris, or the Queen's official re-opening of Leicester Square. Of course, running counter to the notion that these events are recorded as if by chance, is the definite implication that none of *London* is accidental (it all being pre-scripted) and that, in these political sequences, Keiller's viewpoint is clearly discernible. As with the rest of *London*, these sequences are shot mute. In these instances, narration is then imposed, some of which repeats verbatim comments that were being made at the time of filming. The lack of sound over the Major sequences represents the distanciation and alienation Robinson and the Narrator (and Keiller) experience. In the Queen Mother sequence, the Narrator replays the disruption of her speech by a rowdy crowd shouting 'murderer, mass murderer'; likewise, the Narrator relays the cry of 'pay your taxes, you scum' to the Queen in Leicester Square. These focused moments of political and social commentary are, more than narrative digressions, tonal disruptions; the lush, honeyed tones of Paul Scofield uttering criticisms of the

Royal family becomes a deeply anarchic act. For all the ambling through *London*'s lost past, this is a journey through the present.

A facet of the angry political sequences is that, however dialectical the use of sound and image, they are inherently logical. For most of the time, *London* charts a journey that has only a tenuous coherence, and certainly no all-encompassing logic. Like Peter Greenaway's obsession with numbers or the importance of Sei Shonagon's lists to Chris Marker's *Sunless*, Keiller is intrigued by non-narrative forms of grouping and structuring. In response to this, Mike Hodges calls *London* a 'film mosaic' made up of 'eighty-four minutes of memorable moments' (Hodges 1997: 166). London's collage of 'moments' is comparable to the *portmanteau* film's bracing together of internally coherent but often tenuously linked shorts (*Paris vu par*, for example). Hodges' memorable moments – the rearrangement of the lines of guardsmen in the Trooping of the Colour or the Polling Station shots – are personal, arbitrary selections that then prompt an equally personal game of image-association, recalling what these moments make Hodges think of (as Shonagon's 'List of things that quicken the heart' does in *Sunless*). Lists permit alternative and extraneous associations to invade the completeness of a larger unit such as a journey and suggest associations that both complement and disrupt the overall structure. The predominance of the list invariably makes *London* appear more formally random than *Shoah*, and its journey less focused; it also makes the film more intellectual, self-conscious and distant. The list, though, is the appropriate complement to the journey's 'and then, and then, and then' structure. Consequently, each spectator's journey whilst watching *London* (as Hodges' response intimates) will necessarily be different from another's. This divergence would not be the intention behind an Aristotelian narrative.

Like the Surrealist game of consequences or the collation of facts about lightning in Greenaway's *Act of God*, a linking system or data organisation can coincidentally be logical but it will preclude such ordering factors as motive and determinism. Take the Strawberry Hill sequence of *London*:

> Over an image of Walpole's house the narrator relates that Robinson tells him that this is where Walpole wrote *The Castle of Otranto*, the first English gothic novel; then, simply because it is nearby, the two visit Teddington lock and then go on to Twickenham, which is illustrated by a sign for a pub named 'Pope's Grotto'. Though we might expect a mention of the poet, none is given. Over shots of Marble Hill, the Narrator tells us he and Robinson encountered some Peruvian musicians whom they stay with overnight and accompany to Brentford in the morning. The image then cuts to black and over the subsequent shot of a woody path the Narrator remarks cheerily, 'When we awoke it was spring'. Peruvian music then starts up over the image of a cow grazing at the base of Richmond Hill; over the same image, the Narrator then interjects 'he told me Turner used to walk along the river here' before cutting to the view down the same valley from Joshua Reynolds' house. After shots of West London bridges Robinson and

the Narrator arrive in Isleworth, represented by another pub sign, this time for the 'Coach and Horses' on the old road to Bristol, 'a notorious haunt of highwaymen' the Narrator divulges, before recounting that he and Robinson are sworn at by the pub's landlord and go onto Kew.

A sequence such as this is comprehensible but it is not cumulative; there is no motive besides geography for going from one part of West London to another and the information we are given about each location does not follow a set pattern. There is also the disruption of Robinson and the Narrator's excursion by the accidental encounter with the Peruvian musicians, whom we do not see. The final mental image is of Robinson and the Narrator hopelessly out of step with modernity, imagining themselves transported back to an era of coach inns and highwaymen. This is a prime example of a list: the spectator accumulates facts, but these are fairly random except for being linked by one or two crucial factors: that they pertain to both the characters we have been following and to a limited geographical area. There is no causal progression through this part of Robinson and the Narrator's journey, and it is further fragmented and broken up by a number of formal devices, the most notable being the use of intertitles and black leader to separate images. A key feature of a list and of the journey undertaken in *London* is that the images and words are not prioritised, that no image is emphasised over others, but similarly none is thrown away; a lingering close-up of the grubby Thames, overlaid with snatches of Rimbaud, is treated as reverentially as images of the last fragment of the London stone. Likewise, the framing of the actual images is consistent: few close-ups, precisely composed, detached and certainly unemotive as if emulating the impersonality of a tourist snapshot or picture postcard. A correlative of this non-hierarchical treatment of image, is *London*'s editing style. Cuts appear at regular intervals, there are no excessively long takes, nor are there any strikingly rapid montage sequences (although there are several instances where Keiller ends a stage in the journey with a selection of images edited together slightly more rapidly, often without narration over them). Such structuring – which presupposes each spectator will absorb the film differently as Hodges' observations suggest – could be viewed as an ironic intellectualisation of direct cinema's notion of ostensibly leaving the driving to us. The ultimate irony is that *London*, for all its highly wrought self-consciousness, is a much looser and more liberating film than much observational documentary.

Despite such freedom, *London* also displays masochistic tendencies, this time ironically and playfully related to the images Keiller collates, how they are assembled and how they are framed. London in *London* is defined by its 'looked-at-ness', it is fetishised and made strange by even familiar images being looked at with such an obsessively static, photographic gaze. Keiller comments that, although the Narrator is pessimistic, 'the whole point of making the film is rather optimistic in that the idea is to make everybody value the place. It is to say: LOOK' (Barwell 1997b: 165). This compulsion to look at each image afresh imbues *London* with a timeless quality, as the images the film comprises, like the events in the chronicle, follow each other but are not causally linked. This lack of an underlying narrative context or a sense of development ensures that the journeys in *London* appear to have no depth or structure in time, they lack priority or a sense of progression and thus inhabit a repetitive, still everpresentness. It is interesting how both *London* and *Shoah*, two quite different uses of the journey structure and metaphor, nevertheless share the same central ambiguity: that despite being about progression and motion, they engender in the spectator a feeling of motionlessness which, in turn, prompts a sense of existing exclusively in the present tense. Keiller's images are beautifully superficial; they are also extreme in their self-consciousness and are meticulously, almost perversely planned, conveying the idea that they have been expertly staged – that the best possible view has been carefully selected, for example, the view from Reynolds' house in Richmond down the valley and the bend in the Thames. (This is in stark contrast to Lanzmann's use of generic shots of trains, for instance, in *Shoah* in which, if the specifics of each train used are important, then the film fails to make this apparent.) This characteristic measuredness exposes the degree of control (from Keiller) that runs through *London*, a control that inevitably contradicts the supposed spontaneity of the digressions that send the journeys awry and the lucid though meandering quality of much of the narration. Each shot is unspontaneous, not reacting to its subject but framing, composing or confining it. Claire Barwell, who was Keiller's camera assistant, recounts how he took an entire morning to re-shoot a single shot, each element (a train, a flag, etc.) needing to be precisely as he had envisaged it (Barwell 1997a: 158). Because personal and idiosyncratic, the gaze in *London* is furtive and voyeuristic; it is not what we are looking at (for the film's images are public and ostensibly unfurtive) but how we are made to look. As Iain Sinclair remarks, 'Keiller's *London* is not your London, it's not the city of the commuter, the person who knows where s/he is going. His discoveries belong to the stalker' (p. 301).

The ultimate perversity is that *London*, a film that so assiduously maps out journeys, is composed of a series of tripod shots that never move, whether through tracking, panning or zooming. In contrast to *Shoah*'s constantly moving, roaming camera drawing the spectator in, *London* represses the motion any physical journey necessarily entails. There is much motion implied through the film, but never by the images; tantalisingly, the stages of the physical journey occur only between the shots; there are not even any edits suggesting movement or the passage of time, just hard cuts between images and cuts to black or subtitles. *London* refers to but denies the sense of dynamic, active movement by using an amalgam of self-contained still shots, fetishistic in their precision. In contrast to *Shoah*, we never see the acts of departing, of going to or arriving at destinations, we are just given images connoting having stopped or having reached a destination. Keiller's editing style is again influential here, as the repeated use of black leader, hard cuts as opposed to more fluid forms of editing such as fades, function as interruptions, hesitations, mimicking the lack of fluidity in the main journey itself. *London*'s is a motionless journey; even the often full and elaborate voice-over, which is the primary mechanism by which the details of the journey are divulged, only talks in retrospect after the Narrator and Robinson have arrived somewhere – we never experience the journey directly. This, in a journey film, is a supreme, excessive act of denial.

London thus also includes a repressed journey, a dialectical movement between what it shows and what it subliminally implies. *Shoah* represses the archive footage of the Holocaust and the implication that its journey would have only achieved logical completion by the total annihilation of the European Jewish population; *London* represses the act of journeying itself and the characters who undergo that journey – Robinson and the Narrator. The lack of character identification means that we almost invariably invent a scenario in our heads to complement the unpeopled images on the screen, probably of two prickly, elderly camp men (at times, I imagine, attired in eighteenth-century garb) indignantly adrift in contemporary London. A further incongruity is that Robinson and the Narrator most characteristically walk to places (another indication that they are out of touch). Likewise, although *London* pictures every conceivable modern mode of transport except the underground – red Route Master buses, cars, boats, planes – these are only looked at, never mounted or used. The perversity of the film stems from its continual masochistic reminder that journeys, if physically experienced, can be sensual and pleasurable; the actual journey *London*'s images keep at arm's length is never entirely obscured. Running counter to the unconventional journey *London* actually follows is the repressed potential for a journey more traditionally conceived, a physical journey involving people and transportation, travel and motion. This, ironically, would also have been Keiller's journey; the spectator's masochism is further enhanced by the awareness that the filmmaker must have travelled to each location, endlessly scouring the city.

Conclusion

London, like its sequel *Robinson in Space,* is a self-consciously intellectual film that poses questions about the process of compiling and receiving images, narrative and the intersection between accidental and predetermined events that a journey is predicated upon. Its journey is reflexive, involving the spectator in the debate the film initiates about the nature of the documentary journey and the documentary category itself. Keiller, for example, never defines the relationship between the ambiguous, quasi-fictional characters of the Narrator and Robinson and the factual, personal content of the voice-over and images. *Shoah* is a journey film that emphasises the moment of encounter on screen between Lanzmann and his witnesses over the author–spectator dialogue. It is a personal quest, most obviously on Lanzmann's part, whose journey through the film embodies the notion of searching, of physically seeking out the stories of the Holocaust. This, in turn, is instrumental to the audience's comprehension of the historical journeys (of the Jews to the camps) that the film concerns, and our journey is facilitated by Lanzmann's use of camera techniques that convey these. Conversely, *London* is not a collective journey but a highly idiosyncratic one; it plays with the idea of travel and journeying, as in its use of distancing camera techniques, editing and anonymous protagonists. It is an intentionally stilted film; Keiller wrote it in two halves, one that comprised sample shots and the voice-over, the other that was a list of journeys (Barwell 1997b: 164), so, despite the enactment of the journey encompassing accidental encounters, there is nothing left to chance. It also complicates the fact–fiction divide. Neither the Narrator nor Robinson, as Keiller says, is a real person as anyone would conventionally understand the term (Barwell 1997b: 161), and yet their journeys are composed of locations and facts that are not imaginary. *London* thereby raises further questions about performance within the context of documentary, as does *Shoah*.

Performance is part of *London*'s reflexive collage, a composite of real images and observations, pre-scripted accidents, cryptic characters, an ambiguous relationship between words and image, author and text, author and spectator. Within the context of *London* and Scofield's role in particular, 'performance' denotes fictionalisation, acting, elements that are not conventionally held to be unproblematic in a documentary context. Lanzmann's film addresses and engages with many of the issues raised by observational cinema that this section of the book began by addressing – namely, the supremacy of events unfolding in front of the camera over and above less spontaneous, more didactic features such as voice-over or the use of archive. What occurs at the time of shooting is the essence of the film; built into *Shoah*, as into classic observational documentary, is the idea that documentaries are inherently unstable entities constructed from unpredictable elements. Conversely, *Shoah* is not a film that simply observes, but one that is made up almost exclusively (one would omit here the filming with a hidden camera) of performances: Lanzmann's, of course, and those of his interviewees, many of whom are asked to re-enact, not merely recall, events from the past. This raises an issue fundamental to the last part of this book: the notion that a performance, far from being merely a fictionalisation or falsification, can possess an authenticity – or reveal a truth – no less valid than the 'truth' revealed by a person when the camera is absent. *Shoah* is one example of how the modern documentary has come to terms with, and integrated into its films, the acknowledgement that any non-fiction film is always the result of a complex negotiation between the filmmakers and reality when it is not being filmed. Although the representation of that reality will never be an interchangeable equivalent of that reality, what is revealed through the filming process is what constitutes a documentary: the performance of reality.

Part III

Performance

The logical conclusion to an analysis preoccupied with the idea that a documentary film can never simply represent the real, that instead it is a dialectical conjunction of a real space and the filmmakers that invade it, is the non-fiction film explicitly focused on issues of performance. The two chapters that follow – a discussion of the American presidential image in documentaries and television broadcasts and the companion discussion of performative documentaries, principally in Britain in the 1990s – tackle the issue of performance from different angles. Performance has always been at the heart of documentary filmmaking and yet it has been treated with suspicion because it carries connotations of falsification and fictionalisation, traits that inherently destabilise the non-fiction pursuit. This suspicion – as so many problems with documentary history and its theorisation – stems largely from the advent of observational cinema in America in the early 1960s (direct cinema), a movement that denied – except in its performer-based documentaries – the role performance played in their films. The essential dilemmas posed by direct cinema have been examined at greater length in the introduction to Part II of this book, but this marginalisation of the issue of performance within documentary is fundamental to how non-fiction film has been and is to be interpreted. As this book's Introduction suggests, direct cinema practitioners were misguided when they ignored the issue of how their intervention into real situations altered those situations irrevocably. Despite this, it is precisely this intervention that continues to be one of the most enduring aspects of observational documentary and why, as a mode, it has continued to be influential: that it can capture the moment at which subjects make the transition to performer for the sake of the cameras.

Because the advocates of direct cinema persisted in making the unrealisable claim for observational documentary that the filmmakers' intrusion made a negligible difference to how the films' subjects acted, the previously more relaxed acceptance of the role performance has always played in documentary has been sidelined. It is not just Robert Flaherty, the founding father of dramatic reconstruction, who incorporated performance into documentaries; in the work of filmmakers as diverse as Dziga Vertov, Georges Franju, Emile de Antonio, Chris Marker, Claude Lanzmann and Marcel Ophuls repeated uses are made of performance not as a means of invalidating the documentary pursuit but of getting to the truth each filmmaker is searching for. The historical and theoretical perception of documentary would, one feels, have been different if the French counterpart of direct cinema – the *cinéma vérité* of Jean Rouch (*cinéma vérité* itself being a term coined by Vertov) – had prevailed instead. *Chronique d'un été* is an exemplary performative text, one whose truth is enacted for and by the filmmakers' encounters with their subjects for the benefit of the camera. This remains the essence of the documentaries and broadcasts to be examined in the following chapters.

An additional intention of these discussions of the performative possibilities of the factual image is to bring to bear on the area of documentary more contemporary and heterogeneous theoretical perspectives than is usually the case, to bring documentary up to date, for instance, with the concept of gender and identity as mutable rather than fixed states. In his final autobiographical documentary, *Mr Hoover and I*, Emile de Antonio comments to the camera filming him: 'Who am I? I suppose I'm the ultimate document.' These final chapters examine and extend this notion of the performance for the camera as the 'ultimate document', as the truth around which a documentary is built.

5   The president and the image
Kennedy, Nixon, Clinton

The focus of this chapter will be the role of the performances by three American presidents in documentaries and factual television broadcasts. There is, however, a fluidity and diversity of material available when it comes to considering the presidential image, which encompasses fiction films and drama-documentaries, the reason being that there have always been discrepancies between the actual presidents and the myths pertaining to the presidency. The role played by performance has been crucial, from John Kennedy's affinity with the observational camera, to Nixon's manipulation and suspicion of broadcast television and finally to the creation of Clinton's image by spin doctors and media advisers. A corollary of this progression has been the erosion of not just trust in the presidency but also a desire to idealise the office; by the era of Clinton, the media can dominate presidential politics to such a degree because there is little respect left for the incumbent. There is also a discernible developing relationship between each incumbent president and documentary; it is no coincidence that John Kennedy's image was cemented by his real appearances in early direct cinema films such as *Primary* and *Crisis*, appearances that made him both accessible and idealised. Conversely, Nixon, though associated very much with the live television broadcast, was suspicious of media representations not under his control and, as a consequence, did not willingly become the subject of documentaries. Although many documentaries, from *Millhouse* to the series *Watergate*, have been made about Nixon, they form part of the political tradition of assembling critical portraits of politicians by editing together out-takes and juxtaposing, for ironic effect, official and unofficial pieces of film, a tradition that includes Santiago Alvarez's *LBJ* and Kevin Rafferty's and James Ridgeway's *Feed*, about the 1992 Clinton campaign. A telling point of comparison with Kennedy's championing of documentary can be found in another documentary about the 1992 campaign, *The War Room* – an observational film made by direct cinema pioneer Donn Pennebaker and Chris Hegedus in which Clinton appears, but only fleetingly. The absence of Clinton from official documentary texts comes at a time when, primarily after the Monica Lewinsky scandal, the public's veneration of the actual president is at an all-time low but its desire for a mythic, idealised presidential image seems undiminished; hence the number of recent Hollywood films (such as *Air Force One*) featuring larger-than-life presidents. With reference to these three American presidents whose images have raised the most questions about performance, representation and history, this chapter will examine the shifting relationship between performance and the reality it relates to.

Kennedy

John F. Kennedy was arguably the first candidate to get elected (in 1960) on the strength of his media presence. His presidential career can be charted via images, from the direct cinema film *Primary* (Drew Associates, 1960) following him and his rival for the Democratic nomination, Hubert Humphrey, through the Wisconsin primary to Zapruder's film of his assassination in November 1963. The end result of this close relationship between the president and the image is the accrediting of Kennedy, despite the attempts of historians to reveal the tawdriness of his 'Camelot', with mythic status,[1] made more significant by such idealisation being the result of real rather than fictional representations of him. The moment that cemented this image of Kennedy in the public consciousness was the first of his televised debates (after he had beaten Humphrey) with the Republican candidate, Richard Nixon.

By 1960, nine out of ten American families had a television set, so the live debates were bound to be influential. Oddly, despite his previous use of the direct television address (notably for his career saving Checkers speech of 1952) Nixon, in 1960, underestimated its power, thinking its novelty value might have worn off; Kennedy on the other hand effectively crammed for the debates. Nixon, despite being the more experienced politician, seemed unable to gauge the requirements of television – what the cameras would pick up, what reactions would be strong and appropriate; so, when Kennedy was answering questions, he either looked away or appeared to agree with his opponent's statements. When it came to his turn to proffer answers, Nixon seemed more intent on eliciting Kennedy's approval than that of the television or studio audiences, only infrequently (unlike Kennedy) looking into the camera. Nixon had also been in hospital for three weeks, had lost a substantial amount of weight, wore a slightly crumpled and ill-fitting grey suit and – because Kennedy had refused make-up – he refused make-up except for some clumsily applied Max Factor 'Lazy Shave' intended to conceal his heavy beard (Berry 1987: 35). In contrast to this, Kennedy was bronzed from having spent days campaigning in sunny California (and hence did not need make-up) and, in the gushing words of the CBS director arrived, 'tanned, tall, lean, well tailored in a dark suit … he looked like an Adonis' (Matthews 1996: 148). The majority of those who saw the debate thought that Kennedy had won on points (some 43 per cent to 29 per cent), whereas those, such as Lyndon Johnson the Democratic vice-presidential nominee, who had only heard the debate on the radio, gave it to Nixon. As Sargent Shriver, Kennedy's brother-in-law, attested, it had been Kennedy's 'body language, more than anything he said, that decided the results of the

Great Debates', and as one Nixon aide muttered at the time 'the son of a bitch just lost the election' (Matthews 1996: 155), a view confirmed by Nixon, who refused subsequently to ever look at the tapes. In terms of poll figures, after this first debate (on domestic policy) Kennedy had climbed from 47 per cent to 49 per cent, whilst Nixon had dropped from 47 per cent to 46 per cent. The margin remained tight and the first debate disproportionately significant, as Kennedy went on to win the presidential election by the narrowest margin in history. [2]

This first debate now functions as a shorthand for the importance of the image to any aspirant to public office, and to the success of those who seek the presidency in particular.[3] Theodore White comments that 'American politics and television are now so completely locked together that it is impossible to tell the story of the one without the other' (White 1982: 165). 'Medialities' or 'events that take place mainly to be shown on television – events that, in the absence of television, would not take place at all or would take place in a different manner' (Ranney 1983: 23), have supplanted unmediated contact between politicians and the electorate. The significance of this move away from more traditional forms of electioneering signals the shift towards a more perfor-mative idea of the politician: one who is constructed with the spectator in mind and whose media image is not automatically presumed to be a direct correlative of his off-screen personality. As the chief of staff in Rob Reiner's Hollywood film *The American President* (1995) speculates to the fictional President Andrew Shepherd, the wheelchair-bound Franklin D. Roosevelt – a radio President – would not have been voted in if the American electorate had been confronted with daily reminders on television of his disability.[4] There is thus a direct correlation to be found between John Kennedy's astute manipulation of the media and the mythic significance attributed to his image both during his presidency and after his death. The very endurance of the Kennedy image-ideal suggests a serious dislocation between fact and desire. Despite the debatable accomplishments of his three-year administration – the Bay of Pigs, the collapse of the Vienna conference with Krushchev, the US entry into Vietnam – and the subsequent revelations about his private life, it is still the case that 'If there is any enduring monument on the ever-changing landscape of contemporary American politics, it is the people's affection and esteem for John F. Kennedy' (Brown 1988: 1). One inevitably asks 'why?', and is confronted with the realisa-tion that such veneration is not rational but emotive. As Brown continues, Kennedy's canonisation is largely due to his being 'cut down in the prime of manhood' (p. 44) but is also due to the diversity of his appeal so that Americans 'have projected upon him their deepest beliefs, hopes and even fears' (p. 5).

This is in direct contrast to the way in which both Kennedy's immediate successor, Lyndon Johnson, and his most enduring rival, Nixon, have been perceived. Although there was considerable continuity between the Kennedy administration and the Johnson years, and despite Johnson's very tangible successes in implementing a liberal and enduring domestic programme during his years in office,[5] he is largely remembered as the usurper, the intruder.

Santiago Alvarez's *LBJ* (1968) epitomises the discrepancy between the public perceptions of Johnson and Kennedy. This short avant-garde film constructed out of photographs, archive film, cartoons and movies, casts Johnson as the villain of the 1960s and John and Robert Kennedy, Martin Luther King and Malcolm X as his martyred adversaries. Although he falls short of direct accusation, Alvarez's hatred for Johnson is evident in many of the film's montage sequences, the most vitriolic of which depicts JFK's funeral through a series of images, the clear inference of which is that Johnson was not only indifferent to Kennedy's death but was implicated in it: stills of the funeral procession to Johnson on a horse to archive film and more stills of the funeral to Johnson digging a hole in the ground, smiling. That this is the 'right' point of view is repeatedly implied by *LBJ*'s use of a close-up of an owl (symbolising wisdom and omniscience presumably) observing all the key deaths that are catalogued through the film. The most protracted sequences in *LBJ* to feature Johnson himself are the opening montage of stills showing his daughter Luci's wedding and its concluding counterpart which focuses on him as a doting grandfather, both of which serve to trivialise and undermine their subject when juxtaposed with Vietnam and assassinations. Conversely, goodness in the documentary is represented by the Kennedy brothers and the Civil Rights leaders, particularly Robert Kennedy whose 1968 assassination is a recent event. The contrasting responses to Kennedy (and his brother) and to Johnson are more emotional than rational; JFK is a figure of desire, LBJ a figure of hatred.

As mentioned, the durability of the Kennedy myth is in part the result of Kennedy's own skilful use of the media and his ease in front of the camera compared to either Johnson or Nixon. John Kennedy learnt to entrust the glorification of his image to documentary following his perceived success of *Primary*. Although the film fails to give a rounded account of the election and the electoral process as Theodore White, Jean Luc Godard and others observe (Mamber 1974: 40), it nevertheless captured the essence of campaigning and elicits from its audience an emotional identification with the candidates. The film's most expressive image, 'the *locus classicus* of the direct cinema "follow-the-subject" shot' (Winston 1995: 152), is Albert Maysles' 75-second hand-held tracking shot following Kennedy through a dense crowd and into a packed hall where he and Jackie address a gathering of Polish voters. The fluidity and casualness of this shot mirrors Kennedy's apparent ease and, like many others in the film, serves to forge a strongly empathetic relationship between spectator and 'star'. Indeed, despite dedicating equal time to each candidate, *Primary* forges a greater affinity with Kennedy than it does with Humphrey. Whilst Richard Leacock's camera[6] observes with tangible closeness the tension and fatigue in the Kennedy camp on election night, the parallel sequences following Humphrey are (with the notable exception of Leacock's shot of Humphrey falling asleep in his car) more formal and reserved. *Primary* invites those watching to take sides, to engage with one 'character' over another. This process of identification detracts from *Primary*'s political bite (although it is debatable that this is what the film is after). Brian Winston (1995: 153) comments that

Rather than representing a breakthrough in the cinema's ability to illuminate the nature of the 'real' world, *Primary* flags the onset of one of the most significant media failures of our time, certainly in the USA – the failure to control, and effectively explicate, the political image.

For Winston, *Primary* demonstrates the need for 'spin', indicating that, whilst some politicians (like Kennedy) are adept in front of the camera and effectively wrest control of their image from the filmmakers, others, like Nixon or Humphrey, are instead controlled by the medium. It was John Kennedy's ability to look as if such a struggle was not taking place, as if nothing could be further from his mind, which cements the power of his performance.

Although eschewing any conventional notion of performance (acknowledging the deceit, playing a part or acting up for the cameras), direct cinema establishes an alternative: the documentary about performance. In performance-based observational documentaries (*Meet Marlon Brando*, *Don't Look Back*, even *Salesman*), the subjects' rapport with the camera is vital, and their success as film performers predicated upon their ability to appear natural and at ease when being filmed. This was John Kennedy's greatest asset. Despite the lack of analysis or direct political commentary in a film such as *Primary*, the benefit to the photogenic or 'cinegenic' subject is that he or she becomes accessible to the spectator, to the electorate through an ability to turn in a non-performance, to affect a casual disregard for the camera that just happens to be pursuing them. Towards the end of *Primary*, there is a lengthy election night sequence in which the film intercuts footage of both candidates awaiting the early returns and projected results. The Humphrey material is much tighter, more formal and coldly edited, as if the crew are no closer to him now than they were at the outset. The Kennedy sequences are considerably looser, the editing is more relaxed, the camera focuses on him not only doing things, but also observing and listening to others. Far from coming across as 'uncontrolled', the relaxed quality displayed in this footage serves to establish control with the subject, in this instance John Kennedy, whose responsive and engaged style mirrors that of observational documentary itself.

Likewise in *Crisis: Behind a Presidential Commitment* (1963), Kennedy, the then president, exudes a measure of authority and calm as he is captured on camera in long, reactive close-ups not doing very much except absorbing the advice being proffered by others and rocking gently in his familiar Oval Office chair. *Crisis* is another Drew Associates film, this time charting the build up to the integration of the University of Alabama, a move that Robert Kennedy, then Attorney General, supports and which George Wallace, the Governor of Alabama, opposes. *Crisis* sides with Robert Kennedy over Wallace, just as *Primary* sided with John Kennedy over Humphrey. Characteristic of this inequality are the two opening 'politicians at home in the morning' sequences. Whilst Bobby Kennedy is followed gently by a hand-held camera as he eats breakfast with his children, urging his daughter Kerry to drink up her milk, answering the telephone, George Wallace is, quite literally, kept at a distance, as a far more static camera captures him greeting his child (who has just left the arms of the black maid) and then is led by Wallace on a grudging, formal tour of his collection of oil paintings of Civil War leaders.[7] Not only does this shift in style display bias on the part of Drew Associates (but then, contrary to conventional opinion, the exponents of direct cinema were never entirely averse to or oblivious of subjectivity),[8] it demonstrates again the power that stems from establishing an affinity with the documentary camera, something the British Prime Minister Tony Blair had clearly learnt by the time he commissioned Molly Dineen to make Labour's most memorable broadcast of the 1997 election: a relaxed, informal interview with him in a car and in his family kitchen. In *Crisis*, Robert Kennedy's casualness is arguably contrived. Towards the conclusion of the film, as the crisis is coming to a head and as the Attorney General's office is still facing the very real possibility of having to arrest the Governor of Alabama for stopping two black students from enrolling at university, Robert Kennedy has been visited in his office by three of his children, all running around freely. When on the telephone to his deputy Nick Katzenbach, Kennedy is pestered by Kerry, to whom he then hands the receiver so she can say hello to (a surprised) Katzenbach. The implications of this one action are several: that Robert Kennedy is cool in a crisis; that he is a tender, loving father, that he can focus on more than one thing at once; that he treats his colleagues as friends. The effect of this sequence is highly beneficial to Kennedy, but has he manipulated the situation so that his image is subtly enhanced?

In both *Primary* and *Crisis*, the films' emphasis on character and personality over issues ironically enhances rather than detracts from the successful politicians' credibility. The Kennedys' non-performances in front of the cameras project a naturalness that makes them appear accessible and, as their counterparts in fictional narrative film, to behave as if there are no cameras present. John and Robert Kennedy become automatic points of identification, the documentaries' emotional focuses and 'characters' imbued with an amalgam of fictional and historical significance. It is worth proposing that this ability to appear 'natural' in front of camera complicates the commonly held opinion of direct cinema's overwhelming significance to the evolution of documentary filmmaking. It could be that the chosen subjects in these early documentaries (films that, in turn, made the filmmakers' reputations) happened to be so at ease with the filmmaking process that they simply reflected well upon the new observational style. Perhaps it is these ground-breaking performances and not merely the arrival of lightweight cameras and portable sound recording equipment that revolutionised documentary; if the direct cinema crews had only had Wallace, Humphrey and the like at their disposal, the course of documentary history might have been quite different.

Aware that he could make the media work for him, John Kennedy consolidated this image of the controlled, effective, accessible politician by allowing subsequent crews to film at the White House and by initiating such things as the regular presidential press conferences. He embraced image-makers. A concomitant of this (and of his untimely death) was that he as a figure became mythic in his own right, symbolic (however erroneously) of a successful, liberal presidency. If one looks briefly at the fiction films that appeared in the 1960–3 period or later features that invoke Kennedy as an ideal presidential figure, the extent of the veneration of his image becomes clear. Apart from *PT 109*, a fictional account of Kennedy's wartime experiences which he as president endorsed (even intervening to suggest Warren Beatty for the part),[9] other feature films being made or released during the Kennedy administration (*Advise and Consent, Dr Strangelove, Or: How I Learnt to Stop Worrying and Love the Bomb, Fail Safe* and *Seven Days in May*) present fictional presidents of lesser romantic stature than Kennedy himself. Although liberal and 'good', these fictional presidents are ineffectual, weakened or ageing. Kennedy's own abilities as a charismatic performer likewise explain why the many posthumous fictionalisations of his own life (as in the television movies *Missiles of October, Kennedy* or *A Woman Named Jackie*) seem particularly deficient.

In the spate of presidential films to appear in the 1990s, Kennedy was again idealised, made into a national ego ideal. J. Michael Riva, the production designer on *Dave*, comments that, in reconstructing the White House, he 'wanted to mirror the Kennedy administration as much as possible, because he was my favourite recent president' (Glitz 1993: 35), using primarily the absurdly genteel Jackie Kennedy-narrated guided tours as research material. Likewise, Lilly Kilvert, production designer on *The American President*, 'picked the White House of the JFK years' (McGregor 1995: 84). Reiner's film further mythologises JFK by twice using the pensive portrait of Kennedy that hangs in the White House (significantly more informal than those commemorating the majority of his fellows), once in the opening title sequence in which images of presidents past are intercut with symbols of Washington power, and once when a dejected President Shepherd walks past it at the film's final moment of crisis. The latter makes explicit the desire to forge an identificatory pattern with the dead JFK. In Oliver Stone's *Nixon* the same JFK portrait figures more ostentatiously as a quasi-relic, the destroyed Nixon musing as he contemplates the image: 'When they look at you, they see what they want to be; when they look at me, they see what they are.' Here, the gulf between ego and ideal is clumsily enacted on the screen; Kennedy, *Nixon* suggests, remains the one president to have successfully integrated the two. People are still prepared, in Kennedy's case, to invest even the real image with positive connotations; so the image is activated in order to suppress any knowledge of the negative aspects of the Kennedy history. The glorified image of John Kennedy is thus mobilised to mask the lack that both the filmmakers and the audience are potentially aware of, and becomes a performance of a falsifying history.

The president's image is an effective metaphor for the state of the presidency within public consciousness, and the Kennedy–Nixon binary that has come to dominate the representation of American political history exemplifies the essential opposition. Whereas Kennedy's image symbolises cohesion and stability, Nixon's more ambivalent image symbolises disunity and instability. The essence of this differentiation lies in the relationship between performance and the narrative of history. In an essay on Oliver Stone's *JFK*, Robert Burgoyne discusses the 'tension between the film's formal innovations and its explicit aim to articulate a narrative of national cohesion' (Burgoyne 1996: 113). Although Burgoyne's analysis of Stone's tortuously inconsistent style as expressive of 'the fracturing of historical identity' (p. 113) is too predictable, he rightly identifies the enduring significance of John Kennedy as representative of a nostalgic desire for the refiguration of a 'unified national identity' (p. 115). Burgoyne's argument is in part based on Timothy Brennan's analysis of nations as 'imaginary constructs that depend for their existence on an apparatus of cultural fictions' (Brennan 1990: 49), the idea of nations as mythic, allegoric entities invented as a social necessity rather than being the inevitable result of historical events. In his discussion, Burgoyne pins these ideas onto the nation's 'nostalgic desire ... for a unified national culture' destroyed by 'the memory of discontinuity emblematically figured in the death of Kennedy' (p. 123). Is it not conversely possible that the death of Kennedy – far from destroying the illusion of national cohesion – was the point at which this illusion became cemented in the social consciousness? If the link between nationhood and cultural fictions is to be sustained, the determining factor in Kennedy's continued symbolic presence as icon for national stability seems to be that, by remaining perpetually a figure of tragedy fixed in the memory by the real images of him up to and including his assassination, he represents the moment at which the myth of national unity took hold rather than the moment at which it was destroyed. Because of the defining event of his death, Kennedy's image is consistent, unchangeable; his real persona has become synonymous with the mythic significance it is fancifully identified with.

Nixon

Whereas Kennedy's composite image has been assembled through documentary, live broadcasts, home movies (his own family's as well as Zapruder's) and fiction films, Nixon's image is forever associated with his televised appearances. Although he has featured in a multitude of films, documentaries such as *Millhouse* or *Watergate* make extensive use of Nixon's televised images. Nixon chose the television broadcast as his preferred mode of address because he assumed he would find it easy to control; he was not intent upon giving the public unprecedented access to him as an individual as Kennedy had done, but on addressing them in a more confrontational manner, often in times of crisis. Unlike Kennedy's rather deftly understated performances in *Primary* and *Crisis*, Nixon's appearances show him quite overtly acting, thus adding to the pervasive perception of him as the 'bad' presidential alter ego. One sees with Nixon a severance as opposed to a reinforcement of the ties between reality and fiction, between the image and the ideal; instead of posing as the embodiment of a mythic presidency, Nixon represents the moment at which a belief in such a myth became untenable. While JFK has become part of American and Hollywood mythology, Nixon has been airbrushed out of the picture, and is conspicuously absent from the montage of past presidents at the beginning of *The American President*. This negativity is not simply the result of Watergate, it was innately linked to Nixon's own public persona, his inability to convincingly mask the cracks between who he was and what he sought to represent. Although he understood the media, Nixon never won it over, seeking the approbation of an institution that he distrusted and knew would never like him (see his self-pitying acknowledgement to the press upon his defeat in the 1962 Gubernatorial race in California and his supposed resignation that he is a national joke: 'Just remember, you won't have Dick Nixon to kick around any more').

Nixon's media performances exemplify a growing disillusionment with reality. An early example is the Checkers speech, Nixon's 30-minutes long televised plea (transmitted 23 September 1952 on NBC and funded by the Republican National Committee) to persuade Eisenhower to keep him on as his running mate for the forthcoming presidential elections following revelations that he accepted illegal gifts and misdirected party funds. The Checkers speech (so called because of the family dog Checkers Nixon cites as being the one unsolicited gift that he will admit to and intends to keep) has had a complex history. At the time of its broadcast it was deemed successful, as Republicans called in droves asking for Nixon to be retained as the party's vice-presidential nominee. The television station's copy was subsequently buried, assumed lost, until it was delivered anonymously to Emile de Antonio, after which it was used

Figure 5.1 Millhouse: A White Comedy
Source: Courtesy of BFI Stills, Posters and Designs

at length in his satirical documentary *Millhouse: A White Comedy* and acquired sufficient cult status to be released as a short to accompany Robert Altman's *Secret Honor* (1984). Similarly, the Checkers speech is open to analysis from various different perspectives: as an example of a primitive political use of television; as illustrative of Nixon's general phoniness and corruption; as an example, post-Watergate, of how Nixon's career was based on sleaze, rule-bending and getting out of scrapes by adopting desperate measures, often the televised broadcast. Now, it is hard to see how the Checkers speech was ever a success. Nixon himself later admitted that the entire broadcast was staged, that Pat (who sat beside him) was as much a prop as the American flag in the background, and in keeping with this, Hollywood producer Darryl F. Zanuck reputedly told Nixon the Checkers speech was 'the greatest performance I have ever seen' (Monsell 1998: 18). Nixon's tactic was to prove his innocence through an excess of detail, offering his viewers a 'complete financial history' and itemising with preposterous precision his meagre inheritance. Nixon's evocation of his 'poor man made good' alter ego seemingly knows no bounds; with a flourish Nixon adds that Pat does not own a mink coat but instead wears, with pride, her 'respectable Republican cloth coat'.

Nixon's quality of performance is very different to that of the Kennedy brothers in *Primary* or *Crisis*. All are, in the broadest sense, acting – they are behaving in a way that directly acknowledges and is compromised or altered by the presence of cameras – but whereas the Kennedys' 'acting' expresses ease with the unreal dynamic created by the filming process and an ability to mirror the ostensibly relaxed style of direct cinema, Nixon's comparable performances, even the successful ones, are forever tinged with desperation. It seems inconceivable that the Checkers speech saved Nixon's career, because as one American journalist comments in 1972, Nixon is always an actor, 'he is conscious of the role he is playing and he has tried to train himself to his needs' (Walter Kerr quoted in Monsell 1998: 9). Perhaps it is easy to say this with hindsight (and certainly one of the most effective and entertaining ways of viewing Nixon's television addresses is through what one subsequently finds out about his infinite corruptibility) but in the Checkers speech Nixon's performance appears fraught with conflicts and barely conceals cracks. His mannerisms are stiff and perfunctory, such as coming round to the front of the desk whence he begins in mock conviviality and informality, his protestations of goodness and innocence so extremely dull that, to a modern viewer, they convey precisely what Nixon wants to disguise, namely his untrustworthiness. Nixon's performance is brittle, self-righteous and painstaking to excess; it is so tempting now to interpret the success of the Checkers speech as the result of the Republican faithful feeling pity for a man so utterly desperate for power that he would open himself up to contempt and ridicule, brandish Pat his wife as a token of his ordinariness, make cheap jibes at his opponents, plead with the viewing public to change Eisenhower's mind about him. Much of this interpretation stems from the manner in which Nixon addresses the viewers directly, imploringly, trapping them with an obdurate stare. Pat, meanwhile, hovers rigidly on the edge of the strategic sofa, fixing her husband with the same weary, wary grimace that we now recognise from the Watergate period and Nixon's ignominious departure from the White House in 1974. Although Nixon survives repeated 'crises'[10] throughout his political career, it is often touch and go, a precariousness echoed by the catalogue of gestures and postures around which Nixon's uneasy performances are built. Unlike Kennedy, Nixon would never have exposed himself to the invasive approach of direct cinema, he sought broadcast situations that he and his aides could control. He never wanted to be caught in an unguarded moment – even the out-takes from his television appearances reveal a person wary of potential viewers.

Through the course of his career, Nixon came to symbolise the decline of any idealistic belief in the presidency as institution or indeed in the veracity of factual images related to it. These schisms are most evident in the appearances during the Watergate period. On 30 April 1973 Nixon made a televised address countering the rumours of his own implication in the Watergate scandal. In his essay 'Strategies of lying' Umberto Eco comments that, in this speech, having been branded a villain by the hostile media, Nixon reconstructs himself as the hero, adopting classic narrative strategies to enforce a specific trajectory culminating in the hero's re-evaluation once the facts are fully known and equilibrium is restored. Nixon transforms himself from villain (which is 'the tale told by the press' [p. 8]) into hero, and his speech becomes 'the confession of a man, himself, struck down by great misfortune and nevertheless capable of rising up again for the common good' (p. 8). The president thus admits to the 'imprudence' of Watergate (p. 8), thereby, in characteristically equivocal fashion, acknowledging guilt whilst simultaneously exonerating himself from blame. This is very much Nixon's strategy in the earlier Checkers speech, and indeed remains his master strategy throughout his career. In the 1973 speech he is at the mercy of the 'collaborators' John Dean, John Ehrlichman and Bob Haldeman, whose resignations he is in the process of announcing, and so, by extension, a system over which he – the little man – has no control. Eco concludes his analysis of the 1973 address with the observation that, 'Before the televised speech, a small percentage of Americans distrusted Nixon, yet after it the figure increased enormously and exceeded fifty per cent' (Eco 1985: 11), offering as a reason for this failure the fact that this otherwise masterful use of narrative construction is a *visual* not a written text:

> Every muscle on Nixon's face betrayed embarrassment, fear, tension. Such a fine story, with the benefit of a happy ending, told by a frightened man. Frightened from start to finish. Nixon's speech was the visual representation of insecurity, acted out by the 'guarantor of security'.
>
> (p. 11)

In essence, it is Nixon's performance, his clumsy body language rather than his laborious self-justifications, that expose his lack of integrity; television is in control of him rather than *vice versa*.

The speech where the discrepancy between words and implied truth is most acutely manifested is Nixon's resignation speech of 9 August 1974. A defiant Nixon (reputedly willing to face impeachment rather than accept Gerald Ford's promise of a pardon, who maintained he did not fear jail as Gandhi and Lenin had done much of their writing there[11]) stands flanked by his family, stoically staring on as he addresses the assembled White House staff. Once again Nixon constructs a grand narrative around himself as the tragic figure. At the outset, the identification of himself as a flawed but great man is merely implied in an impersonal dialogue with those watching:

> When the greatness comes and you're really tested, when you take some knocks, some disappointments, when sadness comes – because only if you've been in the deepest valley can you ever know how magnificent it is to be on the highest mountain.

Through this grandiloquent portion of the speech Nixon avoids the direct gaze of both audience and cameras, until he reaches the description of the 'highest mountain' at which point he looks up and half smiles, as if recalling that feeling. The manner in which Nixon delivers this obscure dramatisation of his fall and rise (it is interesting how the sentence's structure puts the two in that order, as if the action is already in the past) both mirrors his words and exposes the denial inherent within this formulation. Nixon, by transporting himself to the 'highest mountain', denies that he is in the 'deepest valley'; his rhetoric distancing his immediate situation from the parabolic transition he evokes. Having thus perked up, Nixon continues:

> always give of your best, never get discouraged, never be petty, always remember others may hate you, but those who hate you don't win unless you hate them, and then you destroy yourself.

Once more this achingly inelegant sentence contains a double narrative. The superficial text presents a buoyed Nixon issuing wise words to those listening (another defiant disavowal of the predicament he is in), and suggests that he himself has acknowledged the obstacles cited and has learnt how to surmount them. This main text is confirmed by Nixon's more confident smile and a greater engagement with those present; this renewed surety stems from the characteristic tactic of having detached himself from the negative connotations of what he is saying by deflecting guilt and the necessity for self-awareness onto the impersonal narrative.[12] The subtext of this speech becomes the narrative that Nixon's words and gestures repress: that he is a hated man, that he has lost. Nixon then resorts to the narrative he knows and performs best:

> I remember my old man, I think they would have called him a sort of little man, a common man. He didn't consider himself that way. You know what he was? He was a streetcar motorman first, and then he was a farmer, and

then he had a lemon ranch. It was the poorest lemon ranch in California, I can assure you. He sold it before they found oil on it. ... Nobody will ever write a book, probably, about my mother. Well, I guess all of you would say this about your mother: my mother was a saint. ...

This piece of sub-Arthur Miller contains Nixon's classic emergency exit, the diversion he takes when refusing to admit he is wrong: to talk about life before he entered politics. Paradoxically, it is sections such as this that most manifestly signal Nixon's failure to achieve his aim. Emile de Antonio comments that, 'the real history of the United States in the Cold War is the out-takes' (Weiner 1971: 4). In fact, history arguably exists in the tension between the official and unofficial histories it comprises, and Nixon (whose specific television out-takes de Antonio is discussing here) is revealed through a similar conflict between how he ostensibly presents himself through words and gesture, and the very different way in which these mannerisms are received.

Nixon's lack of straightforwardness has meant that he has become not a hero like Kennedy but a symbol of untrustworthiness and instability, Watergate still being the most ignominious moment in American presidential history. As an event, it engendered scepticism on a widespread scale, and has resulted in two oppositional approaches to the issue of the presidential image in general and to Nixon's image in particular: the impulse to reinstate a historical continuum via narrative and representation, and the acknowledgement that such a continuum is irretrievably lost. As George Herbert Mead, writing in 1929, notes, 'When a society is confronted with a seemingly novel event that disrupts the meaningful flow of events, the past must be rewritten to repair the discontinuity' (Johnson 1995: 37, 38). The former tendency is epitomised by Oliver Stone's *Nixon* which, for all its emphasis upon Watergate and Nixon's demise, nevertheless offers the view that Nixon was not that bad, a view sustained only by the prioritisation of personal and psychological character analysis over political scrutiny. To cement this view, the film concludes with real archive of Nixon's funeral (which all living ex-presidents attended) over which a voice-over lists his achievements since Watergate: his pardon, his six books, his work as an 'elder statesman', his view that, if he had not been 'driven from office', North Vietnam would not have overwhelmed the South in 1975. *Nixon* is an exercise in what could be termed the collective remembering and collective forgiveness of a moment of national trauma, as Stone's Nixon becomes one who loves not wisely but too well, a strange metamorphosis indeed for Tricky Dickey. Rather than excise Nixon from American political history, Stone conforms to the revisionist trend to reinvent him as a quasi-hero and concomitantly to reimpose historical stability on the very events that ruptured the illusion of a continuum in the first place,[13] opting to incorporate him and Watergate into a unified image of the recent past that provides continuity between that past, the present and the future.

The alternative tradition where Nixon's representation directly follows on from the corruption suggested by Nixon's own chaotic, ambivalent performances. In the immediate aftermath of Watergate, there was a spate of different texts all of which were deeply critical of the Nixon administration and cynical about presidential politics, for example, films such as Altman's *Secret Honor* and Pakula's *All the President's Men* (1976) or books such as the entirely blank *The Wit and Wisdom of Spiro Agnew*. A more recent documentary series that tackled the corruption of Nixon and his administration is Norma Percy's series *Watergate* (Brian Lapping Associates/BBC, 1994). *Watergate* has, as its opening premise, Nixon's unquestionable guilt, placing right at the start of its first episode John Ehrlichman's comment that White House staff were always 'carrying out Richard Nixon's instructions, day to day'. The five-part series unpicks in great detail the events that made up Watergate, from the establishing of Nixon's own paranoid political intelligence and surveillance systems to his departure from office. Perhaps it is because for so long we had been subjected, especially through the 1980s, to a romantic reassessment of Nixon's career that Percy's intricate series is so refreshing: it reminds us – through the replaying of the White House tapes, through interviews with all the main Watergate protagonists and through archive – of the infinite corruption of the Nixon administration. The series gains extensive interviews with Bob Haldeman, Nixon's Chief of Staff (who died very soon after), John Ehrlichman, his chief domestic adviser, James Dean, his counsel, and the White House Intelligence organisers, Howard Hunt and Gordon Liddy. The sense, particularly as Nixon's illegal tapes are played and memos (many assumed destroyed) get passed from one witness to another, is of reliving Watergate. Although the series concludes with the comment that Nixon died in April 1994 still denying he had broken the law, *Watergate* testifies against this. For example, John Dean (with the obvious relish of Nixon's scape-goat avenging himself) talks of how he plucked from the air the figure of $1 million to be paid to Hunt and Liddy to hush them up – a sum that, to Dean's amazement, Nixon said he would find. Likewise there is the replaying of the 'smoking gun' tape of 23 June 1972 on which Nixon blatantly orders a cover-up and from which someone in the White House erased 18 minutes. Nixon may deny his guilt, but history does not. *Watergate* conveys the extremity of the events leading to Nixon's resignation, albeit imparted by a series of educated, well-dressed men (Gordon Liddy, interviewed in front of a highly polished table on which is carefully arranged his gun collection, stands out here). Such an intricate historical series painstakingly enacts the development of what John Dean, on a tape recorded 21 March 1973, terms a 'cancer … close to the presidency that's growing'. Unlike *Nixon*, which buries the unpalatable truths of these recordings under the romantic notion of fluid political progression, *Watergate* does not let us forget that this was the event that most conclusively wrecked the ideal of not only a historical continuum, but also dispelled the myth of the good president. In the words of Jonathan Rauch in *The New Republic*, Nixon was 'easily the worst president of the post-war era, and probably of the century' (Johnson 1995: 7).

Robert Altman's *Tanner '88*, a fictional 6-part television series in which fictional and real political figures intermingle, exemplifies the post-Nixon shift towards distrusting the idea that truthfulness and politics are in any way closely related. *Tanner '88* was written by political cartoonist Garry Trudeau and broadcast by HBO throughout the 1988 presidential campaign. The series' focus is an idealistic but ineffectual democrat candidate, Jack Tanner; it is shot on video in a fly-on-the-wall style reminiscent of direct cinema and pastes the fictional Tanner into the events of the real campaign. The blurring of the distinction between real and fictional presidential politics has since been much copied, most directly by *Bob Roberts* (Tim Robbins, 1992). Jack Tanner is an innocent abroad whose image is created, distorted, used by the sassy throng that surrounds him. In the opening episode, 'Dark Horse', his first campaign video is shown to a group of sample New Hampshire voters who unanimously declare it to be disastrous. The only aspect of the video these punters like is

Figure 5.2 Tanner '88

Source: Courtesy of BFI Stills, Posters and Designs

Tanner's face, adamantly rejecting quite plausible campaign ploys such as the woolly fireside address to camera in which Tanner (a single father) – dressed in a chunky cardigan (Figure 5.2) – talks about having to interrupt his political career because of his daughter's Hodgkin's disease, or introduces a 1960s montage juxtaposing Kennedy's 1961 inaugural speech ('Ask not what your country can do for you ...'), his assassination, Neil Armstrong's 'Giant leap for mankind' and the album cover of The Beatles' *Sgt. Pepper*. To replace this unsuccessful video Deak, the increasingly uncontrollable cameraman in the Tanner entourage, makes a new one out of secretly shot footage of Tanner's spontaneous, impassioned monologue that closes the first episode in which he admits, 'real leaders have always stepped forward ... it's time for that leadership now. I'm not sure it's me, but I'd like the chance to find out'. Filmed through a glass table and thus shaky and indistinct, this new video is aired on television at the outset of Episode 2 and concludes with the new campaign slogan in the corner of the screen: 'For Reel' crossed out and replaced by 'For Real'. The response from the barmen watching this bemusing exercise in hidden camera television is to ask: 'What the fuck was that?'

The replacement of the first stilted, derivative attempt to the 'For Real' video is representative of Tanner's metamorphosis from a carefully constructed candidate overly aware of the correlation between political success and image manipulation, to one who recognises the power of naturalness and honesty; as one aide comments, 'Tanner is about as real as Reagan is unreal'. This is, of course, out of step with the times and fatal to Tanner's credibility as a presidential candidate. Between 1968 and 1992, Jimmy Carter was the Democrat party's only president, and it is to the maligned Carter that Tanner is compared. In a piece of fake news footage, he is seen carrying his own bags, after which an aide remonstrates with him that this signals 'you can't or won't delegate. It says Jimmy Carter. People may want you to be for real Jack, but that doesn't mean they want you to be like him.' It was not until Clinton's victory in 1992 – when even Dan Quayle, the Republican nominee for Vice-President, remarked that, if Clinton runs the country the way he ran his campaign, things will be all right – that the Democrats fully engaged with the importance of slick image-making.

Tanner is an eminently plausible 1980s Democrat loser (compared to George McGovern as well as Carter) who is woven seamlessly into the 1988 campaign. He is shown meeting a wary Bob Dole, a real Republican contender, and declares, in a speech at a Waylon Jennings-led gala evening, 'I've become Al Gore's worst nightmare'. Even Tanner's partner Joanna is seen in conversation with her 'friend' Kitty Dukakis after the Democrat convention, being asked whether or not Jack will come out in support of her husband Michael, the real Democrat nominee. At the convention itself, Tanner goes to the floor (the first candidate – however unreal – to do this during the vote itself), canvassing support after taking a stance (alongside Jesse Jackson) against the system of block 'super delegate' voting.[14] Tanner's invasion of the real political arena does two notable things: it problematises the boundaries between the factual and the fictitious and it makes one view with great cynicism the values of real presidential politics. Unlike *Forrest Gump* or *Zelig*, films that graft the fictional onto the documentary for essentially comic effect, Tanner's realness is equivocal. *Tanner '88* draws attention to the distinction between the composite, pastiche character of Jack Tanner and his real counterparts, at the same time as it renders *him* a highly plausible Democrat candidate and *them* equally plausible fictional entities. The struggle within Tanner is the struggle between possessing and relinquishing an identity, and so functions as a metaphor for the ailing, compromised Democrats of the 1970s and 1980s. Tanner's progressive pro-environmentalist, anti-racist stance is at odds with his shameless promotion as the unknown outsider who attends small town barbecues and drops in on a Ladies Auxiliary quilt-making afternoon. Inevitably it is his progressiveness that is repressed.

Tanner '88 has a perpetually accidental quality that mirrors the meandering nature of the Democratic party at the time. In terms of its narrative structuring, apart from generally leading up to the convention and the conclusion of Tanner's failed bid for the presidential nomination, the series maintains a veneer of formlessness – journalists get stranded on the press bus on the way to the Waylon Jennings evening and so miss the bungled assassination attempt on Tanner; Tanner unwittingly gets arrested at a 'Free South Africa' rally. This in turn is mimicked by the observational filming style, exemplified by Deak's increasingly extreme and clandestine shooting for his alternative campaign film. Tanner's campaign is pursued by a lazy, unbothered and uncritical camera that frequently gets diverted (at times onto something interesting, such as Tanner emerging with Joanna from a room when no one yet knows they are an item). The style of filming, therefore, is an inherent component of the series' pretence at realness, its eavesdropping quality replicating the essential direct cinema paradox of constructed, ordered chaos. The filmmaking style pioneered by the direct cinema exponents of the 1960s has become the common shorthand mechanism for giving a piece of fiction a documentary edge, of legitimating its claim to reality. In *Tanner '88*, Altman utilises this technique ironically, overemphasising and so complicating the notion of the real, both through Deak and through the persistent references to Tanner or his image as real.

Tanner '88 is an ambiguous, hybrid text: both in its filmmaking style and its narrative it advocates truthfulness; it also signals that, in the 1980s political climate, Tanner's attachment to such values lacks political credibility. What the appositely named Jack Tanner lacks is Kennedy's ability to perform naturalness, to be both politician and real at the same time. This deficiency has altered by the time another Jack – Stanton in *Primary Colors* – appears in another semi-fictional campaign film. Altman's series, rather than merely accept the necessity of the Kennedy paradox, ridicules the political allegiance to a concept of fabricated realness, within this undermining the idea of 'a cinema of truth'. The transition from natural idealistic candidate to victorious politician is simply made in an earlier film, *The Candidate*; in *Tanner '88* the neat progression is substituted by a polemic on realness. Within the very different documentary context of Jennie Livingston's *Paris is Burning*, realness is understood as a performance that cannot be 'read' or deciphered as false by others. Tanner's dilemma, and the one that Altman's unflinchingly observational style underlines, is that he can too easily be 'read'. By the 1980s we no longer believe the transparency of observational documentary, nor do we any longer, since Nixon, believe the politician and his image are meaningfully correlated. A gag that runs through *Tanner '88* is that no one knows who he is; from an early encounter with a pair of New Hampshire autograph hunters who enquire 'Jack Tanner, who's he?', to the perplexed responses to the 'For Real' campaign film, Tanner the candidate is a nonentity. The central struggle contained within *Tanner '88* between realness and manufacturedness is enacted through the more specific conflict within Tanner (that is in turn echoed by the series' style) between wanting to forge an identity and realising that, once he enters the political arena, his identity must be relinquished; hence the attempt at suppressing any intimations of progressive politics as well as the bemused, uncertain smile that adorns Tanner's face.

Clinton

The real Democrat candidate who most closely resembles Jack Tanner is Bill Clinton: the child of the 60s Democrat whose liberalism is endlessly compromised by the necessities of politics and the intrusions of scandal. There is also an ironic stylistic similarity between *Tanner '88* and the actual documentary examinations of the 1992 campaign, *Feed* (Kevin Rafferty and James Ridgeway, 1992) and *The War Room* (Chris Hegedus and Donn Pennebaker, 1993), both of which depict a similar blend of hypertension and mundanity. By the time of Clinton's election in 1992, the cynicism that pervades *Tanner '88* has come to dominate representations of both the real and fictional presidential image, so media stories and communication strategists or 'spin doctors' dominated the campaign. Whereas *Primary* was elegant and evocative, suggesting that there was still a mystique surrounding the presidential fight and that the filmmakers had been granted privileged, unprecedented access to the candidates, a modern equivalent such as *Feed* indicates that now there is limitless media access to the American electoral process, that the candidates are mere cogs in a system that comprises dull, trivial, ugly television images. As if acknowledging this loss, the anonymous novel *Primary Colors* (later identified as the work of journalist Joe Klein), which tells the very thinly veiled story of the Clinton 1992 election campaign, opens with a conversation between the idealistic Henry Burton and Susan Stanton (assumed to be George Stephanopoulos, Clinton's communications director, and Hillary Rodham Clinton respectively). Burton, contemplating joining Jack Stanton's presidential campaign, says:

> The thing is, I'd kind of like to know how it feels when you're fighting over … y'know – historic stuff. I'm not like you. I didn't have Kennedy. I got him from books, from TV. But I can't get enough of him, y'know?

Can't stop looking at pictures of him, listening to him speak. I've never heard a president use words like 'destiny' or 'sacrifice' and it wasn't bullshit. So, I want to be part of something a moment, like that. When it's real, when it's history I. …

(Anonymous 1996: 24)

Susan Stanton simply replies: 'It's good. History's what we're about, too What else is there?' By 1992, the bubble has burst as far as creating history and myth through politics is concerned. Reading or watching (in Mike Nichols' film of *Primary Colors*) Burton's naïve vision of what is real and what is history also touches upon our collective awareness that such mythologisation is 'bullshit' anyway, and that what links Kennedy and Clinton perhaps more than anything else is their womanising, not their rhetoric. Those watching Clinton on television are too knowing to accept his rhetoric at face value, so the myth is created elsewhere – by the spin doctors, the media, the multitude of Hollywood movies featuring heroic presidents that the 1990s spawned.

The War Room is most clearly illustrative of this loss as it is made within a comparable observational style to *Primary* and *Crisis*, especially the loose, eaves-dropping camera work much of which is Pennebaker's own. As suggested by its title, which refers to the Arkansas 'war room' from which Stephanopoulos and James Carville, campaign manager, masterminded Clinton's victory, the documentary observes the entourage responsible for that victory. Clinton himself is marginal; what is foregrounded is the relationship with the media covering the campaign. *The War Room* contains a few inevitable but somewhat sardonic echoes of *Primary* (on which Pennebaker worked as a cameraperson), for instance two lengthy hand-held tracking shots in pursuit of George Stephanopoulos that are reminiscent of Albert Maysles' shot following John Kennedy in 1960. The second is particularly emblematic of the shift in political representation that has taken place. Following the first televised debate (of which we only see bites on the television sets that Stephanopoulos, Carville and others are fixated upon) Stephanopoulos runs out clapping, his arms in the air, convinced that Clinton has won the night. The jubilant communications manager is not running to congratulate his candidate (in fact, any communication between the two is strictly limited to telephone conversations in which Stephanopoulos imparts information to Clinton) but towards the press to reiterate his point that Bush has lost.

Whereas *Primary* draws us in and forges an affinity with Kennedy in particular, *The War Room* invites its audience to experience electioneering vicariously: we are doubly removed from Clinton by gaining access to him second and third hand from, firstly, the media and, secondly, his campaign team who are constantly analysing that media coverage. Direct cinema in the 1960s emphasised and followed individuals – *Primary* boiled down to a contest between the two candidates with party politics taking a back seat, *Crisis* offered a portrait of how a political crisis impinges on the people involved – *The War Room*, with its twin stress upon process and party politics, lacks the emotive pull of the earlier films precisely because it lacks Clinton. Throughout the film there is an overwhelming sense of Clinton engulfed by throngs of people or being coached and guided by a string of minders; once he has gained the nomination, he becomes even more marginal, effectively disappearing altogether whilst Carville and Stephanopoulos think up soundbites and evolve strategy. Clinton is depicted as the team's figure-head, in itself a necessary comment upon the manner in which power has shifted away from the individual candidate – of Clinton's victory address to the Democratic convention, for instance, the film includes only the last phrase ('I still believe in a place called Hope'). The real power resides with Carville and Stephanopoulos. Stephanopoulos' role, more than anything else, is to patch up Clinton's fragile image, to stem leaks, to divert dangerous exposés: on the eve of victory he is shown aggressively fielding a call concerning allegations (later disproved) that Clinton fathered an illegitimate mixed-race child. The culmination of his and Carville's success is Clinton's emphatic victory, and yet, dressed in evening wear, Stephanopoulos is still amending the now President's victory speech and, just before we cut to the party, there is a final phone conversation between the two in which Stephanopoulos advises the president-elect to 'say what you wanna say – this is your night'. In this context, this deference to the President is deeply ironic, for the entire documentary has stressed Clinton's lack of power and independence. This is a documentary about the team that manufactured Clinton's victory. Clinton himself is not necessarily the emblem of that victory and the film's downbeat conclusion (two shots of the empty 'war room') serves as a reminder that the political process is ongoing, that, unlike the romantic 'crisis' narratives of direct cinema, closure is not granted by the victory celebrations as those celebrations are simply part of the process.

It is tempting to agree that *The War Room* reveals simply 'the amoral and ultimately apolitical attitude of approaching political communications solely as a battle of images, waged through the mass media' (Diamond and Silverman, 1997: 108), although the film seems more complex than this; what it signals, more than pure cynicism, is a sense of what has been lost by this inevitable shift towards media-dominated politics. *The War Room* does not only offer evidence that Carville and Stephanopoulos created the electable candidate Bill Clinton through their dual manipulation of his image and the media, it raises the suspicion that the main task of the two advisers, having saturated the media with pictures of their candidate, is perversely to shield him from view. Despite its direct cinema pedigree, *The War Room* does not (and presumably was not permitted to) show Clinton or the others in many undirected situations (although there is what looks like a hidden camera shot of Carville fixing a date with Mary Matalin, deputy manager of the Bush campaign). Towards the beginning of the documentary, there is a brief sequence showing Clinton on the telephone in baseball cap, T-shirt and shorts, he looks at ease and comfortable. As *The War Room* progresses, there are fewer and fewer glimpses of him, the implication being that the spin doctors do not want to run the risk of exposing their candidate to unpredictable encounters with a documentary crew. The motto of modern politics is 'always be on your guard'.

The observation that politics has become solely a battle of images could more legitimately be made about *Feed*, a documentary that appeared in art-house cinemas on the eve of the 1992 election and comprises unofficially collated footage from the networks' satellite transmissions of the Democratic New Hampshire Primary campaign. Emile de Antonio's remark that the real history of post-war America is to be found in television out-takes seems witty and plausible until one sees *Feed*, much of which dwells on out-takes so vapid and mundane they fail to expose a meaningful hidden history. Punctuating *Feed* from start to finish is a series of shots of George Bush waiting behind his desk to begin a television address; Bush looks bored and vacant, and the most inter-esting question raised by this material is what precisely is he doing with the hand that repeatedly drops behind his desk? More pertinent to *Feed* than de Antonio's comment concerning the importance of out-takes is his comment that nightly news coverage is deliberately unanalytical. *Feed* offers no answers, just a by now conventionalised 'collage junk' of media images from the non-stop coverage of all aspects of the opening Primary campaign. Much of this (such as the press conference at which Gennifer Flowers repeats her allegations of a 12-year affair with Bill Clinton) is highly familiar, but is juxtaposed with plenty of material that is less so and funnier for it such as Paul Tsongas (recently recovered from cancer and keen to prove his fitness) posing for the cameras in his swimming trunks, Jerry Brown lecturing some college students for not knowing who Marshall McLuhan was before offering a rather inept account of his ideas himself, and Bill Clinton suppressing giggles as he is about to go on air.

Feed achieves two notable things: it demonstrates that the presidential poli-tics is so image-dependent that who the candidates are (in terms of character, the man behind the mask, etc.) has become an irrelevance; it also suggests that the business of politics has become a puerile joke. Is the election for President of the United States worth taking seriously if the most important aspect of a candidate is whether or not he or she gives good sound-bite or performs well on 'soft format' television such as chat shows? *Feed* answers no, but with this inevitably comes a nostalgia for an era when the presidential election procedure did not flaunt its tackiness quite so brazenly. *Feed* contains few vestiges of the dialectical editing of an earlier Rafferty film, *Atomic Café*, suggesting more that it is intent on conveying the degree to which modern campaigns are not about candidates but about their multiple, serial representation for a variety of televi-sual purposes. The film's use of unofficial footage ultimately leads to a reassessment of its official corollaries such as the televised address or the docu-mentary which remain environments which the politician can, to some extent, control. What *Feed*, through its intercutting of the official with the unofficial image, proceeds to focus upon is the moment of transition between waiting to go on air and commencing the public performance. Because the unofficial out-take material is not especially revealing, *Feed* inevitably questions the belief in the 'real' person as opposed to the 'performance'. What both *The War Room* and *Feed* demonstrate, therefore, is that the modern candidate is purely an arti-ficial construct.

Is the 1992 presidential election to be remembered as the one that admitted that standing for office is a performative act? At a White House dinner to commemorate the film version of *Primary Colors*, Bill Clinton invited John Travolta, who in the film plays Jack Stanton, his fictional alter ego, to impersonate him for the assembled guests. Travolta declined, but both Clinton's action and the accuracy of Travolta's rendition of Clinton's mannerisms in Mike Nichols' film demonstrate the corrosion of the distinction between the real and the performed. *Primary Colors*, the film, is a historical enactment, a narrative representation so close to the actual events and individuals portrayed that it, on several occasions, collapses the differences between them. Included in it is a quasi-re-enactment, or re-presentation of the Gennifer Flowers episode, although Flowers' name has been altered to Cashmere McLeod – now Susan Stanton's hairdresser rather than a nightclub singer. The fictionalised version of events shares many components with the original news story: Cashmere sells her story to a magazine, the Stantons go on television to deny the allegations and Cashmere retaliates with a press conference at which she plays a tape (later discovered to be faked) of an alleged conversation between her and Stanton. Although not a verbatim rendition of the Clintons' appearance on *60 Minutes* to refute Flowers' claims, the version in *Primary Colors* is an accurate paraphrase, simulating not just the narrative situation but also the couple's deliberate and studied body language (sitting very close to each other, clasping hands, Hillary/Susan gazing fixedly at her husband as he admits there have been problems in their marriage). The proximity of reconstruction to historical original renders the performance transparent. *Primary Colors* lacks the critical distance of *Tanner '88*; whilst Jack Tanner was a credible pastiche of an 1980s Democrat, Jack Stanton is merely a pseudonym for Clinton, a 'readable' but accurate citation.

There exists a contrast between Clinton's de-mythologisation by constant media exposure and the mythologisation of Kennedy's image via the same means. Kennedy was venerated at a time when his ease in front of the camera, his accessibility still signified his realness – and the realness of an idealised, glamorous presidential institution. Post-Nixon, the straightforward belief in the realness of the factual image has been replaced by cynicism about politics and a disillusioned knowingness about the infinite corruptibility of the real, an insinuation enacted in *The War Room* with the focus upon the shaping of Clinton's public persona. More frequently the spin doctors or 'handlers' (disguised as 'public relations consultants' and 'communications advisers') are more discreet, their string-pulling less in evidence because their 'manipulations are intended to be subliminal' (Diamond and Silverman 1997: 109). *The War Room* and *Feed* transgress these rules, thereby exposing the fraudulence of the conceit that, by focusing on the candidate alone, the spectator can and will repress the realisation that their image is artificially created. What both films show is the assembly of the performance, so undermining its false integrity. Clinton's actual media appearances complicate the issues surrounding such an awareness; his presidency is predominantly perceived as one extended performance and, as such, examples of the president's lack of honesty have ceased to precipitate a national crisis.

A case in point is Clinton's video testimony to the Grand Jury (17 August 1998) concerning his sexual liaison with White House intern, Monica Lewinsky, and his alleged lies about this affair whilst testifying under oath during the Paula Jones hearing. Although the video of Clinton's Special Prosecutor, Kenneth Starr, was intended for private Grand Jury use only, copies of it were soon leaked and a commercial edited version quickly became available. The quality of the four-hour video is poor, with Clinton just to the left of the fixed camera looking towards a screen that links him to Starr. What makes the video such compulsive viewing is that it is indeed the incumbent president who is compelled to answer questions about cherry chocolates, cigars and what constitutes sexual relations. This Grand Jury interrogation is crude, explicit but highly amusing, in substantial part because Clinton, unable to automatically control the situation as he would be able to do in a scripted broadcast, cannot hide behind rhetorical flourishes and convoluted impersonal fantasies as Nixon could under similar threat of impeachment. The American president is grilled and ridiculed in equal measure. Starr's error of judgement is arguably that Clinton's crimes are so trivial by comparison with those perpetrated by the Nixon administration that his testimony is a spectacle that serves to indict Starr rather than expose Clinton as unworthy of the office he holds. Clinton is witnessed being asked whether he touched Ms Lewinsky's breasts, whether he used a cigar as a sexual aid and whether he participated in masturbatory 'phone sex'. To all these questions Clinton responds by reverting to his prior statement: that his relationship with Lewinsky was not sexual as defined by the particularly circumlocutory and obfuscating Paula Jones deposition which Starr is querying, thereby avoiding the need to specifically redefine these acts as non-sexual or to have to respond to each question explicitly. What is built up through the often mundane and superfluously detailed cross-examination is the unspoken text suggesting why people are interested in watching the testimony in the first instance: that perhaps Clinton *did* do all these things that the dominant, overt text is mindful to repress. Whilst the text of his Grand Jury testimony states that Clinton did not have sexual relations with Lewinsky, its barely masked subtext implies, in great detail, otherwise.

Much of our pleasure from viewing this material stems from the knowledge that this was not intended as a public broadcast. Arguably, as a result of this, much of Bill Clinton's performance has a relaxed, casual and spontaneous air: he often leans towards the prosecutors as if to be more engaged and helpful; he crosses his arms and gesticulates for emphasis; he does not altogether disguise in his voice his tenderness towards Lewinsky. We, as furtive viewers, are party to this intimacy and side with Clinton during an interrogation fixated upon questions about breasts, lovers' presents, secret messages and the like. This is a moment of ignominy, but also of proof that this material will not defeat Clinton, for the Prosecutors' main problem is that he rarely relinquishes control, but shows himself able to handle the pedantry of the cross-examination with wit and humour. The one time that Clinton looks genuinely shocked (as opposed to awkward, embarrassed, frustrated) is when Starr enquires whether or not he used a cigar as a sexual aid. At this point, Clinton's eyebrows arch, his eyes widen and he takes a moment to restore his composure. Here, several factors intersect: the acknowledgement that the President of the United States is being asked about his intimate sexual conduct on tape; that this treatment of the president is indeed without precedent; that Clinton is momentarily disempowered. Such a moment is the antidote to the mediated, engineered image created by Clinton's spin-doctors and strategists, its spontaneity signalling the inherent precariousness of the manufactured political image – its deficiency, as opposed to efficiency, as a controlling device. Clinton's performance is, for all the outward casualness, poise and authority, inherently unstable; the truth that it reveals is only in part defined by the structure he has sought to impose on his responses – namely that he is innocent of perjury and is telling the truth about the extent of his relationship with Lewinsky.

It is perhaps the openness this discrepancy admits that saves Clinton, for these moments of disruption are also the moments at which Clinton is addressing his non-legal audience more directly. Direct cinema documentaries such as *Primary* are predicated upon the notion that behind a public image there is a private and, by implication, 'real' person, a presumption openly challenged by later films like *Feed*. Even within the far less explicit parameters of the Grand Jury testimony, Clinton reiterates the idea that, far from being distinct from it, the performance is the reality. Who Bill Clinton 'really is' is an irrelevant question when 'Bill Clinton' – the composite image created by spin, cover ups, scandal and himself – is all there is to see. This returns the argument to the current de-mythologisation of the image of the president, for it is these fissures that indicate not only that Clinton is more accessible but also that he has been divested of the mystique that a figure who remains detached and aloof would possess. Clinton is too familiar, he has been plagued by publicly acknowledged financial and sexual crises throughout his two terms in office, and, as a result, images of the mythic president have been transferred to fictionalised film figures – figures that can be both controlled and idealised. When the president can be asked, on video, about whether or not the insertion of a cigar into someone's genitalia constitutes sexual relations, there is little respect left.

This loss of respect exists alongside the loss of belief in the 'real person' underpinning the public performance and signals a growing acknowledgement that, whilst the incumbent's image is not inherently valuable or worthy, the desire for idealised presidential images can only be satisfied by the creation of fantasy characters, hence the appearance of so many fictional images of the presidency during the 1990s. With the documentaries and broadcasts that deal directly with Clinton and the presidency, what has become evident is that there is now no attempt to mask over the cracks between man and ideal, no attempt to create a false historical continuum. Instead, there is an acknowledgement of Clinton's ambiguity (that he partook of a joint but did not inhale; that he dodged the draft but denied it; that he had an improper but not a sexual relationship with Monica Lewinsky) not as a source of collective national trauma (as was the case with Nixon) but as the normative state of affairs. The unification of man and myth and the creation of a tenable iconic image has been irretrievably lost; in its place is the cynical suggestion that, under Clinton, the idea of the president has become little more than a blank archetype to be drawn and redrawn at will. The Clinton years have witnessed the emergence of increasingly extravagant films that accept the irrelevance of the president (*Wag the Dog*), create an implausibly good presidential figure (*Dave, The American President*), an action movie hero (*Independence Day, Air Force One*) or an exaggerated villain (*Absolute Power, Clear and Present Danger*). Cinematic archetypes are thus being mobilised to mask the panicked realisation that the presidency as an idea is so bankrupt that we are invited to fill the gap between reality and the fantasy figure of our imagination with ideals made familiar by escapist fiction. As if to legitimate these fantasies, real politicians and public figures appear in these films, such as Newt Gingrich, Oliver Stone and Senator Paul Simon in *Dave*, and concomitantly there are echoes of real presidential policy in even the most romantic fictions – President Andrew Shepherd in *The American President*, for instance, talks of a Johnson-esque Great Society.[15] These fictional presidents are cartoon characters, most obviously the Boy's Own heroes – Presidents Whitmore and Marshall – in *Independence Day* and *Air Force One*, respectively. Emmerich's film (America against the alien invaders) has the simplicity of a B movie, Whitmore looking uncomfortable with diplomacy but, being a war hero, proving much more effective as a combat pilot leading his troops. Marshall like-wise enacts the fantasy of the derring-do commander-in-chief who wrests control of the hijacked presidential aircraft from pro-Soviet fanatics and ejects their leader single-handedly from an open hatch whilst uttering, 'Get off my plane'. This spate of films share several characteristics – the marginalisation of the real president; the reassertion, within the framework of fiction, of the progressive, socially responsible leader; the implication that the presidency is so debilitated that the president can be easily impersonated – all of which have both real and fictive antecedents. The realisation permeating these feature films – that the severance of the actual president from the iconic ideal is irreversible – has led to dual impulses towards both greater satirisation of the plausible presi-dential figure (as occurs in *Wag the Dog* and *Primary Colors*) and, conversely, the accentuation of the fantasy characteristics in the more romanticised figure.

Conclusion

Although the number of fictional presidents to appear during the Clinton administration is indicative, as has been argued, of a loss of respect for the holder or the office of president (and thus a further indication that, in the age of spin, Clinton himself is a figurehead whose victories were the results of slickly managed campaigns) they also reflect back upon the role performance plays in the construction of the real politician's image. What has been revealing through the decades has been the way in which different presidents have negotiated the interaction with the camera, for it is at that moment that the politician comes into being. What has altered since Kennedy featured in *Primary* and became president is not the politicians' awareness of the importance of the media and of performance, but the spectators' acknowledgement that the politician is an artificial construct. It was the nature of Kennedy's performance, his ease and affinity with the observational camera, which repressed knowledge of falsification and media manipulation. As a result of this, Kennedy's image – for all the shortcomings of his presidency – has remained idealised. This faith in the president's image was irreversibly undermined by Richard Nixon's subsequent use of the televised address (and the concomitant eschewal of the potentially more intrusive documentary form) as a platform for lying repeatedly to the public. How this discussion approached Nixon's media manipulation was to suggest that the very quality of Nixon's performances – the discernible tension in his face, gestures, words – proclaimed their untruthfulness. With this, it became impossible to deny that Nixon was performing, and for a considerable time after Watergate (Altman's series *Tanner '88* being the prime example discussed here) both documentary and fictional treatments of the presidency became overtly preoccupied with the distinction between the real and the performed. By the time of the 1992 election, however, with the growing significance of television and image-making, Clinton's varied and contradictory televised appearances – particularly during the Monica Lewinsky scandal – have effectively signalled the redundancy of that distinction, because a video performance as un-slick as the Grand Jury testimony does not reveal a tangibly different or more authentic Bill Clinton to the one who made the earlier categoric denial of the affair or the one who appeared on daytime television with Hillary by his side. These broadcasts serve as reminders that to try to enforce the distinction between the 'real' person and the performance is futile, the politician is necessarily performative. In the last chapter of this book, this notion will be discussed in relation not merely to those in front of the camera but also to the performative documentary, films that in and of themselves acknowledge the inherent instability of representing reality.

6   The performative documentary
Barker, Dineen, Broomfield

This final chapter will discuss the performative documentary, a mode which emphasises – and indeed constructs a film around – the often hidden aspect of performance, whether on the part of the documentary subjects or the film-makers. When one discusses performance and the real event, this fusion has more usually been applied to documentary drama, where a masquerade of spontaneity can be seen to function at an overt level. It is useful to note the discrepancy between performative documentaries and dramas that adopt the style of a documentary by using, for instance, hand-held camera work, scratchy synch sound recording and ad-libbed dialogue as one finds in Ken Loach's *Cathy Come Home*. Loach, the exponents of Free Cinema at the end of the 1950s (Lyndsay Anderson, Karel Reisz and others) and the British tradition of gritty drama that ensued – for instance BBC social issue dramas such as *The Spongers* (1978, directed by Roland Joffé, written by Jim Allen) or Granada Television's docudrama output of the 1970s to early 1990s – all approach 'realness' from the opposite perspective to the filmmakers to be discussed here, assuming proximity to the real to reside in an intensely observational style. The docudrama output of the past thirty years is predicated upon the assumption that drama can legitimately tackle documentary issues and uncontentiously use non-fiction techniques to achieve its aims. It thus becomes possible for drama to perform a comparable function to documentary: *Cathy Come Home* raised public awareness of homelessness and prompted the founding of Shelter, whilst Granada's *Who Bombed Birmingham?* (1990) led directly to the re-opening of the case of the Birmingham Six. Continuing in this tradition, Jimmy McGovern's more recent *Dockers* (1999), about the Liverpool dockers' strike, confused the boundaries between fact and fiction further: dockers and their wives collaborated with McGovern on the script and some appeared alongside actors in the cast.[1] Within such a realist aesthetic, the role of performance is, paradoxically, to draw the audience into the reality of the situations being dramatised, to authenticate the fictionalisation. In contrast to this, the performative documentary uses performance within a non-fiction context to draw attention to the impossibilities of authentic documentary representation. The performative element within the framework of non-fiction is thereby an alienating, distancing device, not one which actively promotes identification and a straightforward response to a film's content. There is, however, an essential difference between films that are performative in themselves and those that merely concern performative subject matter (arguably some straddle the two), and this discussion will distinguish between them. The argument posited throughout this book has been that documentaries are a negotiation between filmmaker and reality and, at heart, a performance. It is thereby in the films of Nick Broomfield, Molly Dineen or Nicholas Barker that this underlying thesis finds its clearest expression.

Bill Nichols in *Blurred Boundaries*, a little confusingly (considering the familiarity of the term 'performative' since Judith Butler's *Gender Trouble* was published in 1990) uses the term the 'performative mode' (following the didactic, the observational, the interactive and the reflexive modes)[2] to simply describe films that 'stress subjective aspects of a classically objective discourse' (Nichols 1994: 95). Conversely, this discussion will focus upon documentaries that are performative in the manner identified by Butler and others after J.L. Austin – namely, that they function as utterances that simultaneously both describe and perform an action. Austin's radical differentiation between the constative and performative aspects of language (the former simply refers to or describes, the latter performs what it alludes to) has been expanded upon and relocated many times in recent years, but rarely with reference to documentary.[3] Examples of words that Austin identifies as being 'performative utterances' are 'I do', said within the context of the marriage ceremony, or 'I name this ship the Queen Elizabeth', said whilst smashing a bottle of champagne against the vessel's side, his reasoning being that 'in saying what I do, I actually perform that action' (Austin 1970: 235). A parallel is to be found between these linguistic examples and the performative documentary which – whether built around the intrusive presence of the filmmaker or self-conscious performances by its subjects – is the enactment of the notion that a documentary only comes into being as it is performed, that although its factual basis (or document) can pre-date any recording or representation of it, the film itself is necessarily performative because it is given meaning by the interaction between performance and reality. Unlike Nichols, who finds it hard to disguise his latent wariness of the performative documentary mode, supposing that the more a documentary 'draws attention to itself', the further it gets from 'what it represents' (Nichols 1994: 97), this chapter will view the performative positively.

The traditional concept of documentary as striving to represent reality as faithfully as possible is predicated upon the realist assumption that the production process must be disguised, as was the case with direct cinema. Conversely, the new performative documentaries herald a different notion of documentary 'truth' that acknowledges the construction and artificiality of even the nonfiction film. Many theorists would view this reflexivity as breaking with documentary tradition – but this is only valid if one takes as representative of the documentary 'canon' films that seek to hide the modes of production. This, largely, has been the way in which the documentary family tree has evolved, with the relative marginalisation of the more reflexive documentary tradition exemplified by early films such as *Man with a Movie Camera*, *A propos de Nice*, *Land Without Bread* and continuing into the work of Emile de Antonio, Jean Rouch and French *cinéma vérité*, Chris Marker. Just as legitimate is the view that the new performative documentaries are simply the most recent articulation of the filmmakers' unease at this very assumption of what documentaries are about, that, like the previous films discussed in this book, the films of Broomfield, Moore and others have sought to accentuate, not mask, the means of production because they realise that such a masquerade is impossibly utopian. The erroneous assumption that documentaries aspire to be referential or 'constative' to adopt Austin's terminology (that is, to represent an uncomplicated, descriptive relationship between subject and text), is being specifically targeted in performative films, which are thus not breaking with the factual filmmaking tradition, but are a logical extension of that tradition's aims, as much concerned with representing reality as their predecessors, but more aware of the inevitable falsification or subjectification such representation entails.

A prerequisite of the performative documentary as here defined is the inclusion of a notable performance component, and it is the insertion of such a performance element into a non-fictional context that has hitherto proved problematic. If, however, one returns to Austin's speech models, then the presumed diminution of the films' believability becomes less of an issue: what a filmmaker such as Nick Broomfield is doing when he appears on camera and in voice-over, is acting out a documentary. This performativity is based on the idea of disavowal, that simultaneously signals a desire to make a conventional documentary (that is, to give an accurate account of a series of factual events) whilst also indicating, through the mechanisms of performance and Broomfield's obtrusive presence, the impossibility of the documentary's cognitive function. Nick Broomfield's films do this quite literally, as the conventional documentary disintegrates through the course of the film and the performative one takes over. The fundamental issue here is honesty. The performative element could be seen to undermine the conventional documentary pursuit of representing the real because the elements of performance, dramatisation and acting for the camera are intrusive and alienating factors. Alternatively, the use of performance tactics could be viewed as a means of suggesting that perhaps documentaries should admit the defeat of their utopian aim and elect instead to present an alternative 'honesty' that does not seek to mask their inherent instability but rather to acknowledge that performance – the enactment of the documentary specifically for the cameras – will always be the heart of the non-fiction film. Documentaries, like Austin's performatives, perform the actions they name.

Paris is Burning, Nicholas Barker and the performative subject

As indicated earlier, there are two broad categories of documentary that could be termed performative: films that feature performative subjects and films that are inherently performative and feature the intrusive presence of the filmmaker.

Following Judith Butler's discussion of it in *Bodies that Matter*, the most notable single film to fall within the former category is Jennie Livingston's *Paris is Burning* (1990), a documentary about the New York black and Latino drag balls of the late 1980s. As a result of its subject matter, the issue of performativity has dogged *Paris is Burning*, and the film itself has been (wrongly) viewed as performative. For the most part, Butler's own discussion of the film focuses on content, above all the issue of drag and gender problematisation, only touching upon the issue of filmmaking at the end (Butler 1993: 136). Caryl Flinn goes one step further in her analysis when commenting:

> Recent documentaries like Jennie Livingston's *Paris is Burning* (1990) and documentary criticism – influenced by poststructuralist and postmodernist theory – have cast the concept of pre-existing 'reality' and its attendant notions of authenticity, truth and objectivity into permanent question (e.g., Allen, McGarry, Nichols, Rosenthal). In fact, it is no stretch to say that documentary films, in many ways more so than other cinematic forms, reveal the constructed – indeed, performative – nature of the world around us.
>
> (Flinn 1998: 429)

Flinn is here conflating form and content and is asking *Paris is Burning* to perform a dual function: to be both a documentary concerned with performativity and to be a performative documentary, which, in the main, it is not. Flinn then unproblematically lists parallels between *Paris* and Michael Moore's *Roger and Me* such as the manner in which both 'send up ... images and behaviour supported by corporate America' (p. 432), without negotiating the issue that in *Roger* it is Moore and thereby the film that are sending up corporate America, whilst in *Paris* it is the subjects of Livingston's film that are doing so. As Butler observes, *Paris is Burning* would have been a markedly different film had Livingston reflexively intruded upon her subject or implicated the camera in the film's 'trajectory of desire' (Butler 1993: 136) – that is, had it been a performative film in the Moore mould instead of remaining a film observing performative actions.

Paris is Burning remains a documentary about the issues of drag, and as such offers a useful discussion of performativity. Livingston's technique is to juxtapose images of the balls with commentary and interviews with drag queen 'walkers' (those who participate in the balls). The interviewees are aspirational, they dress up under various categories of chic whiteness ('Executive Realness', 'High Fashion Eveningwear', 'Town and Country') which they seek to emulate and be mistaken for. Throughout, there is an ongoing discussion about 'realness' which, in the words of Dorian Corey, one of the more senior drag queens, is 'to look as much as possible like your straight counterpart ... not a take off or a satire, no – it's actually being able to be this'. To be real, therefore, is to pass for straight and to not be open to 'reading' or 'shade' which are differing levels of critical repartee engaged in after having detected and found fault in the 'realness' of someone's performance. The successful performance is that which cannot be read. On this level, *Paris is Burning* plays a game with its audience inasmuch as its interviewees, however convincing, will always be open to 'reading' because we know, by virtue of the interview/performance juxtaposition, that they are performing/taking on another identity when at the drag balls. As a result, the more significant episodes of the film as far as an examination of performativity is concerned are those which occur beyond the parameters of the balls. There are fleeting moments in *Paris is Burning* when the film itself becomes performative, expressing the notion that the documentary – like the drag performances it captures – is ephemeral, fluid and in an unstable state of redefinition and change. One such episode (although rather clumsily self-reflexive) is the film's first interview with Pepper Labeija. Pepper is filmed asking 'Do you want me to say who I am and all that?' to which one hears Livingston reply 'I'm Pepper Labeija … ', a command which is in turn mimicked by Pepper himself as he begins again 'I'm Pepper Labeija ...' with a roll of the eyes. More significantly performative are the couple of forays Livingston makes onto the 'real' streets of Manhattan to film 'real' rich, privileged whites in their designer attire. These sequences, by being intercut with the balls and inserted into the ongoing dialogue about realness and drag, take on a strange, performative quality of their own, throwing into disarray the notion – upheld by the majority of the film – of a 'realness' that can be 'read'. The rich whites (who, in contrast to the interviewees, do not appear to know they are being filmed), through their contextualisation within the discourse of drag, start to look no more authentic than their black and Latino imitators; the difference between originals and mimics becomes hard to 'read' in a film where performing is the norm. For the most part, however, *Paris is Burning* is a conventional film that espouses such stability but just happens to be about a group of individuals who do not.

The performative documentary is the binary opposite of the performer-based direct cinema films. Both feature individuals who are performers and/or comfortable with the idea of performing on film, but whereas the ethos behind the earlier films was to use subjects that were so used to performing that they would not notice the potentially intrusive documentary cameras, the ethos behind the modern performative documentaries is to present subjects in such a way as to accentuate the fact that the camera and crew are an inevitable intrusion that alter any situation they enter. It is significant, however, that several of the filmmakers to be discussed have cited as primary influences the chief exponents of direct cinema or their successors; Nick Broomfield, answering questions at the NFT during a season of his films (in 1996) singled out Donn Pennebaker and Fred Wiseman as major influences on his work (the former being formally thanked at the end of *Soldier Girls*), and Nicholas Barker, when researching *Signs of the Times*, said the series would be an extension of the observational mode. In fact what happened in the cases of both Broomfield and Barker is that they evolved radically different and innovative styles of documentary that replaced the observational with the performative.[4]

The performative element of Nicholas Barker's work stems from the correlation

of a minimalist visual style and the self-consciously constructed performances he elicits from his subjects. At the front of the feature film *Unmade Beds* (1997) there is the apparent oxymoron 'the characters in this film are real', a literalness that arose out of necessity, as those who attended the film's London and New York test screenings 'were convinced they were watching highly naturalistic fiction' (Barker 1999). The ambiguity created by this residual complexity around the nature of performance is a development of Barker's earlier series *Signs of the Times* (BBC, 1992) about interior design and personal taste. Each of the five parts abides by much the same format: a pre-title montage of images and comments, followed by a series of seven or eight interviews with individuals or couples about their homes. The films are episodic and non-narrative; the interviewees are loosely grouped around a theme (couples, mothers and daughters, singletons, those who see themselves as a 'little bit different'), but are not subsequently used to develop a cumulative argument. In this, *Signs of the Times* is quintessentially observational, and yet it differs markedly from the style of classic observational documentary. Whereas observational documentaries remain unreflexive, *Signs of the Times* is analytical of the voyeuristic impulse close observation prompts in its audience and, in its self-conscious visual style, also reflects its subjectivity and authorship. *Signs of the Times* proved hugely influential in terms of the development of British television documentary, BBC2's *Modern Times* (the channel's replacement for the more conventional, people-based *40 Minutes*) being one such 'slavish imitation' (Barker 1999).[5]
Signs of the Times abided by a manifesto of rules that included:

> minimal artifice in lighting; where possible shooting everything frontally and at the height of observation so you never looked down or up at anything; no arty angles, no angles that screamed elegance or style; very few close-ups; no dissolves; everything had to be shot on widescreen; no music.
>
> (Barker 1999)

As Barker now admits, 'whenever anyone gets into manifesto mode they are generally protesting too much' (Barker 1999), but his forensic approach to documentary achieved two notable things: the dissection of his subject matter and the dissection of documentary convention. *Signs of the Times* is minimalist, stylised and possesses a stylistic uniformity that gives it a clear identity and lends it a fetishistic intensity, mesmerised by superficialities, appearance and detail. Although many of Barker's imitators produce films that are simply in themselves superficial and empty, *Signs of the Times* is not. Barker describes, for example, how he juxtaposed image and sound:

> The shot changes [in *Signs of the Times*] were always coming one beat too late ... I also played a very simple trick with film grammar – I would either give you too much to look at and nothing to listen to, so you were invited to be a voyeur and look at [the image] in a very photographic way, or I would give you something spectacularly banal and a rich display of words,

the anxieties and prejudices of the characters we were recording. Here
there was no visual distraction, so the viewer's relationship with the television was rather like participating with radio. ... I consider *Signs of the Times*
to be the bastard off-spring of stills photography and radio drama, it didn't
belong in the documentary canon.

(Barker 1999)

The latent perversity of this method – of upsetting the equilibrium between its
two main constituent parts – is characteristic of the way in which *Signs of the
Times* invites the spectator to engage with new ways of watching and listening,
clearly acknowledging the voyeurism, for instance, that more conventional
documentaries suppress.

Signs of the Times is performative: it challenges notions of fixed identity or
truth and prioritises the moments of interaction between filmmakers, camera
and subjects, capturing the tension between the realness of the documentary
situation and its artificialisation by the camera. Just as it is somewhat perverse to
alienate the spectator through the dislocation of sound and image, so it is
equally perverse to maintain a distance from the series' 'characters'. These 'characters' are performative on two counts: they are performing their words by
being the embodiments of their identified tastes and attitudes, and they
perform their interviews in such a way as to raise questions about spontaneity
and documentary authenticity. These alienating performances stem from how
they are eventually filmed and from the interviewing methods employed. In the
first instance, Barker would record his subjects using a digital video or High 8-
mm camera from which he made detailed transcripts, he would then distil those
transcripts and selecting passages he wanted his subjects to repeat when it came
to the actual recording, returning to them (with Super 16-mm cameras) for the
filming and coaxing them into 're-articulating something they had said before'
(Barker 1999). This is not a completely unusual technique, but one that is, in
Signs of the Times, taken to an extreme, in that the characters clearly signal this
lack of spontaneity through how they interact with each other, look at the
camera and pose for it. In this, the subjects in *Signs of the Times* are, like the
walkers in *Paris is Burning*, playing with concepts of 'realness', giving an
approximation of themselves; the difference being, however, that the scripting is
done very much by Barker, the overtly controlling director. The spectator
remains aware of this fundamental tension between the 'realness' of the image
and the elaborate manufacturedness of the series' style, between freedom on the
one hand and restraint on the other. Our response, therefore, is in keeping with
the perversity of Barker's intention to create television out of incompatible
media elements: we are both as engrossed by the subjects' narratives and observations as we might be within a more conventional framework and are
conscious of the films' reflexivity that requires us to be simultaneously aware of
their construction and authorship.

This duality is at the heart of the series' fetishistic involvement with the image
and its subjects. The close-ups of accessories, ornaments and fabrics function

as weighty metaphors for the conflicts they symbolise: in one of the mini-narratives of the opening film 'Marie-Louise collects bric-a-brac', one woman (Tricia) is accused by her partner of spoiling his spartan mansion flat with her clutter, an invasion illustrated by a montage sequence of Tricia's ornaments gradually encroaching upon the surfaces of an empty shelf unit. Like Freud's concept of the fetish as the indirect purveyor of sexual desire, the series' way of revealing the characters of its subjects is via a perverse interest in minutiae – many interviews start, for example, with close-ups of details such as the subjects' shoes. This fetishistic eye is, by association, applied to the people's performances: the mannered and rehearsed way in which they speak, their direct address to camera and their painterly poses. We are invited not to observe but to scrutinise them, their mannerisms, their words; the effect of this scrutiny functioning as an indication that each time these people speak they are doing so with their audience very much in mind. Just as they are putting their houses on display, so they are presenting themselves for assessment. These subjects are not caught unawares or merely talking about themselves in an unpremeditated fashion, rather they are conscious of their involvement in a performative event, one that is simultaneously a description and an enactment of their lives and lifestyles.

This challenge to preconceived notions of realness is taken further in *Unmade Beds*, Barker's feature film following, over the course of several months, four single New Yorkers (two men, Michael and Mikey; two women, Aimee and Brenda) in their pursuit of relationships. They demonstrate different attitudes to sex and couples, ranging from Brenda's search for men not for sex but for financial security, to the younger Michael's search for a stable relationship. The structure of the film is episodic and non-cumulative in that, by the end, although we have gained intimate insights into the four characters, their stories are not conventionally closed. Instead what is offered is a detailed composite portrait of not just four individuals, but the generalised issue of dating. The primary mechanism for achieving this is the use of interviews with the protagonists spoken directly to camera in which they reveal their insecurities and desires. *Unmade Beds* is less brittle than *Signs of the Times* and builds up empathy between spectators and the characters, all of whom have a preoccupation with which we can sympathise: weight, stature, age, financial insecurity. Although Barker consciously refuses to furnish his spectators with traditional biographical information about the four characters (maintaining that 'as soon as I give you that information, I provide an easy handle for your prejudices' (Barker 1999)) he shows their vulnerabilities and invites us to sympathise with them. *Unmade Beds* is less obsessed with its own style and more responsive to the personalities of the characters being filmed. The younger Michael, for example, who seems particularly self-conscious (about his height) and angry at the world, is often kept at a greater distance than Brenda, who, from the outset, is more than happy to confide in the camera, discuss her maturing body whilst scrutinising it in the mirror or admitting that money is her sole motivation for wanting a man.

The four characters' performativity is reflected in the film's style which, like Patrick Keiller's Robinson films, gives the impression of existing only in the present, giving no historical background and stopping without indicating either closure or a definite future for the four protagonists. The film offers a protracted glimpse at lives that, from an audience's perspective, remain incomplete. In *Unmade Beds*, Barker takes the preparatory techniques used in *Signs of the Times* much further, ending up with 'a formal script which was then negotiated with the principal characters who were then directed under more or less feature film conditions to perform it pretty much as we'd agreed' (Barker 1999). With the performances from the characters he sought an 'illusion of spontaneity' (Barker 1999), thus imposing another perverse marriage between seemingly incompatible elements that, in turn, are reflected in the film's equivocal tone: warm and interested on the one hand, distant and analytical on the other.

Interspersed throughout *Unmade Beds* and functioning as counterpoints to these long interviews are sequences shot, from a distance, through windows, looking in at anonymous New Yorkers as they go about their intimate, daily routines. These montage episodes make explicit the film's voyeurism. Barker re-staged scenes that, 'with or without binoculars' he had witnessed over the seven or eight months he spent in New York researching *Unmade Beds*, scenes that he 'only half understood' (Barker 1999). These scenes (deeply reminiscent of *Rear Window*) were then reconstructed using people who were not those Barker had originally watched. Clearly directed (using walkie-talkies, lights) and filmed over long periods of time Barker maintains that at the times these subsidiary characters forgot they were being filmed. This idea of seeing the details of an intimate scene unfold without fully comprehending their significance is crucial to *Unmade Beds* and to the voyeuristic impulse it enacts. These window sequences are visually quite distinct from the interviews; they are formally laid out on the screen (for example, two windows: one on a horizontal axis the other on a vertical), the window frames act as a physical barrier between us and the people in the rooms, thus illustrating our invasion of their privacy as we are all cast as peeping toms. The strangeness of these interludes makes us reassess (rather like the 'real' Manhattan sequences in *Paris is Burning* do) the remainder of the film. What is being played out here is Barker's discovery of the role windows play in New York:

> The thing about New York is that most people in the city share a window with another window, and one of the really interesting things I discovered when I first started living there, was that there was a social contract between the people who looked onto one another, so that people would be entirely happy to share their nakedness or their daily toilet rituals with the window opposite, because that intimacy was reciprocated, but they all felt that if anybody else should see their daily pattern that it would be a violation of their privacy.
>
> (Barker 1999)

Windows grant access but they also alienate; this duality provides the temptation to construct, out of detailed fragments of people's lives, the fantasy of who they are because 'you don't have enough information to assemble your narrative and so fill in the gaps with your own imaginings and fantasies' (Barker 1999). This has repercussions for how *Unmade Beds* suggests we look at and assimilate the more conventional documentary image: out of snippets we construct whole stories and characters we can identify with and whose 'realness' we find credible.

The formalised use of the camera, framing and self-conscious performances by all the four protagonists in *Unmade Beds* might yield intimate and revealing details, but our knowledge remains compromised by the alienation imposed by such stylistic mannerisms. The performative aspects of *Unmade Beds* suggest that some things will forever be withheld from us. Although Barker describes himself as a portraitist, remarking that the scrutiny of the 'surface texture' can reveal 'certain underlying psychological truths', he does not give an interpretation of those 'psychological truths' and in fact intentionally represses them by, for example, withholding conventional biographical information pertaining to his characters such as age and profession or by keeping back, until late in the film, discussions of issues (such as the weight of Aimee, the woman) that might touch on such 'truths'. This alienation is echoed directly in *Unmade Beds'* style and narrative form. What one retains immediately from watching the film is details of the characters' appearance, sartorial taste and verbal or physical mannerisms. Because Barker himself does not then mould these ostensibly superficial observations into a more rounded portrait, we as spectators are then left to do the contextualisation for ourselves and imagine, as Barker describes he did as he watched strangers through windows, what these details tell us about the characters as a whole. We will never know whether or not our suppositions are correct, and *Unmade Beds* is, in this respect, a liberatingly non-prescriptive film. Its narrative likewise remains open, charting (like many a city documentary before it) a chronological structure whilst not resolving the individual narratives of the characters. There is a fluid progression, obviously, to the way in which time passes in *Unmade Beds* which can be correlated with the consistency of the film's visual style. Although less rigidly conceived than *Signs of the Times* (there is, for example, a richly evocative use of music), *Unmade Beds* still demonstrates a uniformity of style, using a static camera, getting the characters to pose, framing them so we never lose an awareness that these people are being filmed. The paradox of this regularity is that it accentuates the film's fragmentary nature – that it remains most intrigued by surface texture, and elects not to construct out of its assembled detail either a traditionally closed narrative or conventional portraits of its protagonists. Judith Butler articulates in her introductory discussion to *Paris is Burning*, 'There is no subject prior to its constructions' (Butler 1993: 124). *Unmade Beds* avoids being this dogmatic, and instead suggests that what we see in the film is a composite of what the characters bring to the film (much of which might remain hidden) and what the film itself can reveal. The performances in front of the camera are composites of the two. Likewise the film's reflexive and photographic style undermines the notion of a stable 'truth' that underpins the documentary film.

Issues of authorship in the performative documentary

What has occurred within the last decade (and performative documentaries are at the forefront of this) is a shift towards more self-consciously 'arty' and expressive modes of documentary filmmaking. Reflexive documentaries, as they challenge the notion of film's 'transparency' and highlight the performative quality of documentary, will emphasise issues of authorship and construction. Barker makes his authorship explicit. This is not to say that *Signs of the Times* or *Unmade Beds* are highly personalised, subjective pieces of filmmaking, rather that their stylistic idiosyncrasies suggest a controlling, manipulating presence. The question of authorship has traditionally proved a thorny problem for the documentary, as the recognised intervention of an *auteur* disrupts the non-fiction film's supposed allegiance to transparency and truthfulness. As, however, this book has argued against the uncompromised rendition of the real being an attainable goal for non-fiction, the presence of the *auteur* is not so problematic, for one of the corollaries of accepting that documentary cannot but perform the interaction between reality and its representation is the acknowledgement that documentary, like fiction, is authored. As with the theorisation of the *auteur* in the realm of narrative fiction film, what appears to pose particular difficulties where documentaries are concerned is the author-director. A familiar charge levelled at documentary directors – who, through a variety of means such as voice-over, appearance on camera and overt stylisation have signalled their control over their work – is that they are needlessly egotistical in not allowing the subject matter to 'speak for itself'. But as Nick Broomfield has countered, no one accuses Alan Whicker (or other presenter-reporters) of being egotistical. The sign-posting of the documentary author-director or his or her overt intrusion crystallises documentary's fundamental conflict between subjectivity and objectivity. One repercussion of the establishment of a documentary canon that has historically marginalised films emphasising the author's presence is that it has been too readily assumed that the repression of the author has been necessary to the implementation of objectivity.

Culminating in the recent work of filmmakers such as Michael Moore, Molly Dineen and Nick Broomfield, who are active participants in their films, documentary has an established tradition of the performer-director. These filmmakers, to varying degrees, participate in their films because they are interested in discovering alternative and less formally restrictive ways of getting to what they perceive to be the essence of their subjects. The means by which they achieve this are not those conventionally associated with truth-finding post-direct cinema as they entail breaking the illusion of film, thereby interrupting the privileged relationship between the filmed subjects and the spectator. Recently, many more documentaries are emerging that take for granted the existence and inevitable presence of their filmmakers, directly demonstrating the inherent performativity of the non-fiction film. The overt intervention of the filmmaker definitively signals the death of documentary theory's idealisation of the unbiased film by asking, categorically and from within the documentary itself: what else is a documentary but a dialogue between a filmmaker, a crew and a situation that, although in existence prior to their arrival, has irrevocably been changed by that arrival? What author-performer-based documentaries reiterate are the twin notions that a documentary is its own document and that the interventionist documentary filmmaker is a fluid entity defined and redefined by every context in which he or she appears. The author-performer is thereby one constituent of a film's ongoing dialectical analysis. Before discussing the rise of the 'star director' with specific reference to Nick Broomfield, this chapter will focus on the work of Molly Dineen, a filmmaker (director and cameraperson) who signals her presence through the persistent use of her voice off-camera, but who nevertheless leaves her subjects to dominate the films visually.

The second chapter of this book examined the historical rarity of the female voice-over, with particular reference to *Sunless*, a documentary that creates a complex dialectic around its woman narrator. Since *Sunless* (1982) or *Handsworth Songs* (1986) – a documentary by members of the Black Audio Film Collective that is also noted for its use of female narration[6] – the female voice-over has become more commonplace, and yet it is more in the realm of the female authorial narration that a major shift has occurred. In late 1990s British television documentary, the presence of the woman director's voice is widespread (a vogue that probably would not have started had it not been for Dineen); the presence of Molly Dineen's voice indicates a desire to use the voice as commentary, as a means of claiming control of the film.[7] Class and gender issues are particularly significant factors within Dineen's work, hence the interweaving of herself into the concerns of her documentaries. Bill Nichols' use of the word 'voice' to signal both the physical voice and the filmmaker's authorial imprint is strikingly pertinent to the work of contemporary women filmmakers such as Dineen, as what this trend towards the inclusion of their own commentaries and interjections most forcefully suggests is a growing desire to reinstate the personal, subjective aspect of the physical voice.[8] The films of Molly Dineen are manifestly personal visions, inscribed with her subjective presence via the physical intervention of her voice.

With this intervention, a filmmaker like Dineen is also signalling the constructedness (a preferable term to inauthenticity) of all documentary by formulating an alternative 'realness' around her desire to show the nuts and bolts of documentary-making. This standpoint is actually enacted towards the beginning of *Geri* (1999), Dineen's documentary about Geri Halliwell following her departure from the Spice Girls. Soon after she has agreed to make the film, Dineen travels by train with Halliwell from Paris to England. During the course of the journey, Dineen films Geri on the telephone to her lawyers offering assurances that she has 'complete control' over the documentary. Dineen immediately contradicts this, asking Halliwell why she should 'spend months following you round' only to relinquish control of the documentary, subsequently explaining, after Halliwell has interjected that she would stop herself being shown in too much of a 'bad light', that any film is a negotiation between filmmaker and subject. Since *Home from the Hill*, her first full-length documentary which she made whilst still at the National Film and Television School, Dineen's work has been predicated upon this understanding of documentary as a dialogue, although Dineen herself has argued that her documentaries are dictated entirely by the people in them, although constructed around her intrusion into their lives. This mutuality is illustrated by Colonel Hilary Hook in *Home from the Hill* (BBC2, 1985) after Dineen has asked him whether or not he is happy. Hook replies: 'Blissfully, in your presence; otherwise I represent divine discontent.' What so many of Dineen's subjects acknowledge is that however well the filmmaker gets to know them (and Dineen, like Chris Terrill, 'goes native' for the long research/shooting period), the difference between them (without her camera and with it) will remain. Dineen's work is consistently illustrative of this dilemma, although between *Home from the Hill* and *Geri* her approach to the twin issues of performance and authorial control has substantially altered.

Dineen's early style – very much indebted to observational cinema – is exemplified by *Heart of the Angel* (BBC, 1989), a film about the Angel Underground station before its temporary closure and modernisation. The film has no explanatory voice-over and elects, in spite of the decrepit state of the station, to remain apolitical and to focus on the characters Dineen encounters. Because *Heart of the Angel* sidelines political issues (later series such as *The Ark* and *In the Company of Men* tackle bigger establishments and themes) it is exemplary of Dineen's method of interacting with her subjects. Dineen's intrusiveness is kept to a minimum whilst the performances of her subjects are maximised; her authorial control, therefore, remains covert. As with many 1960s direct cinema films such as *Salesman*, *Heart of the Angel* is reliant upon the subjects' performances for and to the camera; as Dineen says, 'People know that they're quirky and eccentric. They *feel* different. It's why we all like watching each other' (Cleave 1991: 26). It is also why we like performing ourselves for others. *Heart of the Angel* opens with one such performance (deeply reminiscent of Paul's monologues in *Salesman*) by the ticket collector in the Angel's lift proclaiming to the customers that they are 'all gonna die – the exhaust fumes from cars are getting very serious'. Unlike the Maysles' film, however, a sense of irony permeates *Heart of the Angel*, and the subjects – including the ticket collector – knowingly act up to and for Dineen and her camera: a group of 'Fluffers' (the women who clean the Underground tunnels at night) sing whilst taking the lift down to the platforms; another 'Fluffer' parodies a striptease whilst changing into her overalls. Likewise Dineen does not hide her own presence, using her characteristic coaxing questions from behind the camera throughout all her films. Whereas some of her contemporaries use similar techniques aggressively, perhaps to catch their subjects unaware (Moore, Broomfield), Dineen does so to enable her subjects to talk more expansively about themselves, asking broad and ostensibly flimsy questions just to get her subjects to open up. Because of this, her films will seldom be political and sometimes her questions appear slightly inane: for example, after the Angel's foreman has said he likes Yorkshire because 'it's so wild', Dineen adds 'do you like wild places?'; she is responsive rather than proactive, and elicits, in this instance, a further description from the foreman of his paintings of Yorkshire landscapes.

The most memorable and emotive of Dineen's conversations in *Heart of the Angel* is with the man in the ticket office who, throughout the film, has been prickly and argumentative, having asked Dineen early on: 'Do you think God put you on this earth to point that stupid little camera?' Dineen could be said to specialise in the mollification of leathery men (most obviously in *Home from the Hill*). Here the ticket man reaches the stage when he too is forthcoming on camera, initiating a dialogue with Dineen by stating, ostensibly unprompted, 'I could do with a change'. Dineen's gentle, general questions subsequently try to coax the ticket seller into expanding upon the significance of 'change' and what he would have liked to have been different. Although he denies being depressed, the ticket man ruminates on death and the meaninglessness of life: 'No-one asks to be born ... you're born, you live, you die.' Dineen's role in this conversation is ambiguous; partly she manoeuvres the situation so the spectator forms a strong identification with the ticket seller (always easier to engineer if universal emotions and desires are being discussed), and partly she maintains her (and our) distance. The mechanism that enforces this equivocation is Dineen's use of her voice. Whilst her voice establishes notions of friendship and intimacy, it remains the tool with which to signal the essential artificiality of the filming situation. The realisation that this moment of revelation takes place in an inherently artificial environment likewise imbues the performances of Dineen's subjects. In the case of the ticket office man, juxtaposed against curious and personal revelations (Dineen: 'What would you actually like to achieve?'; ticket man: 'I don't really know ... I'd like to have been taller ... had a better education') are ironically informal exchanges with Dineen that once again emphasise the formality of the set-up. This conversation (interview being too formal a term) concludes with a short chat that does just this:

> *Ticket man*: 'You think I'm gorgeous.'
> *Dineen*: 'I think you're wonderful.'
> *Ticket man*: 'Can I drink my water now?'
> *Dineen*: 'Yes.'
> *Ticket man*: 'Thank you'.

The ticket man is here doing several things: he is reflecting back at Dineen her use of flirting with men to elicit good answers to her questions; he is indicating that Dineen is ultimately in control of what he says and does in front of the camera and that he, at times, doubts her sincerity; he is shedding doubt through this knowingness on the authenticity of his previous words, prompting us to ponder the multiple levels of his performance. Dineen's documentaries, more clearly than many, are negotiations between the reality before she arrived and intruded and the artificial environment generated by her presence. Within this, Dineen is perpetually oscillating between relinquishing and asserting control.

This is a problem that becomes more apparent in *The Ark* (BBC2, 1993), a series following events at London Zoo at a time when they are threatened with closure, because it is also an issue-led, institution-focused film that ostensibly demands more than a sensitive interaction with personable and eccentric characters. Unlike the comparable BBC series *The House*, that similarly features a grand organisation at a moment of crisis and threat,[9] Dineen does not approach her subject with a critical eye and objects to 'the modern trend for trying to catch people with their trousers down' (Lawson 1995: 10). *The Ark* is less overtly critical of its subjects than *The House*, proving Dineen's point that she seeks to focus on 'the human side' as opposed to 'issues' (French 1989: 4); it also has only a minimal, explanatory voice-over, whereas hanging over *The House* is Jancis Robinson's arch commentary. Through *The Ark* Dineen maintains an unobtrusive position; although we hear her voice from off-screen, what remains memorable about the series is its strength as a piece of observational filmmaking, its use of long sequences with minimal interference (an elephant being moved back to Chester zoo, for example), its slow development of character and its relative marginalisation of the closure crisis. In the battles between keepers and management, Dineen subtly favours the former, intercutting (in the last film of the series, 'Tooth and Claw') the keepers tending to their animals with the Fellows and management's EGM. A keeper feeding a sick koala bear is inevitably more appealing than a hands-off managing body. Having said this, later in that same episode the deterioration and eventual death of the koala is edited in parallel with the demise of the role of General Director and the departure of the current incumbent, David Jones (another Hilary Hook figure). Dineen is most at ease occupying the conciliatory middle ground, which is why, arguably, she repeatedly turns to David Robinson (Senior Keeper: Tropical Birds) who espouses his apolitical, equally anti-management and anti-militant views. In Robinson's opinion the battles with the management are detracting from the care of the animals, a position echoed by Dineen who skirts over the arguments put forward at the EGM to focus on the outcome – the ousting of David Jones.

Although the last of *The Ark*'s three parts is a beautiful, subtle piece of documentary filmmaking, there is a slight listlessness about the series as a whole, stemming from the more pronounced absence of Dineen's actual and metaphoric voice. Subsequently in her career, a significant stylistic shift occurs, as she begins to introduce more of her own voice-over and thereby begins to overtly structure her work around her own sensibilities and observations, a change that becomes very noticeable with *In the Company of Men* (BBC2, 1995), her series about the Prince of Wales regiment during their tour of duty in Northern Ireland. Besides personalising the films to a greater extent, this increased voice has the effect also of making *In the Company of Men* more conventional, not a loose, non-didactic observational documentary series of which Dineen is an instrumental part, but a structured observational series (more in keeping with the 1990s shift towards the formalised formats such as docusoaps) that does the thinking for us. The transition to a more authoritative style with *In the Company of Men* makes Dineen into the series' principal subject as well as its *auteur*, and marks the shift towards a more concrete embodiment of the director-performer. It is significant that with this increased presence comes an increased focus on gender and difference. Still Dineen nudges the soldiers to respond to questions that are personal and apolitical, despite the regiment's role in guarding a border police station and despite Dineen's first bit of voice-over locating the action within the period around the first Northern Ireland cease-fire. The material her interviewees throw up is also more reflective of Dineen and her filming role than was the case in previous films, and the series' title *In the Company of Men* embodies its ethos.

The opening interview is with the regiment's commander, Major Crispin Black, who holds up a copy of *The Tatler*, 'just to conform to stereotype', thereby rapidly establishing the series' linking mechanism to be the soldiers' rapport with Dineen. There are many such reflexive references, such as Major Black urging Dineen to put on weight 'so that we can at least have sexual fantasies about you', or remarking that he would have John Birt (the then Director General of the BBC) 'sacked' from his regiment. *In the Company of Men*, like Dineen's previous films, is an elaborate flirtation with a band of unlikely men who, until *Geri*, have been the most prominent points of interest in her work. Contentiously (particularly considering the time given to the 'Fluffers') Dineen has referred to *Heart of the Angel* as 'a very political film, about male slavery. They'd give over their unopened pay packets to their wives, especially the Irish ones' (Billen 1995: 9). Such an unguarded comment encapsulates her work's essential tendency (epitomised by *In the Company of Men*) towards glorifying and exonerating masculinity. This is so in *Home from the Hill* with its essentially soft treatment of Hilary Hook, *Heart of the Angel*, in particular the interview with the ticket office man and the night-time sequence with the underground maintenance men, and *The Ark* in its uncritical attitude towards David Jones. Dineen, who also operates the camera in her documentaries and creates films that are intensely attuned to issues of sexual difference, clearly does not wish to repress her male subjects' flirtatious references to her, just as she rather obviously treats with greater sensuality and warmth the male Underground workers in *Angel* than their female counterparts the 'Fluffers'. Dineen's films are not often self-consciously stylised, but the use of carefully directed lighting to emphasise the contours of the men's grubby torsos in this tunnel sequence is marked, as is the men's boss's comment to Dineen 'Do you have to stop my blokes from working, eh?' Dineen explains this concentration on men as 'an ego thing – you want to be accepted by the most unlikely people' (Lawson 1995: 11), which makes filming sound like a series of conquests (she did go out with one of the maintenance workers for a time), but is not entirely accurate. She also enjoys engaging with men, not women – which is what makes *Geri* a surprising film.

The self-reflexive referencing of Dineen, her wispy though persistent middle-class voice, her increased presence as the narrator of her films and the fact that she will never (as the cameraperson) appear on screen, have specific gender connotations. Dineen remains an absent, fetishised body constantly evoked by her on-screen (usually male) subjects; she makes use of the camera to forge an intimacy with people, but also to preclude closeness; her subjects are always seen through her eyes and her apparatus, whilst Dineen is represented only by her voice. Whereas this has, at times, been treated as a position of weakness,[10] here it connotes strength. Dineen performs an archetypal femininity that is concerned and curious, coaxing an intimacy and camaraderie out of her willing male subjects whilst never relinquishing her omniscient, camouflaged position. Ironically, however, because Dineen's films are largely driven by her desire to extract compelling performances from her subjects, the audience finds itself compelled to focus upon Dineen's performance as well. As she later also takes on the role of narrator, the flirtatious, feminine voice from behind the camera seems less genuinely curious and more scheming.

In *Geri* the hierarchical relationship between Dineen and her subject, Geri Halliwell is not so much about gender difference but about class. In Dineen's need to spell out that she is in control of the documentary, she is partly compensating for the fact that *Geri* is about a female subject who is far more famous than she is. *Geri* is not simply a biography of an individual, but an examination of celebrity, which includes a certain amount of dialogue concerning Halliwell's image. Dineen has a very definite, simple view of Halliwell, namely that behind her exterior performance as the recently rejected Ginger Spice, there is the 'real' Geri accessible to the filming process. When she films and questions a tearful Spice Girls fan looking over Ginger memorabilia on the eve of an auction at Sotheby's, Dineen asks the girl why she is mourning the effects of Ginger who, after all, was not the real person Geri Halliwell. The girl is sad and confused: to her, Ginger is real. Halliwell herself wants to believe in this basic split between real and fake, forever promoting her 'real', minimally made up self-image and contrasting this with her previous alter ego Ginger, a character she says was 'based on my wild-cat days'. Halliwell comes across as intensely likeable, but wholly unaware of the multiplicity of her performances and of the fragility of her distinction between the real and the fake. As a film, *Geri* substantiates Halliwell's self-perception, treating the post-Ginger Halliwell – whether she be at home with her mum or at a UN press conference following her instatement as ambassador for birth control – as unproblematically 'real'. This places Halliwell in a subordinate position, which, despite her command of the visual image, Dineen does little to dispel or qualify. Instead, Halliwell's inarticulacy concerning her image and her desire for fame is shown in the context of her having lost control to Dineen (the person who is now manipulating her image). Preceding the conversation about control on the train, Dineen comments in voice-over:

> I was becoming intrigued by the situation. I should have realised there'd be complications, though. Geri got on the phone to her lawyer, to tell him that I was taking over the film.

The ostensible purpose of this piece of voice-over is to locate the subsequent conversation; because, however, that conversation is about the struggle for control between filmmaker and subject, the very fact that Dineen prefaces it by telling us what to expect, ensures that the sequence is illustrative of Geri's lack of control over the film. So, Geri's performance of herself and her obsession with how others perceive her is more a manifestation of fragility than of strength. This is deeply ironic, considering Dineen's own preoccupation with how the men in her films view *her*.

Despite her fame, Halliwell's image is filtered through Dineen's perception of it. Geri's relative weakness is, in substantial part, the result of the imposition of a social hierarchy. Through the middle-class tone of her voice, the demonstration of her own articulacy and the critical use of narration, Dineen emphasises her intellectual superiority over Halliwell. *Geri* is a celebration of inarticulacy as it pursues a liberated Halliwell fervently seeking a serious role for herself and trying to define her aspirations, but not having the vocabulary with which to express them. Dineen's focus on this struggle is, in itself, far from generous and Halliwell is set up on several occasions only to be shot down.

Geri is a smug documentary intent on wresting control from its subject without telling her, obviously, that this is the intention. With Dineen's recent move towards claiming her films by adding her own authoritative voice-over to her already prominent conversations from behind the camera, she is moving towards becoming a 'star director'. It is ironic that Dineen's most prominent bid for stardom comes with a film about stardom, for this is a common factor among star directors of documentaries. The more famous Nick Broomfield becomes, for instance, the more famous the subjects of his films. Although they are frequently bracketed together (both British, National Film and Television School graduates, both direct and perform a technical role in their films, both 'author' those films through direct interventions that are not edited out), Dineen and Broomfield offer different types of documentary performances and elicit different performances out of their subjects. During the last British general election, Dineen was brought in to direct the Labour Party's most distinctive campaign film: a casual portrait of Tony Blair, chatting with Dineen and spending time with his kids. Tony Blair comes across as a 'Good Thing', an urbane, intelligent guy who has done ordinary things like play in a band but who now just happens to want to run the country. As Dineen has often stated in interviews, her aim is not to embarrass her subjects or stitch them up, but to take a mediatory stand: 'What I like to do is get people who are fair game and then not make them fair game at all' (Billen 1995: 9). It seems legitimate to speculate that the image- and media-obsessed 'new' Labour Party would have viewed this conciliatory tone (and her femininity) as Dineen's most significant credential: she offers a kind, witty portrait of Blair, but one that is ultimately not threatening, critical or undermining. One senses that 'new' Labour would not have commissioned Nick Broomfield to make a campaign film for them.

The 'Star Director': Nick Broomfield

BBC2's *The Late Show* ran an item entitled 'How to make a Peter Greenaway film' in which mundane clips from *Nationwide* were transformed into meaningful, choreographed moments once they had been set to insistent Michael Nyman music. Greenaway's style is formulaic, so too, it could now be argued, is Nick Broomfield's – so much so that in 1999 he (with the assistance of his original cameraperson/collaborator Joan Churchill) starred in a series of Volkswagen Passat television ads brandishing his distinctive boom and asking his generic awkward questions. Broomfield is British documentary's 'star director', he is a recognisable face, has had a season of films at the National Film Theatre (1997) and has reached the gossip columns. His trademarks are films built around the tortuous chase after elusive subjects and the collapsed interview that sometimes, as in *Tracking Down Maggie*, fails to materialise. When *Kurt and Courtney* was released in 1998, several journalists expressed their disillusionment with 'the Broomfield film', commenting that his 'reputation as a serious filmmaker has suffered in recent years, mainly as a result of his propensity to include himself in his own films' (Spencer 1999: 63).[11] The simple fact that there was an anti-Broomfield backlash is testament to his star status. Since *Driving Me Crazy* (1988), Broomfield has appeared in his films as the hassling director enacting the process of making a documentary, hounding his subjects and wearing them down until they finally give him a story. Broomfield's films (despite his indebtedness to direct cinema) have become supreme examples of the director-performer model; he is the undoubted *auteur* of his films and their very structure proclaims that, without his intervention, there would be no films.

The central issue in how one perceives Broomfield's work is the specific persona he performs on camera. Towards the end of *Driving Me Crazy* – a documentary following the rehearsal period and performance of the all-black musical *Body and Soul* – scriptwriter Joe Hindy exclaims 'I don't think you're adorable any more, Nick', a sentiment echoed in *Heidi Fleiss: Hollywood Madam* (1995) when, once again after some time, Madam Alex, one of the film's three protagonists, shouts at Broomfield down the telephone: 'You're such a greedy f****** pig. I'm so sick of you.' Broomfield's on-screen persona is the sweet, ingratiating, slightly gullible buffoon; it is only late in the proceedings (if ever) that his subjects realise that this is an act, a ploy on Broomfield's part to get the material he wants. In one interview, Broomfield cites an unlikely precursor in Pier Paolo Pasolini, whom he met during the filming of *The Canterbury Tales* in England in 1971. He saw in Pasolini someone who, though ostensibly reserved himself, generated chaos around him, observing that, whilst other film crews 'were always incredibly ordered, almost military, with a clear chain of command', Pasolini's 'seemed to operate with a purposeful anarchy' (Broomfield 1993: 46). Broomfield's particular admiration for Pasolini's 'ability to use chaos to a creative advantage' (p. 46) could be describing his own post-*Driving Me Crazy* films, for all the documentaries that revolve around his on-screen performance are exercises in controlled chaos. The 'control' aspect relates directly to Broomfield's performance of himself: he remains sweet, dogged, usually unflustered, whilst around him his films almost implode. The anger of Joe Hindy and Madam Alex stems from their belated realisation that Nick Broomfield the documentary filmmaker is not synonymous with 'Nick Broomfield' the charming man with Mickey Mouse earphones and boom who extracts information from them. An interesting aspect of how critics and spectators relate to Broomfield's work is that they too sometimes find it hard to accept the dichotomy: after the screening of *Heidi Fleiss* at the 1995 London Film Festival, one member of the audience during the ensuing Q&A session asked Broomfield to expand upon the fact that, whilst he appears a little stupid on screen, he seems intelligent in real life. Broomfield's tactful response was to reiterate that his smiley persona has proved most useful in getting his subjects to open up on camera.

Broomfield's self-performance fuels the debate around 'realness'. Peter Wollen in 1974 used a formula to specifically illustrate this schism in relation to authorship and the fiction film, arguing – from an *auteur*-structuralist perspective – that the *auteur* is only the identity discovered within the text and does not pertain to the individual beyond its parameters.[12] Adopting Wollen's equation, Nick Broomfield ≠ 'Nick Broomfield', the inverted commas signifying the version of the *auteur* to be found within the films. It is over-simplistic to argue that Nick Broomfield, the author beyond the frame, is irrelevant to how one views and interprets the films in which 'Nick Broomfield' appears; rather it is the dialectic between the two that motivates the documentaries and informs our responses to them. The subject 'Nick Broomfield' is constructed on screen from within the documentary frame, whereas Nick Broomfield the *auteur* remains omniscient and detached (a role that is partly articulated through Broomfield's own narration for his films). Complicating matters is that the two are indisputably the same person, they just perform different functions for the purposes of making a documentary and it is this difference and the dialogue that ensues which informs the films. Quite graphically, Broomfield's dual presence articulates the idea that documentaries are the result of a dialectical negotiation between the reality that existed before he arrived and that which subsequently becomes the subject of his films. Why is the performative documentary problematic? Most importantly, it is problematic because it throws into sharp relief previously held notions of fixity of meaning and documentary 'truth'; in a film in which all reliable significance is generated by and through 'Nick Broomfield' the performer-director, there is necessarily a tension between the subjects before and after his arrival that is never fully resolved. The true stories upon which Broomfield's documentaries are based are compromised, filtered through the structured chaos on the screen.

Nick Broomfield's films could not always be characterised thus, and it is illuminating to compare the later documentaries with those he made with Joan Churchill. Although it is in *Driving Me Crazy* that Broomfield first appears on-screen as his films' *agent provocateur*, it is the earlier *Lily Tomlin: The Film Behind the Show* (1986) about the American comedienne which proved to be the catalyst for a change of approach. Despite its title, *Lily Tomlin* is a straight-forward film in the direct cinema mould that follows a performer, in this case Tomlin, preparing her one-woman Broadway show *The Search for Signs of Life in the Universe*. Subsequently Broomfield describes the 'nightmare' that filming *Lily Tomlin* became when, following an exchange of writs, the resulting film was severely compromised:

> The film was a very pale reflection of what had been a very miserable experience. But it occurred to me that if we'd had the miserable experience on film it would have at least been amusing.
>
> (Brown 1996: 42)

Prior to this, Broomfield had collaborated on several observational documentaries, many of which – such as *Tattooed Tears* (1978), about the California Youth Training School, and *Soldier Girls* (1981), about women US Army recruits of Charlie Company, Fort Gordon, Georgia – followed in the Fred Wiseman mould of showing the workings of institutions and official organisations. The films are serious, politically motivated and subject-driven, concentrating on material that is still the standard fare of observational documentaries. Even though (as in both films cited above) Broomfield and Churchill single out a handful of individuals to focus upon, such figures are used as representative characters through whom the workings of the institution/organisation can best be conveyed, so – in a generic sequence repeated eighteen years later in *Soldiers To Be* – a brutal, aggressive Sergeant shouts at new recruits for making their bunks sloppily. As with Molly Dineen's early films, the Broomfield–Churchill collaborations use interventionist mechanisms only sparingly and functionally – for example, conveying factual information that assists the spectators' understanding of a sequence through short subtitles. The films' emphasis is on the subjects to such an extent that, at the end of *Soldier Girls* when Private Johnson (one of the film's principal characters) is leaving, she spontaneously turns and bids farewell to Churchill and Broomfield. Although the image of Private Johnson embracing Nick Broomfield is caught on camera and is not omitted from the finished film, he is only glimpsed fleetingly in the corner of a frame as if signalling the filmmakers' surprise and self-consciousness at this violation of a key observational rule. For the most part, *Soldier Girls* and *Tattooed Tears* serve as exemplary illustrations of the *vérité*-derived tradition: they feature personalised situations that carry with them more general political connotations; they make statements through observation as opposed to through intervention; they sublimate the filmmakers' opinions to those of the people they pursue, although elements such as editing, a greater identification with the 'victims' rather than the figures in authority and the subjective camera work serve to implicitly convey what those opinions might be.

Both early films contain several moments that could legitimately be termed 'classic *vérité*', when observation becomes synonymous with insight and the acquisition of knowledge. Sequences that dwell upon Ronnie, one of the youthful prisoners in *Tattooed Tears*, being forcibly restrained or Private Alvez in *Soldier Girls* being punished for lack of motivation by having to dig, well into the night, an ostensibly useless grave-like hole both manage to imply criticism of the actions they show simply by the length of time that is dedicated to each and the by the manner in which the filmmakers focus upon the suffering, victimised Ronnie and Private Alvez. Both sequences offer covert commentary on the events they depict.

Broomfield's subsequent style evolved out of a frustrated awareness of the limitations of the observational mode. He articulates this most directly in relation to *Driving Me Crazy* when commenting 'I'd always wanted to examine the documentary form and I'd become sort of disenchanted with the narrow parameters of this style of filmmaking. All too often what you look at on TV is very cleaned up and dishonest' (Paterson 1989: 53). If one examines even the much earlier work, the tensions are visible within the films themselves. During the restraint sequence in *Tattooed Tears*, Ronnie snatches a quick, furtive glance to camera, this transgressive look highlighting the immutable wall between the subjects and the filmmakers of observational films. Similarly throughout *Soldier Girls* there is the suggestion that the film's protagonists are knowingly acting up for the camera and hence unable to mask the film process's lack of spontaneity. Part of the power of *Soldier Girls* results from its enactment of this tension between what should and should not be included in an observational documentary – moments such as Private Hall learning how to perform the role of Sergeant by joining in Sergeant Abing's sustained, personalised attack on Private Alvez following her fit of screaming after being made to dig the hole. Abing begins with the groundless intimidation 'you don't deserve to be out there in society, you might kill someone out there, Alvez' (Alvez, after all, was originally accused of lacking motivation as a recruit) to which Hall adds:

> You know Alvez there's something about you that tells me you might be the type that would take a weapon and go up on top of a building and start just picking off people in the street just for the heck of it, because you're so apathetic, sooner or later it's bound to turn to hate.

Besides contradicting herself, Hall delivers this fanciful diatribe in the deliberate, slow manner of someone who is both assuming an unfamiliar role that she is eager to perfect (in this case the part of the brutalising sergeant) and is trying to sound convincing despite having to make up what she is saying as she goes along. This and other similar performances in *Soldier Girls* imply, through their very awkwardness, that they are striving to seem unaware of the filmmakers' presence but are finding this impossible. It is moments such as these that substantiate Broomfield's contention about 'dishonesty'. Not only are his and Churchill's films characterised by such textual cracks and tensions, but they illustrate the unworkability of the observational ideal by striving too hard to mask the necessity for more formally structuring devices such as voice-over or direct authorial intervention.

Broomfield's transition to a more openly authored style also coincides with the termination of his partnership (both personal and professional) with Joan Churchill, although she has continued to operate the camera on some of his later films such as *Tracking Down Maggie* and *Kurt and Courtney*. If one returns to Broomfield's statement about his growing disillusionment with his methods at the time of *Driving Me Crazy*, what also becomes evident is his frustration at not having been able to show (in *Lily Tomlin*, for example) the mechanics and practicalities of documentary filmmaking. An indispensable corollary of making the shift towards appearing on camera is Broomfield's now proven desire to 'examine the documentary form' by dismantling it. From being good genre films, Broomfield's documentaries become anti-documentaries in which an analysis of the non-fiction film takes the form of a perverse enactment of what a documentary should not be: a film made up of telephone conversations, arguments before and after interviews, discussions between director and crew, chats with incidental characters. In this sense Broomfield's post-*Driving Me Crazy* films, with their formal and physical marginalisation of their central subjects, come to echo the dichotomy between director and performer that Nick Broomfield embodies when appearing in his films. Just as there is a fundamental distinction to be drawn between Nick Broomfield and 'Nick Broomfield', so there is an equally significant differentiation to be made between the documentary and 'the documentary', the former signifying the films' putative subject and the latter the resulting film. The contrast is most graphically illustrated by an unsuccessful film such as *Tracking Down Maggie*, a film, ostensibly about Margaret Thatcher, which contains very little of Thatcher (and certainly no proper access to her) and becomes instead a film about   not just featuring – the peripheral characters such as the neighbour on Flood Street who took Thatcher's old lavatory from the skip in front of her house. *Tracking Down Maggie*, despite amusingly self-deprecating moments like Broomfield's piece of parody documentary commentary 'I'd almost given up when, in a remote spot in the heart of the Essex countryside, we found Francis Wheen', fails because it cannot bring together the two components of the dialectic. The success of Broomfield's performative documentaries is directly dependent upon the collision at some point between the proposed conventional documentary subject (Eileen Wuornos, Eugene Terreblanche, Heidi Fleiss, Madams and clients of a New York fetish parlour) and the unconventional, ostensibly shambolic performance of that subject on film; the documentary and the 'documentary' must meet as must Nick Broomfield and 'Nick Broomfield'. The interview situation is the usual place for these meetings to occur, and films that lack a substantial interview with their pivotal figures (*Maggie* or *Kurt and Courtney*) prove unsatisfying because any serious intent behind the films is lost altogether.

Broomfield's most cohesive and powerful film is *The Leader, His Driver and the Driver's Wife* (1991), a documentary about Eugene Terreblanche, the leader of the neo-Nazi Afrikaner Resistance Movement (the AWB) in South Africa, made at a time when apartheid was crumbling. Still reminiscent of the earlier, more obviously committed films, *The Leader* is the apotheosis of Broomfield's amalgamation of political content and performative style, and so represents another turning point in his career. In subsequent documentaries the balance has shifted more (some would say too far) towards the performative, any serious commentary becoming quite clearly the films' secondary element. Like all of Broomfield's later *auteur*-performer films, *The Leader* parallels the amassing of the documentary story about Terreblanche with the experience of making the film; inevitably, much of the action revolves around travelling and establishing contact with Terreblanche and a variety of intermediaries, most notably his driver 'JP' and JP's wife Anita. Like Michael Moore's performance at the centre of *Roger and Me* (1989) in which he unsuccessfully tries to get Roger Smith, the chairman of General Motors, to come to Flint, Michigan to confront company workers whose jobs are being cut, Broomfield's performance in *The Leader* is successful because it appears rooted in earnest commitment rather than simple egomania. Despite flaunting the comic detail of the story (like so many trophies), *The Leader* powerfully enacts, through the mechanisms of the performative documentary, the real decline of the AWB from sinister, sizeable power to impotent political side show. The documentary opens with Barry Ackroyd, Broomfield's cameraman, being floored by a punch from an angry AWB member at a packed rally, but ends with a counter sequence at an AWB parade that was expected to attract 5,000 but which is attended only by a meagre few (Figure 6.1); it contains several incidental travelling sequences during which Broomfield's voice-over catalogues episodes of AWB brutality, whilst the body of the film shows Terreblanche unable to control his horse, getting angry when Anita points a loaded gun at him and JP leaving the party. The performative elements of *The Leader* ostensibly marginalise the documentary's substantive material, only to reflexively re-invoke it.

This correlation would not have occurred if the interview with Terreblanche had not taken place – if, that is, the conventional documentary had not met its performative counterpart. Although Broomfield encounters Terreblanche on a couple of occasions prior to this interview, these meetings are insubstantial; the interview itself (which comes two-thirds of the way through the film) likewise appears, on the surface, to be inadequate, a 'non-interview' in the words of many critics. To back this up, the interview (in JP's estimation, 'the worst he's ever seen') comprises an argument between Terreblanche and Broomfield concerning the latter's lateness for an earlier appointment and Terreblanche's repeated misunderstanding of one simple question: when had he decided that the AWB would have to go to war against the blacks? Firstly, it appears that turning up a few minutes late for the previous appointment is a ploy to anger Terreblanche, for 'Nick Broomfield' the *provocateur* is heard to mumble sweetly that the reason he and the crew were late was that they were 'having a cup of tea'. Throughout this argument, Barry Ackroyd holds the camera steady on Terreblanche (from a low angle, ironically suggestive of power and superiority). Secondly, whilst the interview may not yield very much substantial discussion of the AWB's policy, it shows Terreblanche, not Broomfield, to be the buffoon of

Figure 6.1   The Leader, His Driver and the Driver's Wife (True Stories)
Source: Courtesy of BFI Stills, Posters and Designs

the encounter (it is significant that, for this sequence, Broomfield remains out of frame), as the leader misinterprets the only question the director is heard to put to him, understanding him to have asked when he will go to war, not when he decided he would have to go to war. Broomfield rephrases the question several times, each time laboriously making it clearer, but Terreblanche obtusely misses the nuances. The essential performative power of *The Leader* is that it spontaneously captures and plays out the disintegration of Terreblanche's power and concomitantly that of the AWB, for however manipulated and preconceived the film might be, Broomfield's way of making films ensures that 'there is never an opportunity to do a second take' (Broomfield quoted in Macdonald and Cousins 1996: 364).

The issue of 'realness' as it pertains to *The Leader, His Driver and the Driver's Wife* is, from the audience's perspective, relatively unproblematic, as the distinction between Nick Broomfield the director and 'Nick Broomfield' the enactment of himself for the benefit of the documentary, appears clear cut. The latter functions as a tool of the former, working to manipulate the figures of the documentary, notably Terreblanche; the persona in inverted commas, therefore, is an accurate simulation that nevertheless remains separate from his real counterpart. If one turns to the performative film as created by the juxtaposition of these two figures, then the identities of the documentary and the 'documentary' are likewise intact. A documentary is deemed performative if it formally illustrates the notion that a documentary is an unpredictable act. The way in which the performative works in *The Leader*, however, ultimately suggests that the pre-existing facts upon which it is based – like the actual Nick Broomfield – do exist. Certain of Broomfield's later films (most notably *Heidi Fleiss*) problematise this simple, reflective interpretation of the performative by not abiding by the simple binary oppositions examined above. Concomitantly, these later films show a move towards the clichéd Nick Broomfield film that is more about him than about his subjects. As the films become more fixated on the 'Nick Broomfield' persona and as that persona increasingly dominates the documentaries' action, so the films subjugate their proposed subject matter to a more focused, insistent interest in the issues of performance and 'realness'. It is also significant that the subjects and situations of these latest films are similarly preoccupied with performance and 'realness': Fleiss is a hooker and madam, the mistresses of Pandora's Box in *Fetishes* enact sadomasochistic scenarios, Courtney Love is an actress. In tandem with these complications, the previously straightforward Nick Broomfield≠'Nick Broomfield' distinction is itself (irretrievably perhaps) problematised.

In *Heidi Fleiss: Hollywood Madam* (1995) all definitions of reality, of what is the truth are thrown into confusion; it is far from clear, by the end, where the boundary between the director and his persona lies (if anywhere), and it is likewise entirely unclear whether the film succeeds in revealing any even superficial truths about its three protagonists: Heidi Fleiss, Madam Alex (for whom Heidi first worked) and Ivan Nagy (her lover and maybe erstwhile pimp). As the confusion mounts, the documentary becomes fixated on this triangular relationship and on Fleiss in particular, leaving virtually untouched the facts surrounding Hollywood's 'Madam to the stars' – the catalysts, essentially, for her arrest (on pandering and narcotics charges) and also for the film. At the outset, and for much of the film, Broomfield appears in control; similarly we, his audience – upon seeing the familiar, formulaic mechanisms in place (the telephone calls, the schmoozing, the dogged pursuit of his subjects, the obtaining of significant access and interviews) – are lulled into a sense that we are indeed, once more, to occupy the privileged position of those whom Broomfield lets in on the act. The chain (one element leading to the next until the filmmaker gets close to his or her main subject) is a fundamental characteristic of the investigative documentary, and the feeling of security remains intact in *Heidi Fleiss* while Broomfield is able to follow leads that take him from one friend or ex-employee to another in his successful endeavour to build up a portrait of Fleiss. Likewise, the manner in which Broomfield subsequently intercuts interviews with two of his protagonists, Ivan Nagy and Madam Alex, suggests that he (as puppet master) is playing one off against the other, thereby controlling them and how they are perceived. If this is suggestive of Broomfield

getting to the heart of his documentary subject, then this confidence is vali-
dated by his arrival at Heidi Fleiss, whom he interviews extensively whilst she is
out on bail and in rehab.

There are also moments, along his relatively trouble-free journey to this
point, when the two Nick Broomfields (the omniscient director and his
bumbling, eager alter ego) seem to merge as they did in *The Leader, His Driver
and the Driver's Wife*, notably in the sequence in Heidi's boutique when he
comes to interview her alongside an American news crew, prior to her agreement to a more substantial encounter. When the US Channel 5 interview has
finished, Broomfield tentatively approaches Fleiss who then turns to the female
news reporter saying: 'They want to film me right in the middle of my trial,
crazy, huh?' After chumming up to Heidi, the woman from Channel 5 grows in
confidence enquiring: 'Who are these people?' A spat ensues between her and
Broomfield focusing on the absurd fact that she has a 5 on her microphone
whilst he has nothing. Broomfield concludes this by saying angrily 'Because
she's got a 5 on her little thing, she's the voice of reason?', pointing out that,
being from the BBC (letters he articulates slowly for maximum stress) he does
not require a number. In winning this bout, Broomfield temporarily appears to
dispense with the distinction with his performative self, provoked into reiter-
ating that he is in the process of making a serious documentary. Usually this is a
moment of strength and control, but in this instance it is not, for it quickly
becomes apparent that Heidi (clearly revelling in the undignified spat) is the
manipulator who has engineered the whole thing. It is at this juncture that the
previously stable documentary is terminally destabilised, the remainder of the
film reversing the familiar concept of authorial control.

From this point on (and perhaps it is a testament to Broomfield's desire to
reveal the truth that he does not disguise this) the Pasolini analogy of the
controlling director surrounded by orchestrated chaos crumbles, so that the
inverse becomes true: that Broomfield is thrown into chaos as order resides
with the subjects he has sought to manipulate. The film's final interviews with
Nagy and Fleiss both suggest that it is they who have been stringing Broomfield
along rather than *vice versa*. Nagy mocks him for being 'an idiot' who 'is not in
the club' and maintains that he is still seeing Fleiss (a statement he substantiates
with a smoochy telephone call to her); Fleiss, whilst denying her and Nagy are
still together, likewise taunts Broomfield by saying 'you're missing something,
Nick … you're way off, Nick. Bye.' This finale, packed with uncorroborated
insinuation, fails to offer any coherent solution to the story of Heidi Fleiss,
instead, none of Broomfield's investigative questions is answered and, in
apparent desperation, he resorts to manufacturing, on insubstantial evidence, a
lame psychological explanation, asking Heidi whether or not any of this would
have happened if she 'hadn't been attracted to the person most likely to destroy
[you]'. Broomfield adopts a particularly flirtatious manner with Fleiss, maintaining that 'We had a very flirtatious game-playing relationship; and if we
hadn't I don't think I'd have got the interview' (Brown 1996: 42), also saying
that, by the end of filming, he had 'a problem with Ivan' and that it was the

film's exposure of their relationship that ultimately precipitated Fleiss' break up with him (p. 42). Is a relationship based on faked flirtation, however, likely to be won by the filmmaker or the madam? There is the possibility, substantiated by Broomfield's rather vulnerable performance, that he is actually flirting with Fleiss but finds himself duped.[13]

Conclusion

The ambiguity at the end of *Heidi Fleiss: Hollywood Madam* encapsulates the idea of documentaries as not necessarily determined or closed, but rather as dialectical and open to reinterpretation. This remains a constant factor linking all the documentaries here discussed. The performative documentary is the clearest contemporary exponent of this book's underpinning thesis that the documentary as prescribed by advocates of observational realism is an unrealisable fantasy, that documentary will forever be circumscribed by the fact that it is a mode of representation and thus can never elide the distance between image and event. It is imperative, however, to acknowledge that this deficiency does not invalidate the notion of the non-fiction film, merely that the non-fiction film is (and largely always has been) aware of the limitations of the audio-visual media. With this acknowledgement, what ensues when examining documentary output is an awareness that it is predicated upon a dialectical relationship between aspiration and potential, that the text itself reveals the tensions between the documentary pursuit of the most authentic mode of factual representation and the impossibility of this aim. The documentaries examined in this chapter express these tendencies through the use of multiple dualities: in *Unmade Beds*, there is the conflict between the invocation of the furtive, unpredictable act of secretly peeping in at strangers' windows represented via a series of precisely framed, lit and performed cameo sequences; in *Geri*, Molly Dineen and her subject Geri Halliwell dispute the question of control of the film ostensibly freely; in *The Leader, His Driver and the Driver's Wife*, Nick Broomfield performs the role of sweet, chaotic investigative reporter as a means of undermining and controlling Eugene Terreblanche's image. From within such a performative framework, the very notion of a complete, finite documentary is continually challenged and reassessed.

Notes

Introduction

1   So the Expository is 'overly didactic', the Observational displays a 'lack of history, context', the Interactive puts 'excessive faith in witnesses' and offers 'naïve history', the Reflexive is 'too abstract' and 'lose[s] sight of actual issues', and the Performative is excessively stylised (Nichols 1994: 95).

1 The event: archive and newsreel

1   The Grassy Knoll is on Elm Street just to the right and front of the presidential limousine as Kennedy was shot.
2   'The Zapruder Footage', *The Late Show* (BBC2, 22.11.1993).
3   The Warren Commission (so called because its president was Justice Earl Warren) was set up 29 November 1963 by President Johnson to investigate the assassination of John Kennedy. Its findings were that Lee Harvey Oswald alone killed Kennedy from the sixth floor of the Texas School Book Depository, a building behind and to the right of the President's car. In order to prove their findings (and thus to refute all claims of a conspiracy) the Warren Commission had to prove that the shots could have all been fired by one person which necessitated what became known as the 'magic bullet theory': the theory that one bullet could have entered Kennedy's neck from the back, exited, changed direction in the air, hit Governor Connally (also in the car) twice before emerging from his body unscathed. The Warren Commission's report omitted certain key frames from the Zapruder film (Nos 208–11), despite asserting that the first bullet struck Kennedy at frame 210, claiming this was an over-sight. Very quickly the report's use of the Zapruder film to substantiate its claims became the focus of conspiracy theorists who believed the Commission deliberately obscured the truth of Kennedy's assassination. In May 1964 the Commission conducted a re-enactment of the assassination based on the Zapruder footage. As Simon comments, 'The re-enactment's production as representation thus came to substitute for the real event but was used in a process that rewrote the event' (Simon 1996: 39).
4   Certain frames from Nix's film disappeared, conspiracy theorists assume because they would have contradicted the Warren Commission Report's findings. Also, in *The Men Who Killed President Kennedy* (Central Television, 1988), Beverly, one of Jack Ruby's ex-employees, maintains that the home movie she shot from just behind Morland was handed over to the FBI but subsequently disappeared.
5   From the introductory commentary of *The Men Who Killed President Kennedy* (Central Television, 1988).
6   *The Men Who Killed President Kennedy.*
7   *The Late Show* (BBC2, 22.11.93).

8 *Don Delillo: the word, the image and the gun* (*Omnibus*, BBC1, 27.9.91).
9 Cf. *The Trial of Lee Harvey Oswald* (David Greene, 1976) and *The Trial of Lee Harvey Oswald* (London Weekend Television, 1986). The former dramatisation of Oswald's hypothetical trial presumes that Ruby did not kill Oswald so the latter was able to stand trial but ends just before the verdict is announced, thereby circumventing the problem of establishing his guilt or innocence. The latter was part of an occasional LWT series in which individuals were put on trial in a studio but using real lawyers, witnesses and jury members; the verdict in this instance was that Oswald acted alone in the murder of President Kennedy. (The other people put on trial in the series were Richard III, Roger Hollis and – using a slightly different format whereby her policies are tried as opposed to her – Margaret Thatcher.)
10 Just such an example of the 'strange incidents' impinges directly on *Rush to Judgement* as one of the eye-witnesses, railway worker Lee Bowers, is killed in a car accident three months after giving the interview. De Antonio does not explicitly make the connection between Bowers' interview (in which he talks of seeing three cars apparently casing the car park behind the Grassy Knoll in the run up to the assassination) and his death, but coupled with Jones' powerful words the implication is obvious.
11 Although often compared to Shub, de Antonio said, early in his career, he had not yet seen any of her work (see Crowdus and Georgakas 1988: 170).
12 Richard Roud, who originally turned down *Point of Order* for screening in New York, only three months later, 'made the discovery that *Point of Order* was a film, after all, and invited it to the London festival' (Weiner 1971: 10).
13 De Antonio refers specifically in this interview to Rauchenberg and Jasper Johns, also to the composer John Cage who appears in *Mr Hoover and I*. Cf. also de Antonio's film *Painters Painting*.
14 Cf. the later discussion of Umberto Eco's analysis of one of Nixon's 1973 television addresses during the Watergate investigations for a further examination of how the public perception of Nixon's character contributed to his downfall (Chapter 5).
15 This footage has appeared in several other films, notably *The Atomic Café*, presumably because of its fine comic potential. Not only is there Nixon, the carved out pumpkin and the piece of film, but also there is Nixon's mute accomplice with his amazingly restless eyebrows.
16 A conclusion pursued to a ludicrous extreme in Oliver Stone's *Nixon* with the president's confrontation with 'the Beast' for example under the Lincoln memorial.

2 Narration: the film and its voice

1 There is also the issue of where the archival material originates (more fully discussed in Chapter 1); for example, that the Nazi footage of Himmler has been appropriated for anti-Nazi purposes.
2 It has often been said that Kenneth Branagh sees himself as the new Laurence Olivier. His narration for *The Cold War* further substantiates this.
3 As in Bill Couturie's *Dear America: Letters Home From Vietnam* (1987), in which it is the actors, and not the GIs whose letters they are reading, whom Couturie lists in the film's title sequence, the presence of Olivier perhaps blurs the issue of how an audience receives the statements he is making. One critic of *Dear America* comments that, in that film, 'Historical context dissolves into subjectivity' (Hoberman 1988: 44), suggesting that the images themselves, through the pre-eminence afforded the actors, uncomfortably become part of a narrativised, mythologised history – one which derives as much of its capacity to move from the mechanisms of drama as it does from the strength of the 'truth' being documented.

4 This is in keeping with the series' 'identity'. *The World at War* did not approach its subject entirely chronologically; instead each episode dealt with a particular campaign, set of events or issues which often spanned several years. 'Genocide' held an ambivalent position within this formulaic structure: it was at once both set apart, more important than the episodes around it (hence the appearance of Olivier at the beginning) and it needed to conform to the series identity.

5 For an explanation of this notion of one primary collision that in turn brings about a series of secondary collisions cf. Part Two of Lukács (1937).

6 Dan White was sentenced on 21 May 1979, having been found guilty of voluntary manslaughter rather than murder. He was paroled 6 January 1985 after serving 5 years, 1 month in Soledad Prison. Although the then Mayor Dianne Feinstein publicly urged White not to return to San Francisco as there had been unrest and several rallies upon his release, White did return and lived 'quietly without incident until he committed suicide by asphyxiation in the garage of his home on October 21 1985' (www.backdoor.com/castro/soledadpage.html).

7 Although this is not emphasised in the film, it is significant that one of the earlier pieces of archive shows Moscone in interview condemning the use of capital punishment.

8 I do not agree with Dai Vaughan that our interpretation is still dependent on how we interpret the soldier's look. Vaughan comments: 'If we assume that he [the soldier] can see the statue, we read pained inscrutability into his expression; if we assume that he cannot, we read irony into the juxtaposition' ('Arms and the Absent', *Sight and Sound*, 48:3, Summer 1979, 183).

9 For the army correspondence relating to *The Battle of San Pietro* see Culbert (1990).

10 I am indebted to Doug Pye for this observation.

11 Cf. Spender (1985).

12 Marker's accreditation of himself as 'editor' is quite common; at the end of *The Last Bolshevik*, for example, appears 'written and edited by Chris Marker'. Either one takes this as a perhaps pretentious self-effacing gesture on Marker's part, or possibly as an indication that he genuinely does not believe in single authorship and wants to emphasise this to his audience. The fact that so many of his films are compilations, using visual material from a variety of eclectic sources, suggests that Marker's concerns are more democratic that didactic. (Cf. also Chapter 2 on archive documentaries.)

13 Cf. William Shakespeare, *Othello*: 'She lov'd me for the dangers I had pass'd, and I loved her that she did pity them' (Act I, Scene iii, ll. 167–8).

14 Cf. Horak (1997: 29ff) for a discussion of Marker's two types of documentaries.

3 New British observational documentary: 'docusoaps'

1 HMS Brilliant was the first Navy ship (in October 1990) to take women to sea, and at the time of filming *HMS Brilliant*, 17 of the 250 crew were women.

2 Bob Hawkins' drag appearance is additionally interesting in terms of how it looks. He wears a dress, a wig, balloons for breasts, but does not attempt to mask his hairy chest, so the overall image is one of intense disruption and potential anarchy.

3 Although the title sequence for *The Cruise* is also strikingly reminiscent of the title sequence for *HMS Brilliant*, as if signalling a certain *auteur*-ist continuity.

4 *The Cruise* likewise followed *Eastenders* when it began transmission in December 1997.

5 Joseph has recently returned to directing *EastEnders*.

6 It is quite interesting that the audience are never given a reverse shot to indicate what exactly Maureen has done wrong.

7   Following *The Cruise*, Jane McDonald released an album, *Jane McDonald*, which
    sold 100,000 copies, went gold and became Number 1 in the British charts in less
    than two weeks. In July 1998 her husband Henrik Blixen became her manager, in
    October–November 1998 McDonald went on a UK tour, since when ITV have
    approached her to do a television series.

4 Documentary journeys: *Shoah, London*

1   For example in Britain, Chris Terrill (cf. Chapter 3 of this book) and Nicholas Barker
    (cf. Chapter 6).
2   Colombat offers a detailed breakdown of this structure (pp. 308–10).
3   It is interesting that in an interview I have seen with Karski since he appeared in
    Shoah, he was far more composed and polished.
4   The issue of ethics is interesting with respect to such a violation of documentary
    'rules' as the hiring of a location with which the interviewee is not associated. In
    addition, there is the hiring of the locomotive Henrik Gawkowski drives into the
    station at Treblinka and the use of hidden cameras (and lies) to extract interviews
    from ex-SS such as Franz Suchomel. Of the last, Marcel Ophuls says, 'I can hardly
    find the words to express how much I approve of this procedure [Lanzmann's
    promise to Suchomel that his identity will not be revealed], how much I sympathise
    with it. This is not a matter of means and ends, this is a matter of moral priorities'
    (Ophuls 1985: 22).
5   Cf. note 4.
6   For a discussion by Lanzmann of this gesture, cf. Lanzmann (1990: 87–9).
7   Although there are recurrent figures in *Rien che les heures* and other city films such as
    the staggering woman who appears sporadically through the Cavalcanti, they do not
    function as characters as such – we are given no extra information about them, for
    example.

5 The president and the image: Kennedy, Nixon, Clinton

1   See Chapter 1 for a discussion of Kennedy's assassination.
2   Kennedy received 303 Electoral College votes against Nixon's 219, whilst the
    popular vote in 1960 was much closer: 34,226,731 for Kennedy and 34,108,157 for
    Nixon – the smallest margin ever recorded (Matthews 1996: 156).
3   The role of the campaign debates in the creation and promotion of a candidate's
    image has continued to be significant; for example, Ford's gaffe of stating that
    Poland and Eastern Europe were not then under Soviet military domination during a
    televised debate against Carter in 1976 made a substantial difference in how the
    candidates were viewed. Whilst a poll taken in the immediate aftermath of the debate
    suggested that, despite the gaffe, Ford had still won the debate, polls taken after
    extended media coverage emphasising the mistake indicated that voters switched alle-
    giance to Carter, giving Ford's statements on Eastern Europe as the major reason
    (Ranney 1983: 25–6). In 1980, Carter's repeated decision not to debate his main
    rival for the Democratic nomination, Edward Kennedy, was vindicated by his victo-
    ries in the primaries, whilst his decision to challenge Reagan, the eventual Republican
    candidate, to a debate only seven days before the 1984 election was considered to be
    the event that converted a slender Reagan lead into a 10% victory margin (Ranney
    1983: 27).
4   Roosevelt himself was aware of the potential effect of his physical frailty, appearing
    for press photographs at the Yalta conference in an ordinary chair.
5   Johnson's most significant domestic legislation came out of the two 'Great Society'
    congresses: the 88th (1963–4) and the 89th (1965–6). These achieved the Civil

Rights Act, major tax cuts, a widespread anti-poverty programme, the Urban Mass Transportation Act, the Medicare Bill for all over 65s and poor, aid to school districts with larger than average numbers of poor families, the Voting Rights Act which abolished literacy tests and other devices designed to keep blacks from voting, an expanded housing programme, a new Immigration Act that ended the 1924 quota system, a permanent food stamps programme, etc. (White 1982: 124–6).

6 There were four photographers on *Primary*: Richard Leacock, D.A. Pennebaker, Terrence McCartney-Filgate and Albert Maysles.

7 As the action in *Crisis* was filmed simultaneously much of the time, there was not time for one crew to do all the filming. The four filmmakers involved were: Richard Leacock, James Lipscomb (who also narrated), D.A. Pennebaker and Hope Ryden.

8 Cf. Richard Leacock's comment (made in 1963): 'Obviously we [the filmmakers] have our own bias and selection, obviously we're not presenting the Whole Truth. I'm not being pretentious and ridiculous: we're presenting the film-maker's perception of an aspect of what happened' (Shivas 1963: 257).

9 In the event Beatty turned the part down and Kennedy was played by Cliff Robertson.

10 Nixon's first of many memoirs was entitled *Six Crises*, a structure that is mimicked by de Antonio's film *Millhouse* (see Chapter 1).

11 *Watergate 5: Impeachment* (1994).

12 Throughout his life Nixon effected this distanciation. In his 1978 memoirs, for example, he talks of 'A president's power begins slipping away the moment it is known that he is going to leave; I had seen that in 1952, in 1960, in 1968. On the eve of my resignation I knew that my role was already a symbolic one, and that Gerald Ford's was now the constructive one' (Nixon 1978: 1077). No acknowledgement, therefore, of the difference between criminality and unpopularity or completion of a second term in office.

13 Watergate was a traumatic break with history and led to the 1974 Presidential Records and Materials Preservation Act which stipulated that papers and tapes should be kept with the National Archives; was the motivation behind the Privacy Act of the same year which extended the provisions of the Freedom of Information Act passed by the Johnson administration and permitted individuals to see personal information in their federal agency files and if need be correct them; led to the Ethics of Government Act, passed by the Senate in 1978 to establish a legal basis for the office of special prosecutor so that he or she could only be removed by impeachment or conviction for a crime (Ambrose 1991: 592).

14 Tanner challenges the 'super delegates' and makes the convention 'open', i.e. allowing each delegate to vote openly rather than have their votes counted as a block state vote, arguing that the 'super delegates' system is not representative of the earlier voting patterns in the primaries. This is a doomed gamble to try to thwart Dukakis who would inevitably win under the 'super delegates' system.

15 See note 5.

6 The performative documentary: Barker, Dineen, Broomfield

1 The actor Ricky Tomlinson who plays the scab in *Dockers* is also an ex-dockers' union leader.

2 Cf. Chapter 2 in Nichols (1991: 32–75) for a discussion of the previous four modes.

3 Cf., though, the mention of Austin in Susan Scheibler, 'Constantly performing the documentary: the seductive promise of *Lightning Over Water*' in Renov (1993: 135–50), and Caryl Flinn, 'Containing fire: performance in *Paris is Burning*' in Grant and Sloniowski (1998: 429–45).

4 Barker's style explicitly informed BBC2's *Modern Times*, the replacement for *40 Minutes* launched by Stephen Lambert in 1995 – cf. Stella Bruzzi (1999: 32–4).
5 A quintessential example is *Lido* (6.12.95), a film made by Lucy Blakstad who was one of the Assistant Producers on *Signs of the Times*. *Lido* adopts many of the same techniques as Barker's series: posed interviews, a formalised and unspontaneous style, an open narrative structure.
6 For a general discussion of *Handsworth Songs*, cf. Corner (1996); for a discussion specifically about its female voice-over, cf. Cook (1987).
7 Cf. Chapter 2 for a fuller discussion of women's voices in documentary.
8 Nichols in 'The voice of documentary' goes on to apply the term voice to 'interactive' documentaries, that is, those which (like the films of Emile de Antonio) formally as opposed to physically suggest their authorship.
9 Cf. Chapter 3 on 'docusoaps'.
10 Cf. the discussion of voice-over in Chapter 2.
11 For a critical response to *Kurt and Courtney*'s depiction of Love, cf. Moran (1998).
12 Cf. *Signs and Meaning* (2nd edition), London: Secker & Warburg, 1972.
13 There have been rumours, strongly denied by Broomfield, that he and Fleiss had an affair, Nagy embellishing this by saying that they were engaged, a further rumour that Broomfield dismisses as 'ridiculous' (Brown 1996: 42).

Bibliography

Ambrose, Stephen (1991) *Nixon, Volume 3: Ruin and Recovery, 1973–1990*, New York and London: Simon & Schuster.

Anonymous (1996) *Primary Colors: A Novel of Politics*, London: Vintage.

Arthur, Paul (1993) 'Jargons of authenticity (three American moments)', in Michael Renov (ed.) *Theorizing Documentary*, London and New York: Routledge.

—— (1997) 'On the virtues and limitations of collage', *Documentary Box*, 11 (October): 1–7.

Austin, J.L. (1970) *Philosophical Papers* (2nd edition, edited by J. O. Urmson and G. J. Warnock), Oxford: Oxford University Press.

Barker, Nicholas (1999) Interview with the author, 10.9.99.

Barthes, Roland (1957) *Mythologies*, London: Paladin [1973].

—— (1973) *S/Z*, Oxford: Blackwell [1996].

—— (1977) *Image/Music/Text* (selected and transl. Stephen Heath), London: Fontana.

Barnouw, Erik (1993) *Documentary: A History of the Non-fiction Film* (2nd revised edition), Oxford: Oxford University Press.

Barwell, Claire (1997a) '*Flâneur* of London', *Pix*, 2 (January): 158–9.

—— (1997b) 'Interview with Patrick Keiller', *Pix*, 2 (January): 160–5.

Bazin, André (1967) *What is Cinema?: Volume I* (selected and transl. by Hugh Gray), Berkeley and Los Angeles: University of California Press.

BBC (1998) Unpublished minutes of editorial policy meeting, Tuesday 8 December.

Bell, Rachel (1998) Interview with the author, 17.12.98.

Benjamin, Walter (1955) *Illuminations* (transl. Harry Zohn), London: Fontana [1973].

Berry, Joseph P. Jr (1987) *John F. Kennedy: The First Media President*, Lanham: University Press of America.

Billen, Andrew (1995) 'Where's Molly?', *Observer Review*, 10 December, p. 9.

Bishop, Louise (1996) 'Is there a producer in the house?', *Television*, 33 (5; July–August): 12–13.

—— (1998) 'Getting real', *Television*, 35 (3; April): 16–17.

Bonitzer, Pascal (1976) 'The silences of the voice'; reprinted in Philip Rosen (ed.) *Narrative, Apparatus, Ideology: A Film Reader*, New York: Columbia University Press [1986]: 319–34.

Branigan, Edward (1992) *Narrative Comprehension and Film*, London and New York: Routledge.

Brennan, Timothy (1990) 'The national longing for form', in Homi K. Bhabha (ed.) *Nation and Narration*, London and New York: Routledge.

Britton, Andrew (1992) 'Invisible eye', *Sight and Sound*, 1 (10; February): 27–9.

Broomfield, Nick (1993) 'Heroes and villains: Pier Paolo Pasolini', *The Independent Magazine*, 6 February, p. 46.

Brown, M. (1996) 'Fetishes', *Daily Telegraph Weekend Magazine*, 10 August, pp. 41–2.

Brown, Thomas (1988) *JFK: History of an Image*, London: I.B. Taurus & Co. Ltd.

Bruzzi, Stella (1999) 'Butterfly on the wall', *Sight and Sound*, 9 (1; January): 32–4.

Burch, Noël (1969) *The Theory of Film Practice* (transl. Annette Michelson), London: Secker & Warburg [1973].

Burgoyne, Robert (1996) 'Modernism and the narrative of *JFK*', in Vivian Sobchack (ed.) *The Persistence of History: Cinema, Television and the Modern Event*, London and New York: Routledge.

Butler, Judith (1990) *Gender Trouble: Feminism and the Subversion of Identity*, London and New York: Routledge.

—— (1993) *Bodies that Matter: On the Discursive Limitations of 'Sex'*, London and New York: Routledge.

—— (1997) *Excitable Speech: A Politics of the Performative*, London and New York: Routledge.

Carr, E.H. (1961) *What is History?* Harmondsworth: Penguin [1986].

Carroll, Noël (1996a) *Theorising the Moving Image*, Cambridge: Cambridge University Press.

—— (1996b) 'Nonfiction film and postmodern skepticism', in David Bordwell and Noël Carroll (eds) *Post-Theory: Reconstructing Film Studies*, Madison: University of Wisconsin Press.

Cavalcanti, Alberto (1939) 'Sound in films', *Films*, 1 (1; November): 25–39.

Cleave, Maureen (1991) 'Molly's hidden depths', *The Evening Standard*, 27 March, p. 26.

Colombat, André Pierre (1993) *The Holocaust in French Film* (Metuchen), New York and London: Scarecrow Press.

Comolli, Jean-Louis (1980) 'Machines of the visible', in Teresa de Lauretis and Stephen Heath (eds) *The Cinematic Apparatus*, London: Macmillan.

Comolli, Jean-Louis and Narboni, Jean (1969) 'Cinema/ideology/criticism', reprinted in Bill Nichols (ed.) *Movies and Methods*, Berkeley and Los Angeles: University of California Press [1976].

Cook, Pam (1987) '*Handsworth Songs*', *Monthly Film Bulletin*, 638: 77–8.

Corner, John (1996) *The Art of Record: A Critical Introduction to Documentary*, Manchester: Manchester University Press.

Crowdus, Gary (ed.) (1994) *A Political Companion to American Film*, Lakeview Press.

Crowdus, Gary and Georgakas, Dan (1988) 'History is the theme of all my films: an interview with Emile de Antonio', in Alan Rosenthal (ed.) *New Challenges for Documentary*, Berkeley and Los Angeles: University of California Press.

Culbert, David (ed.) (1990) *Film and Propaganda in America: A Documentary [Volume III: World War II – Part 2]*, New York and London: Greenwood Press.

Dale, Peter (1998) 'Documentaries in danger', *Broadcast*, 23 October, p. 17.

Dams, Tim (1998) 'Time to move on', *Broadcast*, 23 October, pp. 16–17.

de Beauvoir, Simone (1985) 'Preface' to Claude Lanzmann *Shoah: An Oral History of the Holocaust*, New York: Pantheon Books, pp. iii–vi.

Diamond, Edwin and Silverman, Robert A. (1997) *White House to Your House: Media and Politics in Virtual America*, Cambridge, Mass. and London: MIT Press.

Doane, Mary Ann (1980) 'The voice in the cinema: the articulation of the body and space', *Yale French Studies*, 60.

Doherty, Thomas (1987) 'Representing the holocaust: Claude Lanzmann's *Shoah*', *Film and History*, 17 (1; February): 2–8.

Drew, Robert (1983) 'Narration can be a killer'; reprinted in Kevin Macdonald and Mark Cousins (eds) *Imagining Reality: The Faber Book of Documentary*, London: Faber & Faber [1996]: 271–3.

Dunn, Elisabeth (1993) 'Documentary the Dineen way', *The Daily Telegraph*, 30 January, pp. 18–19.

Durgnat, Raymond (1967) *Franju*, London: Studio Vista.

Eco, Umberto (1985) 'Strategies of lying', in Marshall Blonsky *On Signs: A Semiotics Reader*, Oxford: Blackwell, pp. 3–11.

Edgerton, Gary (1987) 'Revisiting the recordings of wars past: remembering the documentary trilogy of John Huston', *Journal of Popular Film and Television*, 15 (1; Spring): 27–41.

Eisenstein, Sergei (1926) 'Béla forgets the scissors', reprinted in Richard Taylor and Ian Christie (eds) *The Film Factory: Russian and Soviet Cinema in Documents, 1896–1939*, London and New York: Routledge [1994]: 145–9.

Eisenstein, Sergei, Pudovkin, Vsevelod and Alexandrov, Grigori (1928) 'Statement on sound', reprinted in Richard Taylor and Ian Christie (eds) *The Film Factory: Russian and Soviet Cinema in Documents, 1896–1939*, London and New York: Routledge [1994]: 234–5.

Fielder, Mark (1998) Interview with the author, 27.11.98.

Fink, Guido (1982) 'From showing to telling: off-screen narration in the American cinema', *Letteratura d'America*, 3 (12; Spring): 5–37.

Flinn, Caryl (1998) 'Containing fire: performance in *Paris is Burning*', in Barry Keith Grant and Jeanette Sloniowski (eds) *Documenting the Documentary: Close Readings of Documentary Film and Video*, Detroit: Wayne State University Publishing.

Foucault, Michel (1977) 'What is an author?', *Language, Counter-Memory, Practice: Selected Essays and Interviews*, Oxford: Blackwell.

French, Sean (1989) 'Shooting from the heart', *The Observer*, 12 November, p. 4.

Glitz, Michael (1993) 'The house that "Dave" built', *Premiere* [US], 6 (10; June): 34–5.

Graef, Roger (1998) 'The truth is in there', *Sunday Times*, 5 April.

Grant, Barry Kieth and Sloniowski, Jeanette (eds) (1998) *Documenting the Documentary: Close Readings of Documentary Film and Video*, Detroit: Wayne State University Press.

Guynn, William (1990) *A Cinema of Nonfiction*, London and Toronto: Associated University Presses.

Hamann, Paul (1998) 'The Docusoap debate', *European Media: Business and Finance*, 8 (20; October): 5, 6.

Hoberman, J. (1988) 'America Dearest', *American Film*, XIII (7; May): 39–45, 54–6.

—— (1996) '*Shoah*: Witness to annihilation', in Kevin Macdonald and Mark Cousins (eds) *Imagining Reality: The Faber Book of Documentary*, London: Faber & Faber, pp. 316–22.

Hodges, Mike (1997) 'The secret city', *Pix*, 2 (January): 166–7.

Horak, Jan-Christopher (1997) *Making Images Move: Photographers and Avant-garde Cinema*, Washington and London: Smithsonian Institute Press.

Hughes, Robert (1980) *The Shock of the New: Art and the Century of Change*, Thames & Hudson [1993].

Innes, Christopher (1979) *Modern German Drama: A Study in Form*, Cambridge: Cambridge University Press.

Insdorf, Annette (1989) *Indelible Shadows: Film and the Holocaust* (2nd edition), Cambridge: Cambridge University Press.

Izod, John and Kilborn, Richard (1997) *An Introduction to TV Documentary: Confronting Reality*, New York and Manchester: Manchester University Press.

Johnson, Thomas J. (1995) *The Rehabilitation of Richard Nixon: The Media's Effect on Collective Memory*, New York and London: Garland Publishing Inc.

Kellman, Steven G. (1988) 'Cinema of/as atrocity: *Shoah*'s guilty conscience', *The Gettysburg Review*, 1: 22–30.

Kerbel, Matthew Robert (1994) *Edited for Television: CNN, ABC and the 1992 Presidential Campaign*, San Francisco and Oxford: Westview Press.

Kolker, Robert Phillip (1971) 'Circumstantial evidence: an interview with David and Albert Maysles', *Sight and Sound* 40 (4; Autumn): 183–6.

Kozloff, Sarah (1988) *Invisible Storytellers: Voice-over Narration in American Fiction Film*, Berkeley and Los Angeles: University of California Press.

Kuhn, Annette (1978) 'The camera I: observations on documentary', *Screen*, 19 (2; Summer): 71–83.

Lanzmann, Claude (1985a) 'The being of nothingness: an interview with Claude Lanzmann', reproduced in Kevin Macdonald and Mark Cousins (eds) *Imagining Reality: The Faber Book of Documentary*, London: Faber & Faber [1996]: 322–5.

—— (1985b) *Shoah: An Oral History of the Holocaust*, New York: Pantheon Books.

—— (1990) 'Seminar with Claude Lanzmann: 11 April, 1990'; *Yale French Studies, 79: Literature and the Ethical Question*.

Lawson, Mark (1995) 'High flyer on the wall', *The Guardian*, 10 October, pp. 10–11.

Levin, G. Roy (1971) *Documentary Explorations: 15 Interviews with Filmmakers*, New York: Doubleday.

Leyda, Jay (1983) *Kino: A History of Russian and Soviet Film* (3rd edition), Princeton: Princeton University Press.

—— (1996) 'Esther Shub and the art of compilation', in Kevin Macdonald and Mark Cousins (eds) *Imagining Reality: The Faber Book of Documentary*, London: Faber & Faber.

Loshitzky, Yosefa (1997) 'Holocaust others: Spielberg's *Schindler's List* versus Lanzmann's *Shoah*', in Yosefa Loshitzky (ed.) *Spielberg's Holocaust: Critical Perspectives on Schindler's List*, Bloomington and Indianapolis: Indiana University Press, pp. 104–18.

Lukács, Georg (1937) *The Historical Novel* (transl. Hannah and Stanley Mitchell) Harmondsworth: Penguin [1981].

McCann (1998) 'ITV gives new docu-soap prime billing', *The Independent*, 23 February.

Macdonald, Kevin and Cousins, Mark (1996) (eds) *Imagining Reality: The Faber Book of Documentary*, London: Faber & Faber.

McGregor, Alex (1995) 'This old house', *American Cinematographer*, 76 (11; November): 83–6.

Mamber, Stephen (1972a) 'Cinéma-vérité in America', *Screen*, 13 (2; Summer): 79–107.

—— (1972b) 'Part II – Direct cinema and the crisis structure', *Screen*, 13 (3; Autumn): 114–36.

—— (1974) *Cinéma Vérité in America: Studies in Uncontrolled Documentary*, Cambridge, Mass. and London: MIT Press.

Marker, Chris (1984) 'Terminal Vertigo' [an interview by computer with Chris Marker], *Monthly Film Bulletin*, 51 (606; July): 196–7.

Matthews, Christopher (1996) *Kennedy and Nixon: The Rivalry that Shaped Postwar America*, New York: Simon & Schuster.

Michelson, Annette (ed.) (1984) *Kino-eye: The Writings of Dziga Vertov* (transl. Kevin O'Brien), Berkeley and Los Angeles: University of California Press.

Moi, Toril (1987) *French Feminist Thought*, Oxford: Blackwell.

Moran, Caitlin (1998) 'You give Love a bad name', *Time Out*, 1077 (June): 18–21.

Monsell, Thomas (1998) *Nixon on Stage and Screen: The Thirty-seventh President as Depicted in Films, Television, Plays and Opera*, Jefferson, North Carolina and London: McFarland & Company Inc.

Nichols, Bill (1981) *Ideology and the Image: Social Representation in the Cinema*, Bloomington and Indianapolis: Indiana University Press.

—— (1983) 'The voice of documentary', reprinted in Rosenthal [1988]: 48–63.

—— (1991) *Representing Reality: Issues and Concepts of Documentary*, Bloomington and Indianapolis: Indiana University Press.

—— (1994) *Blurred Boundaries: Questions of Meaning in Contemporary Culture*, Bloomington and Indianapolis: Indiana University Press.

Nixon, Richard (1978) *The Memoirs of Richard Nixon*, London: Arrow Books [1979].

—— (1990) *In the Arena: A Memoir of Victory, Defeat and Renewal*, New York and London: Simon & Schuster.

Ophuls, Marcel (1985) 'Closely watched trains', *American Film*, 11 (2; November): 18–22, 79.

Ouellette, Laurie (1995) 'Camcorder dos and don'ts: popular discourses on amateur video and participatory television', *Velvet Light Trap*, 36 (Autumn): 33–44.

Paterson, Elaine (1989) 'Heller let loose', *Time Out*, 1007: 6–13, 52–3.

Pearson, Allison (1998) 'All the world's a soap set', *The Daily Telegraph*, 28 May.

Plantinga, Carl (1997) *Rhetoric and Representation in Nonfiction Film*, Cambridge: Cambridge University Press.

Rafferty, Terrence (1984) 'Marker changes trains', *Sight and Sound*, 53 (4; Autumn): 284 8.

Ranney, Austin (1983) *Channels of Power: The Impact of Television on American Politics*, New York: Basic Books.

Renov, Michael (1986) 'Re-thinking Documentary: towards a taxonomy of mediation', *Wide Angle*, 8: 3–4.

—— (ed.) (1993) *Theorizing Documentary*, London and New York: Routledge.

Rivele, Stephen J., Wilkinson, Christopher and Stone, Oliver (1996) *Nixon* (screenplay, ed. Eric Hamburg), London: Bloomsbury.

Rosenthal, Alan (1978) 'Emile de Antonio: an interview', *Film Quarterly*, 31 (1; Fall): 4–17.

—— (1988) *New Challenges for Documentary*, Berkeley and Los Angeles: University of California Press.

Rotha, Paul (1930) *The Film Till Now: A Survey of World Cinema* (new edition), London: Vision Press Ltd [1963].

—— (1952) *The Documentary Film* (2nd edition), London: Faber (originally published 1935).

Safire, William (1975) *Before the Fall*, New York: Belmont Tower Books.

Sei Shonagon (1971) *The Pillow Book of Sei Shonagon* (transl. Ivan Morris), Harmondsworth: Penguin.

Shearman, Nick (1998) Interview with the author, 26.11.98.

Shivas, Mark (1963) 'Interview with Richard Leacock', in Kevin Macdonald and Mark Cousins (eds) *Imagining Reality: The Faber Book of Documentary*, London: Faber & Faber [1996].

Silverman, Kaja (1988) *The Acoustic Mirror: The Female Voice in Psychoanalysis and Cinema*, Bloomington and Indianapolis: Indiana University Press.

Simon, Art (1996) *Dangerous Knowledge: The JFK Assassination in Art and Film*, Philadelphia: Temple University Press.

Sinclair, Iain (1994) 'London: necropolis of fretful ghosts', *Sight and Sound*, 4 (6; June): 12–15.

—— (1997) *Lights Out for the Territory*, London: Granta.

Sobchack, Vivian (ed.) (1996) *The Persistence of History: Cinema, Television and the Modern Event*, London and New York: Routledge.

Spencer, Megan (1999) 'Sideshow alley: the documentaries of Nick Broomfield', *IF*, 15 (July).

Spender, Dale (1985) *Man Made Language* (2nd edition), London: Routledge & Kegan Paul.

Steiner, George (1972) *Language and Silence: Essays on Language, Literature and the Inhuman*, New York: Atheneum.

Stone, David M. (ed.) (1985) *Nixon and the Politics of Public Television*, New York and London: Garland Publishing Inc.

Sweeting, Adam (1998) 'Lights. Camera. Act natural', *The Guardian*, 10 January.

Terrill, Chris (1998) Interview with the author, 8.12.98.

Titus, Constandina (1983) 'Back to ground zero: old footage through new lenses', *Journal of Popular Film and Television*, 11 (1; Spring): 3–11.

Tretyakov, Sergey, Shklovsky, Victor, Shub, Esther and Brik, Osip (1927) 'Symposium on Soviet Documentary', in Lewis Jacobs (ed.) *The Documentary Tradition* (2nd edition), Toronto: J. McLeod [1979].

Tuchman, Mitch (1990) 'Freedom of information', *Film Comment*, 26 (4; July–August): 66–8.

Vaughan, Dai (1974) 'The space between shots', *Screen*, 15 (1; Spring): 73–85.

—— (1979) 'Arms and the absent', *Sight and Sound*, 48 (3; Summer): 182–7.

Walker, Martin (1996) *Clinton: The President They Deserve*, London: Fourth Estate.

Wasson, Haidee (1995) 'Assassinating an image: the strange life of Kennedy's death', *CineAction!*, 38 (September): 5–11.

Watson, Paul (1998) *The Daily Mail*, 17 February.

Waugh, Thomas (1985) 'Beyond *Vérité*: Emile de Antonio and the New Documentary of the Seventies', in Bill Nichols (ed.) *Movies and Methods II*, Berkeley and Los Angeles: University of California Press, pp. 233–58.

Weiner, Bernard (1971) 'Radical scavenging: an interview with Emile de Antonio', *Film Quarterly*, 25 (1; Fall): 3–15.

Weiss, Marc N. (1974) 'Emile de Antonio', *Film Library Quarterly*, 7 (2): 29–35.

Weiss, Peter (1971) 'The material and the models: notes towards a definition of documentary theatre', *Theatre Quarterly*, 1: 41–5.

White, Hayden (1987) *The Content of the Form: Narrative, Discourse and Historical Representation*, Baltimore and London: Johns Hopkins University Press.

—— (1996) 'The modernist event', in Vivian Sobchack (ed.) *The Persistence of History: Cinema, Television and the Modernist Event*, London and New York: Routledge.

White, Theodore (1982) *America in Search of Itself: The Making of the President, 1956–1980*, New York: Harper & Row.

Williams, Linda (1993) 'Mirrors without memories: truth, history and the new documentary', *Film Quarterly*, 46 (3; Spring): 9–21.

Winston, Brian (1993) 'The documentary film as scientific inscription', in Michael Renov (ed.) *Theorizing Documentary*, London and New York: Routledge, pp. 37–57.

—— (1995) *Claiming the Real: The Documentary Film Revisited*, London: British Film Institute.

Youdelman, Jeffrey (1982) 'Narration, Invention, History'; reprinted in Alan Rosenthal (ed.) *New Challenges for Documentary*, Berkeley and Los Angeles: University of California Press [1988].

Zimmerman, Patricia (1995) *Reel Families: A Social History of Amateur Film*, Bloomington and Indianapolis: Indiana University Press.

Index